ESSAYS IN
ENGLISH ARCHITECTURAL HISTORY

OEVVRE.
DE LA DIVERSITE
DES TERMES, DONT ON
vſe en Architecture, reduict en ordre:

Par maiſtre Hugues Sambin, demeu-
rant à Dijon.

A LYON,
PAR IEAN DVRANT.
M. D. LXXII.

Title-page of Hugues Sambin's, *De la Diversité des Termes*, published in Dijon in 1572, with the signature of the Earl of Worcester (see p. 116)

ESSAYS
IN
ENGLISH
ARCHITECTURAL
HISTORY

Howard Colvin

PUBLISHED FOR
THE PAUL MELLON
CENTRE FOR STUDIES IN BRITISH ART BY
YALE UNIVERSITY PRESS
NEW HAVEN AND LONDON
1999

Set in Bembo by Best-set Typesetter Ltd., Hong Kong
Printed and bound by C.S. Graphics Pte Ltd., Singapore

Library of Congress Cataloging-in-Publication Data

Colvin, Howard Montagu.
Essays in English architectural history / Howard Colvin.
p.   cm.
Includes bibliographical references and index.
ISBN 0-300-07034-9 (cloth : alk. paper)
1. Architecture–Great Britain.   I. Title.
NA961.C6   1999
720'.942 – dc21   98-50532
CIP

CONTENTS

To
Christina

PREFACE

THE ESSAYS PRINTED in this volume are products of a career as an architectural historian that, apart from a study of funerary architecture in Western Europe, has been devoted chiefly to architects and architecture in the British Isles from the Middle Ages onwards. Five of them (numbers 3, 4, 5, 6 and 18) are printed here for the first time. The remainder have been selected from a larger number of published essays and articles listed below (pp. 298–302). They examine themes, episodes or individual buildings that seemed of sufficient importance to justify perpetuating in a separate volume. Three of them (numbers 7, 8 and 13) have been extensively revised, especially 'The South Front of Wilton House', which reviews a problem that has attracted a good deal of attention, scholarly and otherwise, since it first appeared in the *Archaeological Journal* in 1954. I regret that Scotland is not represented, but the fruits of my long and enjoyable involvement in Scottish architectural history were nearly all incorporated in my *Biographical Dictionary of British Architects*.

Once more I am indebted to the Paul Mellon Centre for British Art for sponsoring a book of my writing, and to Yale University Press for publishing it with characteristic efficiency. The sources of those essays that have previously appeared in periodicals, learned journals and symposia are listed below (p. 303). For permission to reprint those that were not my own copyright I am grateful to the editors of the *Archaeological Journal*, *Architectural History* and *Country Life*, and to the publishing managers of Dumbarton Oaks (Washington), the Hambledon Press and the Colston Research Society of Bristol.

For scholarly help generously given or criticism kindly offered I have to thank Dr Giles Barber, Professor Martin Biddle, Dr Ian Campbell, Dr Bridget Cherry, Dr Amanda Claridge, Dr Rosalys Coope, Sir John Habakkuk, Mr Robin Harcourt Williams, Mr John Harris, Dr Gordon Higgott, Dr Emily Kearns, Mr John Newman, Mr John Peacock, Mr Nicholas Purcell, Professor D.A.F.M. Russell, Professor David Walker, Mr Anthony Wells-Cole and Dr Adam White. For access to buildings I am grateful to His Grace the Duke of Marlborough, His Honour Judge Wills, Mr Christopher Rice, Mrs C.R. Sinclair and the Sue Ryder Foundation.

Mr Paul Draper kindly allowed me to reproduce his drawing (fig. 49) of the triumphal arch designed for Temple Bar by Inigo Jones, and I have to thank Mr

Richard Avent, Mr Michael Clifford, Dr John Crook and the late Jill Allibone for taking photographs specially to illustrate this book. Others were lent by Mr Bruce Bailey, Dr David King, Professor Lawrence Stone and Dr Simon Thurley. Dr Edward Impey generously drew figure 17 and figure 127 owes more than just draughtsmanship to Mrs Daphne Ford.

For permission to reproduce drawings belonging to them I am grateful to the British Architectural Library, the Society of Antiquaries of London, the Provost and Fellows of Worcester College, Oxford, the Earl of Harrowby, the Earl of Pembroke and Mr Robin Fryer. Mrs Margaret Jope kindly allowed figure 16 to be reproduced. The sources of the other illustrations are indicated in the captions. Figures 1 and 2 are Crown Copyright, reproduced by permission of the Controller of Her Majesty's Stationery Office. Uncredited photographs are by the author.

C. Rutter del.   S. Howlett sc.

W. Bos: aq fort

I

ROYAL GARDENS IN MEDIEVAL ENGLAND

As a contribution to garden history this paper has limitations that need to be made clear at the outset. It is largely a by-product of research on English royal houses in the Middle Ages, and it is about the structure of the gardens associated with those houses rather than about the plants that were cultivated in them. Its scope will be limited to England because it is the records of the medieval English monarchy that I happen to be acquainted with. They are financial and administrative records, beginning in the twelfth century. They have their limitations, but they are more complete than those of any other European state. What was true of England cannot of course be regarded as necessarily typical of Western Europe, and gardens, more even than other symbols of civilised life, are conditioned by climate and geography. But the monarchy, at any rate from 1066 onwards, was the least insular component of medieval English society. The Norman kings (1066–1154) were not only as much at home in their French duchy as they were in their English kingdom, but maintained close connections with their cousins in Sicily. The Angevins (1154–1216) ruled half of what is now France as well as all England and much of Wales, while the Plantagenets (1216–1399) and the Lancastrians (1399–1461) spent much of their lives trying by diplomacy or war to make good their claim to be kings of France as well as of England. Gardens were, moreover, the especial province of women, and if we analyse the national origins of the twenty-two queens of England between 1066 and 1485, we find that only five of them were born in Britain. Nine came from northern France or Flanders, four from Aquitaine or Provence, three from Castile or Navarre, one from Bohemia. Their taste in gardens must have been even more cosmopolitan than that of their husbands. Some of them indeed brought gardeners from abroad: we have evidence of a Provençal gardener directing the royal garden at Windsor at the time when the queen of England was Eleanor of Provence, and of Aragonese gardeners working for Queen Eleanor of Castile at her manor of King's Langley in the reign of Edward I.[1] When they conferred with their gardeners these foreign ladies would have had in their minds the gardens of sunnier and more exotic climates than that of England. But even in the all-important matter of climate medieval England was, at any rate until the early fourteenth century, less clearly differentiated from the continent than it has been in modern times. In the twelfth century vines grew freely in southern England, and men could pick grapes in what are now the streets of

1. The king's houses 1154–1216 (from *The History of the King's Works*, i, 1963). The stippled areas show the royal forests.

Bloomsbury.[2] The history of climate is still in its infancy, but there does seem to be general agreement that in the twelfth and thirteenth centuries England enjoyed a climate that approximated more closely to that of continental Europe as a whole than it does now. So in studying the royal gardens in medieval England we are studying a type of garden which must have had much in common with contemporary royal gardens in other parts of Europe.

In England, as elsewhere, the royal gardens were attached to the houses and castles that belonged to the king and queen. If we count the number of houses and castles that were at one time or another in the hands of the Crown between 1066 and 1485 it comes to well over 200. But few of these remained permanently in royal possession throughout those 400 odd years: the stock was constantly being renewed, and as constantly depleted, by inheritance on the one hand and by grant on the other. However, at any given time, the King of England had at his disposal a number of residences, some fortified, some unfortified, of whose amenities a garden formed a normal part. In a castle, of course, a garden would have to take

2

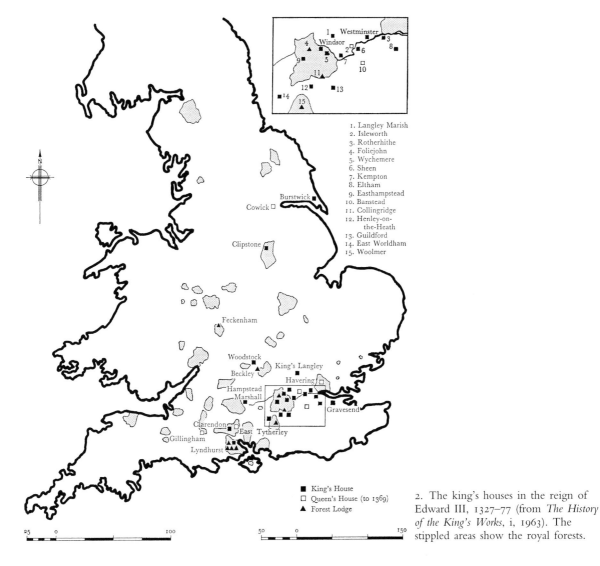

1. Langley Marish
2. Isleworth
3. Rotherhithe
4. Foliejohn
5. Wychemere
6. Sheen
7. Kempton
8. Eltham
9. Easthampstead
10. Banstead
11. Collingridge
12. Henley-on-
the-Heath
13. Guildford
14. East Worldham
15. Woolmer

Burstwick
Cowick
Clipstone
Feckenham
Woodstock
King's Langley
Beckley
Havering
Hampstead
Marshall
Gravesend
Clarendon
East Tytherley
Gillingham
Lyndhurst

■ King's House
□ Queen's House (to 1369)
▲ Forest Lodge

2. The king's houses in the reign of Edward III, 1327–77 (from *The History of the King's Works*, i, 1963). The stippled areas show the royal forests.

25   0   100   50   0   150

second place to the needs of defence. The herbarium 'in front of the king's chamber,' of which we read at Arundel Castle in 1187,[3] was probably quite constricted, and gardens outside the walls, as at Caernarvon,[4] ran the risk of destruction in time of war. In the 1420s, for instance, gardens outside the walls of one of the castles guarding the enclave of English territory round Calais in northern France had to be removed for the safety of the sentries guarding the walls at night.[5] Even at Windsor, by the sixteenth century more a palace than a castle, the young King Edward VI was to complain in 1549 that it was like a prison, for 'here be no galleries nor no gardens to walk in'.[6] Nevertheless a garden was an appurtenance of many of the royal castles, and we know that Edward I 'particularly delighted' in the one at the Tower of London.[7]

Although there was more space for gardens at the unfortified royal houses, it was hunting rather than horticulture that determined their siting. The close relationship between the royal houses and the royal forests is clearly demonstrated by the two maps showing the king's houses in the twelfth century and in the reign of Edward

3

III (1327–77) (figs. 1, 2). Associated with many of these houses was a deer-park, enclosed by paling. Such parks might have their attractions: in 1354 a balcony was constructed at Woodstock outside the window of one of the king's daughters in order to give her a view of the park. The record is explicit that it was built for that purpose.[8] But medieval parks were primarily for the benefit of the deer, and the idea of a park as an extension of a garden was far in the future. Park and garden were separate entities, even when they were adjacent to one another. When a herbarium was made in the park at Odiham in Hampshire for Queen Philippa in 1332, it was surrounded by some 2,000 feet of hedge and there was an inner enclosure protected by a boarded fence with five doors.[9] At a later date such a detached garden would perhaps have been called a 'pleasance'. The word 'pleasance' enjoyed more popularity in the nineteenth century than it seems to have done in the Middle Ages, but the country house that the humanist Duke Humphrey of Gloucester (youngest son of King Henry IV) built at Greenwich in Kent in the 1430s was known as 'the Manor of Pleasance', and his elder brother, King Henry V, built a 'Pleasance' on the far side of the Great Pool at Kenilworth Castle. The quadrangular site was moated and there were towers at the four corners. The centre was laid out as a garden, and there was a dock for boats to bring parties of courtiers on summer outings from the castle.[10]

A king who has a dozen or twenty houses at his disposal cannot occupy them all on a permanent or even on a regular basis. In fact the medieval English court was itinerant, moving round the country from one house or castle to another, and, apart from Windsor and the metropolitan palace at Westminster, only a few specially favoured residences – Clarendon and Woodstock in the twelfth century, Eltham, Sheen and King's Langley in the fourteenth and fifteenth – were regularly occupied for long periods. Most of the royal gardens were therefore only for occasional use. When the court was in residence the garden produce was consumed by the royal household; at other times it was sold. Generally the income from this source was modest, but as early as 1130 the king's garden at Carlisle was being farmed, that is to say rented out, for the then considerable sum of thirty shillings a year.[11] In the 1260s the revenues of the king's garden at Westminster contributed ten shillings to the works then in progress there.[12] The principal royal gardens at Westminster, Windsor, Eltham and Sheen had salaried gardeners in charge, and so did some others. We know the names of some of these men, who have been conveniently listed by John Harvey.[13] They were generally paid two and a half or three pence a day, considerably less than master masons or master carpenters, and although occasionally designated as 'Master', seem normally to have enjoyed an inferior status. Each held an independent post, there was no head gardener with general authority over all the royal gardens, and any major expenditure on gardens was accounted for by the clerks who supervised the royal works. It is chiefly from their accounts, preserved among the records of the Exchequer in the Public Record Office in London, that we know what we do about the royal gardens of medieval England.

And that, it must be emphasised, is very little, for there are no plans, no topographical drawings, no formal descriptions, either in the royal archives or elsewhere. The earliest drawings we have of English royal gardens were made in the middle of the sixteenth century, and they show gardens profusely adorned with heraldic ornament in a manner that cannot be traced before the reign of the first Tudor king, Henry VII (1485–1509). Where Tudor gardens were clearly designed to impress, their medieval predecessors were designed, one suspects, more for relaxation than display. It had not yet been realised that gardens, like architecture, might have their political uses. At any rate, the gardens of the Plantagenet and Lancastrian kings lacked the blatant dynastic advertisement that was so conspicuous a feature of the gardens of their Tudor successors at Westminster, Hampton Court, Richmond and elsewhere.[14]

What were these English royal gardens like? The term most frequently used in the accounts in connection with horticulture is *herbarium*, which has been variously translated by the editors of the Chancery and Exchequer records as 'garden', 'herb-garden', 'lawn' and 'arbour'. The word demands more expert philological exegesis than I can attempt to offer. But to equate *herbarium* with 'garden' is to mistake a part for the whole, for *herbaria* are not infrequently referred to as features of *gardina*, gardens. In 1307–8, for instance, a gardener called Roger of Folkestone was busy, with six assistants, putting in order 'divers *herbaria*, walks and other places in the king's and queen's privy gardens at Westminster'.[15] Often a *herbarium* is spoken of as occupying space between the buildings of a royal house or castle. At Westminster, for instance, we have reference in the thirteenth century to a 'small enclosed *herbarium*' next to the pentice, or covered passageway, between the king's chamber and the neighbouring abbey, in which six pear trees were to be planted in 1262,[16] and to a 'great *herbarium*' made in 1277–8 between the Chapel and the Receipt of the Exchequer on the east side of the palace.[17] It seems clear that the word, as used in the English royal records, need imply little more than a patch of grass or cultivated ground, but if it was enclosed, as it often was, by a wall or fence or hedge, then it might assume the character of a garden within a garden. *Herbaria* were generally grassed, and they often contained benches, as for instance at Clarendon in 1250, when King Henry III ordered a bench to be made round about his great *herbarium* and the wall above the bench to be whitened.[18] These benches were sometimes built of stone, as at Windsor in 1246,[19] but more often they were of less substantial construction, being made largely of turfs (reinforced no doubt by timber or wickerwork), as at Windsor in 1311, when turfs were provided for the repair of the benches of the *herbarium* between the hall and the royal lodging,[20] or at the *herbarium* in the park at Odiham which I have already mentioned. The poet Chaucer, who was Clerk of the King's Works at Westminster from 1389 to 1391, writes in the *Legend of Good Women* of 'a litel herber that I have, that benched was on turves fresh y graven.' Such benches are illustrated in medieval manuscripts, such as a miniature of *c.*1400 in which we see a king and queen seated on turf benches in what is evidently a 'herber' within the walls of a castle.[21]

If we were to visit one of the English royal gardens, what would strike us as the most prominent feature would almost certainly be the vines. There are innumerable references in the accounts to the framework of rods and timber on which they were trained. At the palace of Westminster in 1312–13 we read of Master Maurice the gardener obtaining 700 willow plants to support the vines and to make covered walks (*alaturae*) in the queen's herbarium.[22] When Jean Froissart was at Eltham in 1397 on diplomatic business he walked round the garden with his English friend Sir Richard Stury and found it 'very pleasant and shady, for these walks [*allées*] were all covered with vines,'[23] and indeed payments for 'vynerodds' for the vines of the great garden outside the moat and for the smaller garden within it are duly recorded in the Eltham works accounts at just this time.[24]

For an illustration of such covered walks, or pergolas, we have to turn to the well-known painting of the Palais de la Cité in Paris in the *Très Riches Heures* of Jean, Duke of Berry (1409–16). There is every reason to suppose that such simple constructions were equally to be found in England, especially as vinestocks were replenished from French sources from time to time[25] and French expertise was no doubt made use of too. Master Maurice de la Grave, the head gardener at Westminster in the reign of Edward II,[25] may well have come to England from France or Gascony, and in the reign of Henry III (1216–72) the master gardener at Windsor was, as I have already mentioned, one of the Provençals who came to England as a result of the king's marriage to Eleanor of Provence. In the reign of Edward I (1272–1307) vines were being grown as far north as the royal manor of Burstwick in the East Riding of Yorkshire.[27] Whether, in the more favourable climate of the thirteenth century, they yielded edible fruit we do not know, but further south the royal vines certainly afforded grapes not only for dessert but for making wine. In the 1360s panniers were brought to convey the grapes and other produce from the gardens of the royal manor of Rotherhithe in Surrey to the king wherever he might be, and in 1377 the wine made at Windsor was good enough for the king to make gifts of it to both the queen and his mistress, Alice Perrers.[28] But in the latter part of the fourteenth century the Windsor vines could not be relied upon to produce drinkable wine every year, and their output was often classed only as 'verjuice', an acid liquor suitable only for cooking.[29]

Although vine-covered walks gave definition to many of the English royal gardens, features of a more architectural character were occasionally to be found. At Guildford, for instance, Henry III gave directions in 1256 for a cloister with marble columns to be made in his garden,[30] and in 1444–7 a cloister (certainly not of marble and very likely of timber) was built at Sheen with an octagonal lead cistern in the middle fed by an underground conduit.[31] Whether this cistern was a garden feature of the sort seen in contemporary continental illustrations or the centre of a paved courtyard is not clear. Nothing as fanciful as the 'chapel of glass' or the revolving summerhouse, which were features of the garden at Hesdin in Artois, was to be found in English royal gardens, but the famous aviary in the castle at Hesdin did have its counterparts in England.[32] There was one at Winchester Castle in the twelfth century, and another at Westminster Palace in the thirteenth. The latter was made, or remade, for Queen Eleanor of Castile in 1277–8 by a Master Richard: in 1309–10 there were eighty birds of different species in the 'queen's cage'.[33] There was a summerhouse too, though not a revolving one, at Sheen. It was a small timber-framed building standing on an island in the River Thames and was equipped with benches and trestle tables. Richard II had it built in the 1380s.[34] The

3. View of the royal garden at Richmond Palace, Surrey, drawn by A. van den Wyngaerde *circa* 1558–62, showing the timber-framed galleries that surrounded it (Ashmolean Museum, Oxford).

tiled 'Erberhowse' mentioned in the Sheen accounts in the 1440s was presumably another building of the same sort.[35] Similarly we may see an early example of a gazebo in a building erected in 1440–1 in the garden of the Royal Mews or falconry at Charing Cross in Westminster, for it had plastered walls painted green and was called a 'Spyhouse'.[36]

An important feature of the Tudor royal gardens were timber-framed galleries, sometimes of two storeys, open below and enclosed above, which surrounded or subdivided them and provided covered walks in hot or wet weather. We can see these clearly in Antonius van den Wyngaerde's views of Richmond Palace (fig. 3), and we know that there they dated from the early sixteenth century.[37] Galleries of this sort already existed in the early fifteenth century at the royal Hôtel de St Pol on the outskirts of Paris.[38] How far such galleries in England should be regarded as a Tudor innovation is difficult to say, for the word 'gallery' can be applied to almost any covered walk or passage. Indeed in one manuscript of Froissart the vine-covered walks that he saw at Eltham in 1397 are called *galleries*,[39] and in Du Cerceau's book *Les plus excellents bastiments de la France* (1576) we find classical versions of such walks described as 'galleries'. The earliest use of the word in a British source appears to date from 1447–8, when carpenters were paid for framing and making a gallery ('galr') at the queen's manor of Greenwich. But the way in which it is referred to in the account as 'next to the queen's chamber over the parlour next the great garden' leaves us in doubt as to its function.[40] We cannot tell whether it was in any sense a garden building or not. The gallery ('galry') mentioned at Falkland Palace in Scotland in 1461 was almost certainly part of the

7

house, since two chambers were partitioned off within it,[41] but the gallery 'over the water' (*galeria super aquam*) built by the Fellows of King's College, Cambridge, in 1468–9 was a timber-framed building at the end of their garden overlooking the river Cam.[42] So the record is inconclusive, and we cannot demonstrate that in medieval England any royal garden was surrounded by roofed galleries of the sort the Tudors were so much to favour.[43]

So far I have said nothing about water as a feature of medieval royal gardens. From time to time we read of a fishpond being made in a herbarium at some royal castle or house, but this was probably for practical rather than ornamental purposes. Certainly none of the English royal houses boasted anything so sophisticated as the great circular pool in the garden of the Parisian Hôtel de St Pol, with its encircling balustrade and its lion spouting water in the middle.[44] Lion fountains of various sorts were a feature of Hispano-Islamic gardens,[45] and water was, of course, an essential feature of the famous gardens of Spain and Sicily, where Arabic art and science were put at the disposal of Christian rulers. At Palermo Roger II, the Norman King of Sicily (1129–54), created a vast park enclosed by a stone wall within which he built a series of palaces served by water brought by underground conduits. These were La Favara, La Cuba and La Ziza, through which, in oriental fashion, water was conducted from one pool to another. Outside, in the park, there were kiosks and pavilions, of which one, known as La Cubola, survives intact and others in a fragmentary condition.[46]

To look for such semi-oriental luxuries in medieval England may seem far-fetched, but there was one English royal garden in which water played an important part. This was at Woodstock near Oxford, where there was a major royal house and where, early in the twelfth century, King Henry I (d. 1134) had enclosed a large park with a stone wall and stocked it with exotic animals – lions, leopards, lynxes, camels and a porcupine are specifically mentioned.[47] The place was known in the Middle Ages as 'Everswell', but from the sixteenth century onwards it was called 'Rosamund's Bower'. Rosamund Clifford (d. 1176?) was a celebrated mistress of King Henry II (1154–89), and according to legend she lived here at the centre of a maze, or labyrinth, of which the king alone knew the secret. Although the idea that the king's mistress lived in a maze must be mythical, a labyrinth, or 'house of Daedalus', was a feature of the remarkable garden of the dukes of Burgundy at Hesdin in Artois,[48] and there was another in the garden of the Hôtel des Tournelles in Paris at the time (1431) when it was occupied by the Duke of Bedford as English Regent of France.[49] At Everswell the labyrinth, 'or secret chamber of Daedalian workmanship', is not mentioned until the fourteenth century, and then only in literary sources, never in the royal records.[50] What the royal records do show is that Everswell was built in Rosamund's lifetime and that by the thirteenth century it contained a chamber named after her.[51] Whether or not Everswell was the scene of Henry II's illicit amours, it was certainly unique among the English royal gardens, forming a kind of Trianon to which the king and queen could retire from the formalities of the court at Woodstock.

A payment of £26 9s. 4d. *in operatione fontis* constitutes the first reference to the spring or 'well' after which Everswell was named. This was in 1166. Thereafter

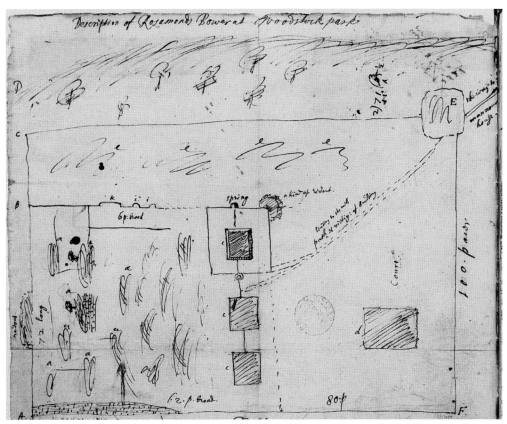

4. John Aubrey's sketch-plan of the ruins of Everswell in Woodstock Park, Oxfordshire, in the seventeenth century (Bodleian Library, MS Wood 176[b], f. 43[v]). The spring and three pools are seen in the middle, with a fourth to the right (d). The ruins marked E (top right) were thought by Aubrey to be 'the ruines of a noble gatehouse or Tower of Entrance' and beyond them he has indicated 'the way to the mannour house'.

there are numerous references to the works here in the royal records. The accounts refer to the 'larger' and 'smaller' pools (*fontes*), the former surrounded by a 'great cloister' (*magnum claustrum*), the latter by benches. The 'cloisters round the pools' were ordered to be paved and wainscoted in 1244. By this date there was a complex of chambers complete with chapel, kitchen and wine cellar, which made Everswell into a self-contained living unit quite separate from the royal house a few hundred yards away. In 1239 Henry III ordered a herbarium to be made round one of the pools. Another was made in 1251–2, and in 1264 Henry ordered a hundred pear trees to be planted in it.[52] The site of Everswell (now in Blenheim Park) was at least partly drowned under the lake created by Capability Brown in the eighteenth century, but a sketch made by John Aubrey shows the three 'baths' as they still existed in the seventeenth century, surrounded by the ruins of the medieval buildings (fig. 4). With Aubrey's help it is not difficult to envisage Everswell as a water garden of the kind that is still to be seen intact in Moorish Spain and in a ruined state at Palermo. It is to Palermo rather than to Spain that we must look for the ideas that may have inspired the layout of Everswell, for the contacts between

9

the English court and the Sicilian one were numerous and of long standing.[53] An Englishman, Robert of Selby, was King Roger's chancellor during the greater part of his reign (1101–54); several Sicilian sees, including that of Palermo, were held by bishops of English origin in the reigns of King William I (1154–66) and King William II (1166–89), and a trusted official called Thomas Brown served King Roger in Sicily for many years before returning to England to become King Henry's almoner and a well-known figure in the Exchequer at Westminster. The marriage, in 1177, of Henry's daughter Joanna to King William II of Sicily was the dynastic consummation of this Anglo-Sicilian entente. In a court where Sicilian affairs were so familiar, the desire to create a Siculo-Norman garden on English soil need cause no surprise. In view of the scantiness of our knowledge the Sicilian inspiration of Everswell cannot be regarded as proved, but it is difficult to account for it on any other basis.

There is, however, another possible dimension to Everswell, a literary one. It is tempting to suggest that the enclosed garden with its chambers and pools was inspired by the twelfth-century romance of *Tristan and Isolde*, a romance of British origin which appears to have had a special fascination for the Angevin royal house; indeed a version of it was probably written for Henry II himself.[54] In this poem the lovers were accustomed to meet in an orchard near the royal castle in which Isolde lived. This orchard was surrounded by a strong palisade, and at one end of it there was a spring from which water first filled a marble pool and then continued in a narrow channel that ran through Isolde's apartment in such a way that Tristan was able to communicate with her by dropping twigs into the stream. Whether at Woodstock the channel actually passed through the room known as Rosamund's chamber is not clear, but the chamber and the running water were undoubtedly in close proximity. Everswell, in fact, provided the complete *mise-en-scène* of the poetic episode: the enclosed orchard; the spring with the stream flowing first into an artificial pool and then into a narrow channel; and the chamber or 'bower'; and finally the lovers, in the persons of Henry and Rosamund. How far the place was intended to be a deliberate evocation of the poem, or the poem of the place, must be a matter for conjecture, but if the two were in some way related, it would help to make sense of the most puzzling and intriguing of the royal gardens of medieval England.

I began by emphasizing the limitations of the evidence I have tried to interpret, and those limitations (as well as my own as an architectural historian attempting to write about gardens) will by now have become evident. Without plans or drawings it is difficult to visualise any of the gardens whose construction and maintenance are recorded in the English royal records, and, with the possible exception of Everswell at Woodstock, none emerges with a clear identity such as we associate with the great gardens of the European Renaissance or of the eighteenth century in England.

What is almost equally serious is that the picture as I have presented it lacks chronological development. In every other artistic sphere the fifteenth century looks very different from the thirteenth, yet in garden history it is difficult to point to any feature, other than summerhouses and possibly galleries, that differentiates a fifteenth-century English royal garden from one of the reign of Henry III. Change there must have been, but without plans or drawings it is hard to diagnose it. I can certainly find no evidence whatever to substantiate a recent assertion that 'from the thirteenth century on, the royal court was a hothouse of experimental gardening.'[55] If experiment there was, it has left little trace in the records, and as for hothouses, whether actual or metaphorical, they are best avoided when discussing medieval gardens. If someone with a wider knowledge of garden history than I can claim were to concentrate their attention on the documentary evidence it is possible that a chronological pattern would emerge. But the only real breakthrough that I can envisage would be through archaeology. Archaeology has already succeeded in revealing not merely the outline but the actual bedding plan of the garden in the Roman palace at Fishbourne in Sussex, and I believe something of the same sort has been achieved on the site of the early eighteenth-century garden at Carter's Grove in Virginia. What can be done for Antiquity and the eighteenth century ought also to be possible for the Middle Ages. In short, what English medieval royal gardens are now in need of is not so much a historian as an archaeologist.[56]

NOTES

1 *Calendar of Liberate Rolls 1267–72*, pp. 217, 224; John Harvey, *Medieval Gardens*, 1981, p. 78.
2 J.H. Round, 'Essex Vineyards in Domesday', *Essex Archaeological Society's Trans.*, NS 7, 1899; R. Lennard, *Rural England 1086–1135*, Oxford, 1959, p. 267, n. 2; E.J. Davis, 'The University Site, Bloomsbury', *London Topographical Record*, 17, 1936, p. 24.
3 *Pipe Roll 33 Henry II*, Pipe Roll Soc., 1915, p. 107. For 'herbarium' see below, p. 5.
4 *History of the King's Works*, ed. Colvin, i, 1963, p. 381, n. and fig. 39.
5 *King's Works*, i, p. 451.
6 P.F. Tytler, *England under Edward VI and Mary*, 1839, i, p. 242. In fact, there was a garden outside the walls of the castle as early as the 13th century (W.H. St J. Hope, *History of Windsor Castle*, 1913, i, pp. 69–70), but it was some distance from the royal apartments. A gallery and a terrace for walking were both built in the reign of Elizabeth I.
7 *King's Works*, ii, p. 723, n. 9. In the 13th century there was a garden 'outside the Tower' (*Calendar of Liberate Rolls 1267–72*, p. 274), but by the 16th century it was within the walls at the south-east corner.
8 *King's Works*, ii, pp. 1016–17.
9 Ibid., pp. 767–8; Public Record Office (hereafter PRO), E 101/478/26.
10 *King's Works*, ii, p. 685, fig. 58; J.H. Harvey, 'Side-lights on Kenilworth Castle', *Archaeological Journal*, 101, 1944, p. 103; report on excavation by W.M. Phelps in *Trans. Birmingham Archaeological Soc.*, 49, 1923, pp. 61–2.
11 *Pipe Roll 31 Henry I*, Pipe Roll Soc., 1929, p. 141.
12 *Building Accounts of King Henry III*, ed. Colvin, Oxford, 1971, p. 425.
13 Harvey, *Medieval Gardens*, pp. 155–8.
14 For the Tudor gardens, see *King's Works*, iv, p. 26 and index; also Roy Strong, *The Renaissance Garden in England*, 1979, ch. 2.
15 PRO, E 101/468/21, f. 35ᵛ: 'Roger de Folkeston' gardinar' operanti circa diversos herbar' alatur' et alias placeas in gardinis privatis Regis et Regine mundand', turband' et reparand' per xij dies'.
16 *Close Rolls Henry III 1261–64*, p. 29: 'in parvo herbario nostro incluso quod est apud Westmonasterium juxta appenticium plumbatum inter cameram nostram et ecclesiam Westmonasterii sex plantas pirorum de Cailhou vel amplius . . . plantari faciatis'.
17 PRO, E 101/467/7(3): 'in factur' magni herbarii inter capellam et receptam'.

18 *Calendar of Liberate Rolls 1245–51*, p. 297.

19 Ibid., p. 32.

20 W.H.St John Hope, *Windsor Castle*, i, p. 92.

21 Illustrated by Harvey, *Medieval Gardens*, plate IIIA.

22 British Library, Add. MS 17361, *anno* vi.

23 *Oeuvres de Froissart*, ed. J. Kervyn de Lettenhove, Brussels, 1871, xv, p. 167.

24 PRO, E 101/502/15.

25 E.g., vine plants brought from La Rochelle to stock the vineyard at Windsor in 1361–2 (*King's Works*, ii, p. 881, n. 4).

26 *Calendar of Patent Rolls 1307–13*, p. 557.

27 *King's Works*, ii, p. 905, n. 10.

28 Ibid., ii, pp. 881, n. 4, 992, n. 9.

29 T.F. Tout, *Chapters in Mediaeval Administrative History*, Manchester, 1928, iv, p. 211.

30 *King's Works*, ii, p. 951; PRO, E 372/104, rot 8ᵛ: 'quodam claustro cum columpnis marmoreis in gardino Regis . . . de novo faciendo'.

31 *King's Works*, ii, p. 1001; PRO, E 364/83, rot. E: 'in factura unius claustri infra manerium de Shene', etc.

32 For Hesdin, see Anne Hagopian van Buren, 'Reality and Literary Romance in the Park of Hesdin', in *Medieval Gardens*, ed. E. Macdougall, Dumbarton Oaks (Washington) 1986, pp. 115–34.

33 *King's Works*, ii, pp. 505, n. 1, 857.

34 Ibid., i, p. 245, ii, p. 998.

35 PRO, E 101/503/15.

36 *King's Works*, ii, p. 551.

37 Ibid., iv, pp. 223–4 and pl. 19.

38 M. Fernand Bournon, 'L'hôtel royal de St. Pol', *Mémoires de la Société de l'Histoire de Paris*, 5, 1878, pp. 99–100.

39 *Oeuvres de Froissart*, xv, p. 167.

40 PRO, DL 28/1/11, f. 14: carpenters 'framyng et factur' unius galr' de novo fact' iuxta cameram Regine supra parloram iuxta magnam gardinam'.

41 W.M. Mackenzie, *The Mediaeval Castle in Scotland*, London, 1927, p. 121.

42 R. Willis and J.W. Clark, *The Architectural History of the University of Cambridge*, 1886, i, pp. 569–70.

43 I say nothing of the remains of a stone-built gallery at Dartington Hall in Devonshire, partly because Dartington was not a royal house and partly because the dating of the gallery is in dispute. See Colin Platt, 'Excavations at Dartington Hall', *Archaeological Journal*, 119, 1962, and A. Emery, *Dartington Hall*, Oxford, 1970.

44 Bournon, 'St. Pol', p. 104.

45 F.P. Bargebuhr, 'The Alhambra Palace of the Eleventh Century', *Jrnl. Warburg and Courtauld Institutes*, 19, 1956, and *The Alhambra*, Berlin, 1968.

46 G. di Stefano, *Monumenti della Sicilia Normanna*, Palermo, 1955, tav. 134, pp. 145–166.

47 A.L. Poole, *From Domesday Book to Magna Carta*, Oxford, 1955, pp. 19–20.

48 For this see Anne Hagopian van Buren (n. 32 above)

49 H. Kern, *Labirinthi*, Rome, 1981, p. 329.

50 *The Works of Michael Drayton*, ed. J.W. Hebel, 1941, v, p. 102.

51 The earliest reference is in the Pipe Roll for 16 Henry III (1231–2), rot. 9. See also *Calendar of Liberate Rolls 1251–60*, p. 464.

52 For further details and references, see *King's Works*, ii, pp. 1013–15.

53 See C.H. Haskins, 'England and Sicily in the Twelfth Century', *English Historical Review*, 26, 1911, and A.L. Poole, *Domesday Book to Magna Carta*, p. 331.

54 See R.S. Loomis, 'Tristram and the House of Anjou', *Modern Language Review*, 17, 1922, pp. 24–30, and 'Vestiges of Tristram in London', *Burlington Mag.*, 41, 1922, pp. 54–60. See also G. Schoepperle, *Tristan and Isolt*, New York, 1913, *passim*, and R. Lejeune, 'Rôle littéraire d'Aliénor d'Aquitaine', *Cultura Neolatina*, 14, 1954, pp. 5–57.

55 Teresa McLean, *Medieval English Gardens*, London, 1981, p. 78.

56 Some medieval English gardens have in fact been archaeologically surveyed (though not excavated): see Christopher Taylor, *The Archaeology of Gardens*, Shire Archaeology, 1983, and notes in *Medieval Archaeology*, 28, 1984, pp. 199–200 and 34, 1990, pp. 155–7.

II

WAS THERE A 'COURT STYLE' IN MEDIEVAL ENGLISH ARCHITECTURE?

IN RECENT WRITINGS on English medieval architecture the concept of a 'court style' has assumed an important place. The expression was, I believe, first used by the late Maurice Hastings in an article published in the *Architectural Review* in 1949,[1] and subsequently in his book on *St Stephen's Chapel* (1955). Geoffrey Webb took it up in his Pelican volume on *British Architecture in the Middle Ages* (1956) and it is frequently met with both in Jean Bony's brilliant book on *The English Decorated Style* (1979) and in John Harvey's complementary volume on *The Perpendicular Style* (1978).

Hastings sought to find a 'court style' exemplified in St Stephen's Chapel (begun in 1292, but not completed until the reign of Edward III), a building in which he also saw the origins of the Perpendicular style, which could thus be connected at its birth with the court. With St Stephen's Chapel he associated other buildings in London and Westminster, including Old St Paul's, the Guildhall, and the Greyfriars' and Blackfriars' churches. What these had in common, he said, was the fact that 'they were the work of, or supervised by, the King's masons.' Geoffrey Webb and Jean Bony both use the term freely in connection with such buildings as the Eleanor Crosses, the Bishop of Ely's chapel in Holborn and Merton College Chapel, which share common stylistic characteristics. For them, as for John Harvey, the 'court style' is simply the prevailing architectural style favoured by the court, which sets the pace for the rest of the country. 'The royal taste,' Harvey says, 'set a fashion which was soon universal and which had a natural growth under a succession of chief architects, the master masons to the Crown, and their pupils.' The fashion which he, like Hastings, is particularly concerned to trace is the one known to us as 'Perpendicular', whose dissemination he attributes to 'the highest levels of the Court', though his account of its genesis differs from (and is to be preferred to) that of Hastings.[2]

As the medieval English kings were, almost without exception, great builders, it is not unreasonable to suppose that, at any given time, there was a recognisable architectural style associated with the royal court. If, however, the idea of a 'court style' is to have any real meaning, it must be demonstrated either that the architectural taste of the court was in advance (or perhaps, since courts are sometimes conservative places, in arrear) of the taste of the country as a whole, or at least that it was marked by some characteristic idiosyncrasy: in short, that it had some aesthetic identity that can be singled out by the architectural historian. And it must be shown that that identity was either consciously fostered by the personal interest of the king or his leading courtiers, or else maintained (perhaps less consciously) by a body of architectural designers – master masons and master carpenters – forming part of the royal establishment. There may be some periods when this is self-evidently true: Henry III's leadership in taste, his leaning towards French architectural forms, is well-known: so is the leadership in Tudor domestic architecture given by the palace-building activity of Henry VII and Henry VIII. But in the two intervening centuries the architectural patronage of the court is less easy to define, much less easy to distinguish from that of the secular lords and the great ecclesiastical corporations. The personal initiative of the king is often difficult to discern, partly because the loss of the Privy Seal records has deprived us of much of the documentary evidence upon which to assess it, partly because building, unlike literature or painting, is to some extent a necessity rather than a luxury, and does not necessarily imply any conscious patronage of architecture as an art. Moreover, at a time when every great lord, whether secular or ecclesiastical, was in some sense a courtier, how are we to distinguish between the court and the courtiers?

The stock of houses used by the court was, moreover, being constantly renewed, and as constantly depleted, by confiscation on the one hand and by grant on the other. Of the eighty-odd houses owned by the Crown between 1066 and 1485, almost half had been acquired from a former baronial or ecclesiastical owner by forfeiture, purchase or inheritance, and very few indeed remained continuously in royal occupation from the twelfth century to the fifteenth: effectively only Westminster, Woodstock and Clarendon.[3] So most royal houses must have been indistinguishable (except, perhaps, by heraldic insignia) from private ones, and only Westminster was normally referred to as a 'palace'.[4] It is above all at Westminster that we must look for signs of a 'court style'. For not only was Westminster the heart of the court, it was the headquarters of the royal works.

Now, as we have seen, the idea of a 'court style' in architecture implies a body of expertise to maintain it, and previous writers have seen the officers of the royal works in this role. It has indeed been natural to suppose that an organisation that in the seventeenth and eighteenth centuries formed the core of the architectural profession in England fulfilled something of the same function in the fourteenth and fifteenth. Such a supposition is explicit in John Harvey's paper 'The Medieval Office of Works', published in 1941,[5] and it has been implicit in much that has been written since. Harvey started with the assumption that there was a central office of works at Westminster from 1256 onwards and that this office was served by a regular succession of master craftsmen holding established posts giving them authority over all the king's works south of Trent. 1256 was the year in which Henry III, dissatisfied with the conduct of his works in the traditional way by sheriffs and other local officials, entrusted them to two experienced craftsmen directly responsible to himself: Master John of Gloucester as master mason and Master Alexander the carpenter for his trade. This was seen by Knoop and Jones as 'marking the beginning of the Office of Works',[6] and Harvey concurred. In a sense this is true, but it must be emphasised that the appointments made in 1256 were personal and perhaps experimental, and did not in fact outlast the lives of the two individuals concerned. Master John died in 1260, Master Alexander probably in 1269, but it is doubtful whether he executed his functions effectively after the king's defeat at the Battle of Lewes in 1264. Thereafter there were no permanent offices held by chief craftsmen with general authority over the king's works in their respective trades until 1336 – nor were there clerks of the works with similar authority. Master James of St George's position as 'master of the king's works in Wales' from 1278 to 1307 was unique and personal to himself. When works were ordered at one of the king's houses or castles the appropriate craftsmen were of course engaged, but even at Westminster there was no regular succession of master masons and master carpenters throughout the reigns of Edward I, Edward II and Edward III.[7]

In 1336, however, another set of appointments was made which in the case of the carpenter (but not that of the mason) did prove to be permanent. But the authority of the craftsmen concerned was formally limited to the Tower of London and to the king's castles south of Trent. For some reason no mention was made of Westminster or of the royal manor-houses. It is difficult to follow Harvey in his assertion that these appointments 'mark the definite assumption of control by Edward III over the architectural establishment'.[8] We know too little of the circumstances in which they were made to justify so large a claim. They may just as well be interpreted as an attempt to make better provision for routine maintenance. But for the Black Death, in which both the mason, William of Ramsey, and his successor, John atte Green, perished, it is possible that they would have *created* an architectural establishment, but as it was there was to be no Master Mason of all the king's works for over a quarter of a century, and it was not until 1378 that a properly constituted office of works was established, with a Clerk of the King's Works at its head, in a form that was to last, with modifications, right up to the era of economical reform in the eighteenth century. This, it may be noted, was undoubtedly an administrative measure attributable rather (to adopt modern terminology) to the civil service than to the court, for it was effected during the king's minority, and at a time when no works of any importance were either in progress or in contemplation. In fact there is good reason to attribute it to the initiative of the Treasurer, Thomas Brantingham.[9] It is, therefore, only from the reign of Richard II onwards that there was at Westminster an established corps of craftsmen who may, by the continuity of their offices, and the prestige of their official appointments, have formed the personnel of a 'court school'. In the twelfth and thirteenth centuries, and for much of the fourteenth, craftsmen were recruited as and when they were required, moving from private to royal service and back again as the king's needs and their own ambitions might dictate. Some, like James of St George and probably Henry 'de Reyns', might be fetched from abroad to serve the king in his works. Others, like John of Gloucester, Robert of Beverley, Michael of Canterbury or William of Ramsey, bore the names of places with famous churches of their own, and are at least as likely to have learned their skill in local ecclesiastical workshops as in the royal yard at Westminster. Once engaged, it is true, some of these men spent most or all of their careers in the king's service. But for others the royal employment was only an incident, however important, in their lives, and the Crown was only one of many possible patrons. The fact that the Crown is also (with one or two exceptions) the only medieval patron of architecture to have preserved the bulk of its administrative records intact means that the careers of many medieval masons and carpenters are known only because at some time or other they served the king. The extent of their work for private patrons can never be known. In these circumstances it is easy to exaggerate the role of the Crown as a patron of medieval craftsmen and to assume that because a man is referred to as 'the king's mason' or 'the king's carpenter', he was a permanent employee of the court. Generally the term has no such significance, and only the granting of a title of office, or the payment of a regular fee, can prove that a craftsman was permanently retained. Even then, the king might have no monopoly of his services. In the reign of Edward III the mason William of Wynford was retained simultaneously by the king and the dean and chapter of Wells.[10] Henry Yevele had a large and flourishing architectural practice that was in no way inhibited by his promotion, in 1378, to be the king's master mason.[11] Yevele, like many other prominent craftsmen employed by the king, was a citizen of London, and the proximity of the city must never be forgotten in any attempt to assess the importance of Westminster as an artistic centre. London was the home of many of the craftsmen employed by the king at his palace, and in the later Middle Ages at least, its gilds and companies would have formed a framework for their lives which must have been at least as important as the royal service.[12] Indeed, when Hastings, and after him Professor Bony, speak of 'the Court Style of London', or of 'the Court Style based in London', they seem to be recognising that the court was only the most prestigious of London's customers, and that what they really mean is 'the metropolitan style', or 'the style in fashion at London and Westminster'. St Stephen's Chapel and the Eleanor Crosses may mark important innovations in Gothic design, but (as Harvey has shown) it was in the City, at St Paul's Cathedral, in the new Chapter House begun in 1332, that William of Ramsey inaugurated the Perpendicular style four years before he entered the royal service as master mason at the Tower of London.[13]

Even in Westminster itself the king was not the only patron of building craftsmen, for the abbey maintained its own works organisation and provided almost continuous employment for masons, some of whom passed from the service of the monks to that of the crown.[14] Westminster Abbey was exceptional because the completion of its nave was a major task that went on intermittently from 1376 almost until the dissolution.[15] But other great abbeys were also nurseries of building craftsmen. When Henry VI began to build King's College Chapel it was Reginald Ely, an East Anglian, not a Westminster mason, who received the commission, and Simon Clerk and John Wastell, who continued his work, were both connected with Bury St Edmund's.[16] At Eton, Henry at first entrusted the works to his Master Mason, Robert Westerley, but by the time the design was completely revised in 1448 Westerley's place at Eton had been taken by John Smyth, a Canterbury mason who had been his second-in-command; and when Smyth became master mason of Westminster Abbey in 1453 the Bury mason Simon Clerk took his place at Eton.[17] Thus the two great royal chapels were effectively designed by masons from outside the office of the king's works, and although in the early sixteenth century there was to be some consultation between the masons employed by the king at Westminster and those at work on the chapel at Cambridge, the building that, as Horace Walpole put it, is 'alone sufficient to ennoble any age', cannot be regarded in any real sense as a product of a 'court school'. If we were to look for a Lancastrian 'court style' the place to find it would have been in Henry V's new house at Sheen, with its satellite religious houses at Sheen and Syon, of which we know little as works of architecture, possibly also in Humphrey, Duke of Gloucester's manor-house at Greenwich, of which we know even less. In King's College Chapel only in the portion built by Henry VII does the elaborate heraldic display directly reflect the taste of a later court and remind us that if anyone deserves to be 'taxed with vain expense' in connection with the building of King's College Chapel it is Henry VII rather than the 'royal saint' his kinsman.

It is by no means my purpose to belittle the importance of the king's works in the history of medieval English architecture. That the Crown sought the services of the most eminent architectural designers is unquestionable, and that it provided many of them with exceptional opportunities to display their skill is obvious. Moreover, by the use, from Edward III's time onwards, of its powers of impress-ment, it sucked workmen from all over the country into its works, giving them involuntary experience of working under its chosen masters, experience which (however unwelcome) must sometimes have transformed the ideas of a provincial mason confronted for the first time with the innovations of a Michael of Canter-bury or a William of Ramsey.[18] The importance of impressment as a vehicle of architectural influence may indeed have been considerable. But the concept of a 'court style' remains ill-defined and requires careful handling if it is not to degen-erate into a mere cliché devoid of any real historical validity.

How far, then, can the idea of a 'court style' in medieval English architecture be regarded as acceptable? Must we reject it as too imprecise to be worth retaining, or can it be redefined in such a way as to serve a useful historical function? Some examples may help to suggest contexts in which the term can be legitimately employed, others where it can not.

As an example of the former I have already mentioned the building activities of Henry III. By his personal enthusiasm and his employment of a master mason with French experience, he was able to build in Westminster a major exemplar of the French *rayonnant* style which had its architectural progeny at Hereford, Hailes, Salisbury and elsewhere.[19] Here the aesthetic initiative undoubtedly lay with the court, indeed with the king himself, and as Hailes Abbey was founded by his brother Richard, Earl of Cornwall, and as Hereford Cathedral was rebuilt under the auspices of Henry's protégé, the Savoyard bishop Peter of Aigueblanche, we can legitimately associate a specific style with Henry III's court. Moreover it was, as we have seen, in Henry's reign that a first attempt was made to establish some degree of central control over all the king's works: an attempt that failed to survive the collapse of Henry's government, but one that may nevertheless serve to underline the connection between a court style and a central works organisation.

Edward I again imported a foreign master to design the castles which were his great architectural achievement, and as the court was for much of his reign on a war footing, the distinctive type of 'concentric' castle associated with Master James of St George might well be regarded as exemplifying the 'court style' of a warrior king. However it is to the exquisitely elegant Eleanor Crosses, with their complex geometrical forms, including ogee arches (the earliest known) that the term has more generally been applied. They were indeed built by masons who, with one exception, all had previous connections of one kind or another with the royal works,[20] and although none of these masons held any specific office at court, and probably met one another quite as often in the London Guildhall as in the Great Hall at Westminster, their workmanship must have received the approval of the queen's executors, one of whom was the Chancellor, the discriminating Robert Burnell, Bishop of Bath and Wells. To that extent the Eleanor Crosses may be said to represent the taste of Edward I's court in the 1290s, though they may equally well be said to represent the decorative style favoured by the leading London masons of the day.

Edward II is, perhaps, more likely than his father to have consciously fostered a court style, for we have evidence of alterations to a ship (the *Margaret* of Westminster that was to fetch Queen Isabella from France) and the building of a new chamber in the palace being done *per proprium divisamentum Regis*, and his critics' complaints of his addiction to base and mechanical arts take on a new significance when we find that he retained a group of twelve to twenty carpenters who travelled round with him everywhere and were responsible both for the maintenance of the household carts and boats and for repairs and minor alterations to the castles and manor-houses visited by the king. They were paid by the Chamber, and much of their work was done at the group of manors directly administered by that household department, notably Burstwick, Byfleet, Cowick, Easthampstead, Hadleigh and King's Langley. As virtually nothing now remains of any of these buildings we are not in a position to judge to what extent Edward II's houses exemplified a recognisable 'court style'. But the employment, in 1325, of eleven of these *carpentarii de familia regis* on the woodwork of St Stephen's Chapel does provide a tenuous link between the most important royal work of the 1320s and the inner circle of Edward II's court.[21]

As for St Stephen's Chapel itself, it was begun by a mason whose background was in Canterbury, and completed by another who had strong connections with Norwich.[22] Though both of them had become established in London before they were engaged on the chapel, they brought with them styles already developed in Kent and East Anglia, a circumstance which serves to demonstrate how far the court was from being the seat of an established 'school' in the reigns of the first two Edwards. Indeed, when Master Michael of Canterbury began work on the chapel in 1292 there was evidently neither workshop nor masons' lodge at Westminster, since one of the first tasks was the erection of these necessary buildings.[23] Moreover, from 1297 to 1320 and again from 1325 to 1331 work had to be suspended as a result of national crises, so (although continuity was maintained by the re-employment of Master Michael of Canterbury in 1320, and of Master Thomas of Canterbury – perhaps his son, certainly a relation – in 1331) Westminster was hardly the home of a continuously active masons' shop throughout the period when it is particularly supposed to have been the centre of diffusion of a 'court style'. It would be nearer the truth to represent St Stephen's Chapel (as at last structurally completed – though not yet glazed or furnished – in 1348) as the showpiece of the London masons of the early fourteenth century.

Edward III's enormously expensive works at Windsor probably deserve more attention in this context than they have received, but so little has survived the successive remodellings of the seventeenth, eighteenth and nineteenth centuries that it is difficult to characterise the architectural style of his new buildings in the Upper Ward. However, the surviving portions of the college of St George which he built in the Lower Ward show that this was an early – though not the earliest – example of Perpendicular design,[24] and had they survived intact Edward III's works in the Upper Ward might well figure more prominently than they do in the history of English medieval architecture. They do at least illustrate the way in which membership of the court could serve to disseminate new architectural ideas, for it was undoubtedly from Windsor that both New College, Oxford, and Winchester College derived important features of their distinctive planning, and their founder, William of Wykeham, was of course the clerk of Edward III's works at Windsor.[25]

Richard II is well known as the rebuilder of Westminster Hall, whose hammer-beam roof is one of the supreme achievements of medieval English architecture. So large and ambitious a roof must have had predecessors, and several possible candidates have been put forward. Among them are the roofs (all destroyed) of the great halls of Arundel Castle, Dartington Hall and Kenilworth Castle. As the first was built by Richard's 'governor', the Earl of Arundel, the second by his half-brother John Holand, Earl of Huntingdon, and the third by his uncle, John of Gaunt, we are perhaps entitled to think of the hammer-beam roof as something particularly favoured by Richard II's court, especially as at Dartington his White Hart badge is prominent in the still surviving porch.[26] Moreover, although we do not know who was employed to build the roofs of the three baronial halls, the master carpenter at Westminster was Hugh Herland, who had been the king's Master Carpenter since the 1370s. He was the successor (and almost certainly the son) of William Herland, who had held the same office from 1354 to 1375 in succession to William Hurley, the designer of the octagon at Ely, an earlier *tour de force* of English carpentry. Here in fact we have an authentic case of the cumulative experience of three generations of men closely associated with the royal works and we can legitimately regard the roof of Westminster Hall as a product of the 'court school' of carpenters.

The tradition of expertise in structural and decorative carpentry was, indeed, a marked feature of the royal works in the later Middle Ages. The timber-framed roof, more or less decorative in character, is as characteristic a feature of English fifteenth-century churches as the stone-vaulted roof is of French ones. It is therefore interesting to find that when Henry V decided to build a royal palace at Rouen in 1419, he employed French masons, but English carpenters.[27] Again it is the roof, rather than the masonry, that marks Edward IV's great hall at Eltham as a major architectural achievement. Here pendants have taken the place of angels as the characteristic decoration of the hammer-beams, and, as Geoffrey Webb observed, when the same effect is achieved in stone, as in the Divinity School at Oxford and later in Henry VII's Chapel at Westminster, it is tempting to see it as a case of the masons emulating the carpenters.[28]

This does not exhaust the episodes in the history of the king's works in late medieval England which might deserve consideration in this discussion, but I hope I have said enough to indicate the degree of caution with which a judicious historian, whether of architecture or of culture, should approach the concept of a 'court style'. There are, of course, other, more technical criteria which also need to be borne in mind. Once it has become institutionalised, a body like the office of the king's works is liable to develop certain tricks of execution that can be recognised as characteristic. Mouldings are a case in point. In recent years a great deal of valuable work has been done on mouldings by John Harvey, Richard Morris and Eileen Roberts, and although much of it has been directed towards the association of specific mouldings with individual masters, rather than with the royal works as such, Morris has identified one moulding whose diffusion can be related to Edward I's works in North Wales.[29] More of this painstaking analysis of mouldings might well help to build up a stylistic identikit of the royal works at particular periods. Meanwhile some characteristic methods of jointing employed by the king's carpenters in the Tudor period have been observed by Cecil Hewitt.[30] I am not aware that any detailed study has yet been made of the brickwork of the Tudor royal palaces, but (although it was not until 1609 that an office of Master Bricklayer was established) the exact specification of the size of bricks to be used at Woking in 1534[31] might suggest that as early as the reign of Henry VIII the officers of the king's works were moving towards some degree of standardisation. Draughtsmanship is another sphere in which a sense of corporate identity can be expressed. In the eighteenth century, for instance, the Office of Works and the Office of Ordnance each had a characteristic style of draughtsmanship that is quite distinctive. The sum total of medieval or Tudor architectural drawings surviving in English archives is too pitifully small for any such office styles to be distinguished today, but throughout the fifteenth century there was in the office of the Clerk of the King's Works at Westminster a 'long oak chest made to keep the patrons [i.e. drawings] and instruments belonging to the chief mason',[32] and if we could inspect its contents it would not be surprising if we could recognise some conventions of presentation, perhaps even some recurrent motifs, as characteristic of the royal works. If we could, we should have gone far towards identifying that 'court style' which it has been the purpose of this paper to confine within somewhat narrower, and, I hope, more intellectually acceptable limits than it has sometimes been allowed to assume in the past.

Notes

1 'The Court Style', *Architectural Review*, cv, Jan. 1949, pp. 3–9.

2 *The Perpendicular Style*, 1978, pp. 14, 44.

3 For the relevant details see *The History of the King's Works*, ed. H.M. Colvin, ii, 1963, ch. xiv ('The King's Houses 1066–1485', by R.A. Brown and H.M. Colvin).

4 Ibid., i, p. 120, n. 4.

5 *Jrnl. British Archaeological Assn.*, 3rd ser. vi, 1941.

6 *An Introduction to Freemasonry*, Manchester, 1937, p. 72.

7 See *King's Works*, i, pp. 105–8, 175–8.

8 *The Perpendicular Style*, 1978, p. 50.

9 *King's Works*, i, pp. 189–90, 210.

10 J.H. Harvey, *English Mediaeval Architects*, 1954, p. 308 (2nd ed., 1984, p. 352).

11 Ibid., pp. 312–19 (2nd ed., 1984, pp. 358–66). Harvey's work on Yevele was the subject of a critical review by A.D. McLees in which the limitations of the documentary evidence were stressed in a salutary manner, though little attention was paid to architectural evidence: *Jrnl. British Archaeological Assn.*, 3rd ser. xxxvi, 1973, pp. 52–71.

12 For the London Masons' Company and its antecedents, see D. Knoop and G.P. Jones, *The Medieval Mason*, Manchester, 1933, reprinted with corrections, 1967.

13 J.H. Harvey, 'The origins of the Perpendicular Style', in *Studies in Building History*, ed. E.M. Jope, 1961, and *The Perpendicular Style*, 1978.

14 Notably William Colchester and William Redman. Redman's father was master mason to the abbey before him, and William had had twenty years' experience in the abbey works before he became the king's Master Mason in 1519.

15 R.B. Rackham, 'The Nave of Westminster', *Proceedings of the British Academy*, iv, 1909–10.

16 See their biographies by Arthur Oswald in J.H. Harvey's *English Mediaeval Architects*, 1954, 2nd ed., 1984.

17 *King's Works*, i, pp. 280, 284.

18 On the exercise of the right of impressment see *King's Works*, i, pp. 180–4.

19 Ibid., pp. 154–5.

20 Ibid., p. 483.

21 Ibid., pp. 179–80, 506.

22 For Master Michael of Canterbury and Master William of Ramsey see Harvey, *English Mediaeval Architects*, and for the latter also Harvey, *The Perpendicular Style*, pp. 47–8.

23 *King's Works*, i, p. 510.

24 See J.H. Harvey in *Report of the Society of the Friends of St George's*, Windsor, 1961, pp. 52–5.

25 On the relationship between New College and Winchester College on the one hand and Windsor Castle on the other, see Harvey, *The Perpendicular Style*, p. 133, and Gervase Jackson-Stops's contribution to *New College, Oxford*, ed. J. Buxton and Penry Williams, Oxford, 1979, pp. 149–64.

26 For the hammer-beam roof see A. Emery, *Dartington Hall*, Oxford, 1970, pp. 237–44.

27 *King's Works*, i, p. 461.

28 *Architecture in Britain: The Middle Ages*, Harmondsworth, 1956, pp. 194, 200.

29 Richard K. Morris, 'The development of later Gothic mouldings in England *c*.1250–1400', *Architectural History*, xxi, 1978, p. 27.

30 In a note appended to Sir W. Addison, *Queen Elizabeth's Hunting Lodge and Epping Forest Museum*, Loughton, 1978.

31 *King's Works*, iv, p. 162.

32 Ibid., i, p. 201.

III

CHURCH BUILDING
IN DEVON IN THE SIXTEENTH CENTURY

THE CHURCHES OF Devon and Cornwall form an exceptionally coherent group. The average village church in these two counties is instantly recognisable. From a distance there is the contrast between the tall west tower and the long, relatively low, roofs of the nave and chancel and aisles. There is no clerestory and the pitched roofs run on to end in a trinity of gables at the east end. On a closer approach the masonry often proves to be of hard granite, sparkling in the sun. Inside, there is no structural division between nave and chancel, and two rows of monolithic granite columns support long waggon roofs. An intricately carved screen, once surmounted by a rood-loft, runs right across from wall to wall, separating chancel and any eastern side-chapels from nave and aisles. Often there are carved bench-ends as well, and sometimes a pulpit to match.

Although relics of earlier periods are apparent here and there, what we see is predominantly the work of the fifteenth and early sixteenth centuries. The standard format, with its characteristic mouldings, window tracery and other details, was, Pevsner wrote in 1951, 'the same in Devon as in Cornwall'.[1] 'They were,' he says, 'certainly established by 1400; but where they came from, and when they were introduced, is not yet sufficiently certain.' Nearly fifty years later the genesis of the Perpendicular church in Devon and Cornwall still remains to be worked out, but there would probably be general agreement that the date by which it can be seen to have been established would now be set a little later than Pevsner's 1400.

It is, however, with the end, not the beginnings, of late medieval church-building in Devon and the neighbouring parts of Cornwall that this essay is concerned. Here, as elsewhere, the history of English church architecture in the sixteenth century is overshadowed by the Reformation. Suddenly, the accumulated riches of five centuries of Catholic piety were arbitrarily rejected by men for whom a new religious conviction meant, as it all too often does, the casting aside of everything that a previous generation had cherished. Monasteries were pulled down or unroofed to degenerate into ruins that a later generation would find picturesque. Chantries were abolished, pilgrimages proscribed, churches stripped of many of their ornaments in stone, wood and glass. A whole culture of piety was brought abruptly to an end.[2]

Architecturally, Protestantism had little to offer in its place. It was not until after the Great Fire of London in 1666 that the Anglican Church found its architectural feet. Before that Anglicans of whatever persuasion all accommodated their differing ideas about the proprieties of religious worship to existing medieval fabrics – removing a screen here or rearranging a chancel there for services in which the sermon had become the principal event. Radical attempts to create interiors suitable for Protestant worship were left to the Calvinist Scots (Burntisland, Fife, c.1592–5), the French Huguenots (Lyon, the Paradis, c.1564) and the Nonconformists, so far as they were allowed to build at all.[3] Piety was not dead, but now it was schools and almshouses rather than churches and chapels that were seen as proper objects for the generosity of the wealthy.

Much of the evidence for post-Reformation church building in England was published by Jack Simmons in 1959 under the title of 'Brooke Church, Rutland, with notes on Elizabethan Church Building'.[4] Although Simmons was able to find over seventy examples of Elizabethan church-building in England, most of them were, like Brooke Church itself, fairly modest and often only partial reconstructions of decayed medieval churches, rarely of much architectural interest. None of them represented any significant new fashion in church-building, nor were most of them motivated by anything more than the necessity of maintaining a place of worship. There are one or two isolated examples of something more ambitious, notably Standish Church in Lancashire (1584–9), externally a complete Perpendicular church of some size with Tuscan arcades within, or the great church which Robert Dudley, Earl of Leicester, began to build at Denbigh in 1578, but never completed.[5] The only other constructions that were not enforced by necessity were the funerary

5. Calstock Church, Cornwall: the Edgecumbe Chapel and vestry built in 1588 at the east ends of the north and south aisles respectively.

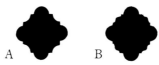

A   B

6. Types of piers characteristic of Devonshire churches in the fifteenth and sixteenth centuries. The simpler type (A) was the one most easily worked in granite, often as a monolith (after Pevsner).

chapels which those gentry and aristocracy who had not inherited a former chantry chapel built to contain their family monuments and sometimes to accommodate their seigneurial pew. Of these, at least a dozen were built in the reigns of Mary and Elizabeth, more early in the seventeenth century, and a few of these were in Devon and Cornwall[6] (fig. 5).

Simmons's list of Elizabethan church buildings included no examples at all from Devonshire and only one (and that merely a porch) from Cornwall, probably because in his excellent book on *Devon*, published in 1954 in a series edited by Simmons himself, W.G. Hoskins had stated that 'The great period of rebuilding and refurnishing of the Devon churches lasted up to the 1540s, and then stopped except for minor changes internally. It seems likely [he continued] that, for the next two or three generations after 1550, many churches were allowed to fall into serious disrepair.'[7] Although in this, as in other periods, there is certainly some evidence of churches falling into decay, a general charge of neglect and disrepair is hardly supported by perusing the random sample of Elizabethan churchwardens' accounts from Devonshire that happen to be in print. They afford ample evidence of repairs to roofs and battlements, to the clearing of gutters, pointing of walls and mending of windows throughout the second half of the sixteenth century.[8] Moreover, in many churches both in Devon and in Cornwall, finely carved bench-ends with Renaissance detailing show that the needs of a congregation listening to a sermon rather than praying to an image soon attracted the attention of churchwardens and sometimes the generosity of private benefactors. As Pevsner noted, and as a recent study by Joanna Mattingly confirms, such benches continued to be made throughout the sixteenth and on into the early seventeenth century.[9] Still, it would hardly be surprising if, after the successive attacks on traditional religious practices in the 1530s and 1540s and the vandalism that so often accompanied them, the enthusiasm that had built so many towers and aisles and rood-screens in late medieval Devon was not sustained. Although, as I hope to show, there may have been a little more post-Reformation church building in Devon than Hoskins, and more recently Whiting,[10] have allowed, it does not amount to enough to alter the general picture of a church-building slump in the second half of the sixteenth century compared with the pre-Reformation boom.

The architectural results of that boom have, however, never been critically examined. For Whiting church architecture was incidental to his main theme, the state of popular religion before and after the Reformation, and although Hoskins had an intimate knowledge of Devonshire churches, his priorities were social and economic rather than ecclesiological. Pevsner, faced with a relatively humble architecture of almost vernacular character, succinctly analysed its principal features (especially the two characteristic types of pier, fig. 6), but did not put them into a

7. Tiverton Church, Devon: the chantry chapel built by John Greenway, a wool merchant, in 1517.

chronological framework. What follows is basically an attempt to do just that and in so doing to facilitate further study of a highly distinctive region by both architectural and ecclesiastical historians.

To the three most famous examples of Tudor church-building in Devon: the Greenway Chapel at Tiverton (1517) (fig. 7), the fan-vaulted Dorset aisle at Ottery St Mary (c.1520–30) and the similarly vaulted Lane aisle at Cullompton (c.1526) (figs. 8, 9), I shall not devote much attention, as these were all sophisticated works which must almost certainly have been designed by masons from outside the county, and which had little influence within it. The Lane aisle at Cullompton and the Dorset aisle at Ottery St Mary do, however, conform to local convention in one respect: assuming that they were both intended to house chantries (though at Ottery there is no evidence that one was ever actually established), they take the form of aisles rather than of self-contained chapels, something that is very common in Devon in the fifteenth and sixteenth centuries. Just as chancel and nave were normally separated only by a screen rather than by a stone arch, so the distinction between private and parochial space tended to be defined by parclose screens rather than by structural features. When such screens survive, they are sometimes decorated with the arms of the families who paid for them, as at Kentisbeare and Ugborough.[11] The legal status of such semi-private aisles could be equivocal. Only a year after his death, John Lane's widow was outraged to find that other parishioners were presuming to use his newly-built aisle for their own burials.[12] The proprietary rights in aisles built wholly or partly at private expense often persisted after the Reformation. Over two centuries later, Dean Milles of Exeter, in his manuscript survey of Devonshire churches, noted a surprisingly large number of aisles as belonging to local estates, presumably because their owners had inherited burial rights from their medieval or Tudor predecessors.[13]

In Devon, as elsewhere, the evidence of church-building is partly architectural and partly documentary. Here the documentary evidence is rather scanty, for although sixteenth-century churchwardens' accounts are preserved for a number of parishes, few of them come from churches where building was in progress during the years covered by the accounts. Wills, the Exeter diocesan records, and one or two lawsuits provide some valuable evidence here and there. There are also a few inscriptions, chiefly on capitals, where it was a local custom to record the names of those who had paid for the work. Good examples, dating from the late fifteenth or early sixteenth centuries, can be seen at Berry Pomeroy and Honiton. Dates are occasionally added: 1547 at Instow, 1564 at Morwenstow, 1593 at Northam. At Parkham, near Bideford, the south aisle can be approximately dated by initials carved in a script similar to that used at Launceston Church, built between 1511 and 1524, while the initials GR on a respond of the north aisle or chapel confirm the statement of the seventeenth-century Devonshire antiquary Tristram Risdon that this part of the church was built by his grandfather Giles Risdon, who died in 1583, aged 90.[14]

Because of the conservatism of Tudor church architecture in the south-west, purely architectural evidence needs careful handling. The characteristic forms of piers, arches, roofs and other architectural features, including towers, tend to remain

8. Cullompton Church, Devon: Lane's aisle, built by John Lane, a cloth merchant, *circa* 1526.

9. Cullompton Church, Devon: plan adapted from one of 1844 by Harold Brakspear. The south porch was originally an internal porch at the west end of the fifteenth-century south aisle. The south wall of the aisle was removed to build Lane's aisle *circa* 1526 and a new west tower was built on the north side of the porch in 1545–9.

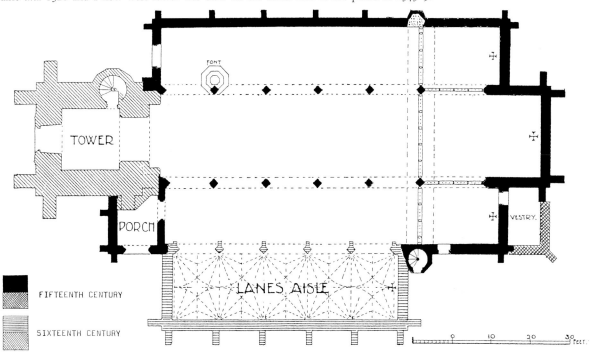

10. Throwleigh Church, Devon: the west tower.   11. Christow Church, Devon: the west tower, dated 1630.

essentially unchanged not merely through the sixteenth, but well into the seventeenth century too. This can be illustrated by two pairs of almost identical church towers, both of characteristic local types: one at Throwleigh, reputedly of *circa* 1500, and Christow, dated 1630 by an inscription (figs. 10 and 11); the other from the South Hams, with a prominent stair-turret in the middle of one side, at South Milton (medieval) and Stockenham (dated 1636).

One feature does change, however, and that is window tracery. Although conventional Perpendicular tracery persists, especially in east windows, two new forms of tracery are found in Tudor Devon and Cornwall. One of these is the square-headed window with two, three or even four uncusped lights, widely employed in Tudor architecture, both ecclesiastical and secular, throughout England. The other is a type of window peculiar to Devon and north-east Cornwall and so common in the South Hams that it may conveniently be called the 'South Hams window'.

To take the square-headed window first: it had probably reached the south-west by the reign of Henry VII, but so far the earliest reliably datable examples that I have found in church architecture are those lighting the walls of the chantry chapel at Coldridge, built by John Evans in about 1510[15] (fig. 12). It also occurs in another, grander, chantry chapel, the Bourchier Chapel added to the south aisle of Tawstock Church by John Bourchier, 2nd Earl of Bath, between 1539 and his second marriage in 1548[16] (fig. 13). There are other, more or less precisely dated, examples

28

12. Coldridge Church, Devon: the chapel built *circa* 1510 by John Evans, keeper of Coldridge Park.

13. (*below*) Tawstock Church, Devon: the Bourchier Chapel built by John Bourchier, 2nd Earl of Bath, in the 1540s.

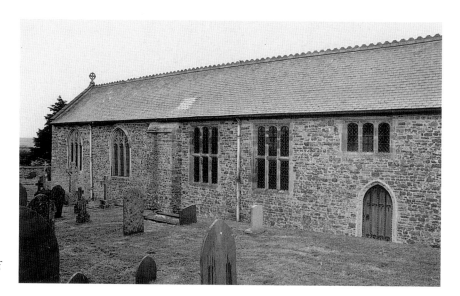

14. Atherington Church, Devon: sixteenth-century windows on the north side of the nave.

at Thornbury, a church burnt down in 1524 and rebuilt with the aid of an indulgence,[17] in an aisle at Littleham built in 1528,[18] at Woodland, near Newton Abbot, and in the north aisle of Instow Church near Barnstaple. Woodland Church was built to serve a newly created parish and was consecrated in 1536.[19] It consists of a four-bay nave-cum-chancel and a north aisle. Here, as often in Devon, the windows in the eastern gables are ogival with Perpendicular tracery, while those in the lower side walls are of the square-headed kind. At Instow a new north aisle was built in 1547 by Richard Waterman and his wife, as recorded by an inscription on the capitals of the arcade.[20] Here too, the windows are square-headed. At Sampford Courtenay windows of this kind still contain glass which must be pre-Reformation, since it depicts the Virgin Mary, but is presumably early sixteenth-century because there are Renaissance motifs in the borders. There are a good many other examples of this sort of window in Devonshire churches, and some of these, as at Lustleigh and East Ogwell, may well be of similar date.[21] But elsewhere in England, for instance at Stoke Poges in Buckinghamshire, windows of this type are found in chapels built thirty or forty years later in the reign of Queen Elizabeth I, and some of those in Devon may be Elizabethan too, for instance at Westleigh, where the absence of buttresses tends to support a late date, and at Alwington, where not only are there no buttresses, but the mullions run straight up without any arched lights between them. Nor can there be much doubt about the late date of the mullioned and transomed windows on the north side of Atherington Church (fig. 14): similar windows are a prominent feature of Blundell's School at Tiverton, built in 1604.[22] But without documentary or other evidence the dating of other examples of this simple type of window remains problematical.

I now turn to what I have called the South Hams window. Unlike the square-headed window it is a speciality of Devon.[23] It exists in both three- and four-light forms. In the three-light version the upper side-lights may or may not be cusped,

30

15. Throwleigh Church, Devon: the north aisle lit by four windows with 'South Hams' tracery. The central lights are not arched.

and there is often no arch to the central light (figs. 15, 22). Typologically it is tempting to see here the progressive simplification of a conventional late Gothic window, which loses first the cusping in its central light, then in its subsidiary lights and finally the central arch, but it is difficult to demonstrate this in practice. Ultimately the side-lights droop feebly, as at Loddiswell (fig. 25). Needless to say, these windows were regarded with distaste by nineteenth-century ecclesiologists: 'an ugly kind of window often found hereabouts', noted Sir Stephen Glynn in 1870.[24] 'The very worst style of debased Perpendicular' was the verdict of the local antiquary Charles Worthy in 1875.[25] Mostly, though not invariably, made of hard moorstone granite (fig. 16), their simplified form was no doubt designed to mitigate the difficulty of working this intractable material. They also had the merit of admitting plenty of light into the naves of aisled churches which, in the absence of clerestory windows, would otherwise have been rather dark.

South Hams windows occur in well over thirty churches in Devon and in at least three in north-east Cornwall.[26] Although they are to be found all over the former county except in the east, by far the greatest concentration is in the South Hams (fig. 17). Rustic and debased though many of them are, they may nevertheless be useful evidence for the chronology of church building in Tudor Devon and Cornwall.

A valuable clue to the dating of these windows is provided by Marldon Church. Marldon belonged to the Gilberts of nearby Compton Castle, and the church was largely built by Otho Gilbert, who was sheriff of Devon in 1475 and died in 1494. Originally it was a chapelry of Paignton, but later it obtained parochial status. In his will, dated December 1493, Otho expressed his wish to be buried 'in the north part of the chapell of Marldon under the foote of our lady, the which chapell partely I have builded'.[27] The church was probably newly built in 1485, when he obtained a licence to found a perpetual chantry at the altar of St Mary in Marldon Church.[28]

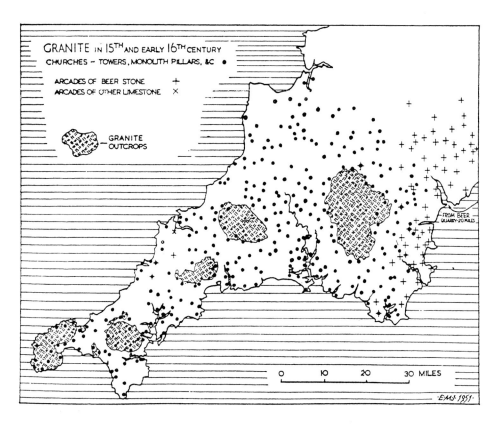

16. Map of Devon and Cornwall showing churches with arcades and other features built of granite, drawn by the late Professor E.M. Jope.

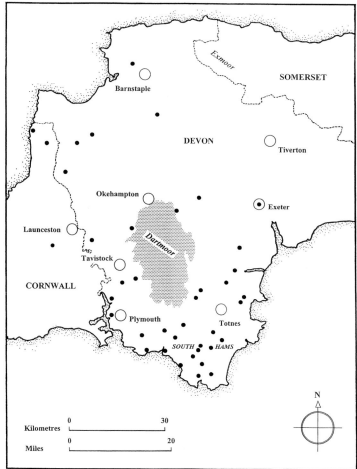

17. Churches in Devon and Cornwall with 'South Hams' windows (drawn by Dr Edward Impey). The churches marked are listed on p. 48.

18. (*above*) Marldon Church, Devon: the north aisle built by Otho Gilbert (d. 1494).

19. Marldon Church, Devon: the south-east chapel built by John Gilbert (d. 1539).

20. Buckland Monachorum Church, Devon: 'South Hams' windows with cusped side-lights in the north chancel aisle.

Then in 1532 his son, John Gilbert, directed that his body should be buried 'in the church of Marledon within the Chapell late by me bilded'.[29] Now the north chapel of Marldon Church, where Otho was buried (and where his curious miniature effigy was placed), has conventional Perpendicular tracery in its windows, but the south chapel, evidently the one built by John, has South Hams windows with cusps in their upper side-lights (figs. 18, 19). Here, therefore, Perpendicular tracery was

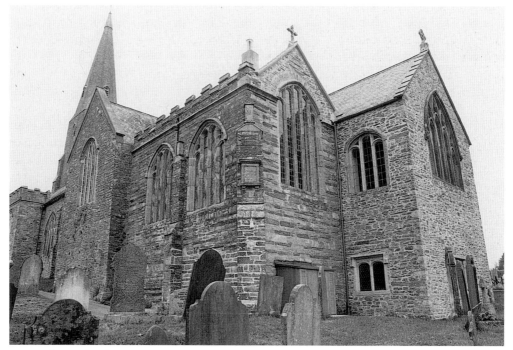

21. Modbury Church, Devon, from the south-east, showing 'South Hams' windows with and without cusped side-lights. The buttresses were added early in the eighteenth century.

still in use in about 1485, but by the late 1520s, when we may suppose John Gilbert was building his chapel, South Hams tracery had been invented.

Other examples of the South Hams window with cusped upper side-lights are (or were) to be seen in the churches of Buckland Monachorum (fig. 20), All Hallows, Exeter (demolished in 1906),[30] Halwell, Modbury (fig. 21) and Ugborough (north-east chapel). At Modbury and Ugborough the windows in question lighted what must have been chantry chapels, built probably by the Champernowne and Fowel families respectively. At Modbury the Champernowne arms were still to be seen in the east window of the south-east chapel in the eighteenth century.[31] Unfortunately no licence to endow chantries in either of these churches can be found. By this time legal devices to evade the Statute of Mortmain were available; chantries were apt to be established in ways that did not attract unwelcome attention from the Crown, and that consequently left no trace in the public records.[32] So here we have no documentary evidence to date the building of the chapels. At Ugborough, where the north-east chapel is lit by South Hams windows with cusps, the south-east chapel has South Hams windows without cusps. The latter chapel is separated from the chancel by a screen with a shield of arms identifiable as those of the Fountain family of Bowcombe in Ugborough parish, but the date remains uncertain.[33]

There are, however, several South Hams windows without cusps to which approximate dates can tentatively be assigned. One is the west window of the north aisle at Heanton Punchardon near Barnstaple. This aisle appears to be one built in about 1540 by a mason called Robert Terell from a neighbouring village.[34] Only the west window is of the South Hams type, the others in the low north wall being square-headed. The aisle was intended to serve as a gild chapel. Just over the county boundary at Morwenstow in Cornwall both north and south aisles are lit by windows of the South Hams type. These, like the tower, may date from the late 1540s, when some valuables were pawned by the churchwardens 'for the finishing of the tower and windows'.[35] At East Allington in the South Hams, where the screen is said to be dated 1547,[36] a general Tudor rebuilding, unfortunately obscured by the insertion of Victorian tracery in all but two of the windows in 1875, may date from the same period. The two surviving windows are of the South Hams type, and the round-headed south doorway is of a decidedly unmedieval form. The set of uncusped South Hams windows which light the north aisle of Blackawton Church (and appear to be an original feature of it) must, however, be somewhat earlier, for one of the capitals of the associated north arcade bears the arms of Torre Abbey, a major landowner in the parish, which was dissolved in 1539, and the screen, which extends into the aisle, has the initials H and A on two of its panels, for Henry VIII and Catherine of Aragon, whose marriage lasted from 1509 to 1533.[37] At Modbury, where virtually every window has South Hams tracery, the churchwardens' accounts show that a new window was made in 1547/8. Described as 'the wyndowe by the processyon dore', it can perhaps be identified as the one in the north wall of the north transept.[38]

So it looks as if the South Hams window, with or without cusps, was in vogue from the 1520s onwards, and that it can probably be regarded as a characteristic

22. Chudleigh Church, Devon: the south aisle built in 1552. The doorway of the original internal porch can be seen in the westernmost bay. The doorway in the third bay from the west is a recent insertion.

23. Chudleigh Church, Devon: sketch-plan showing the south aisle and porch added in 1552.

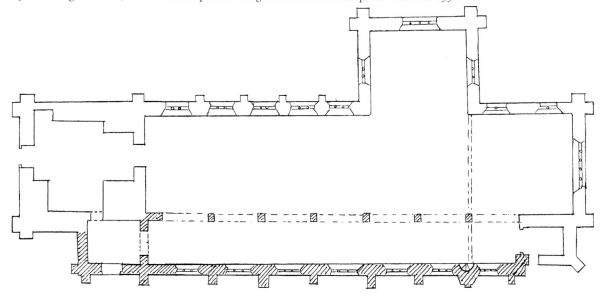

feature of Devonshire church architecture in the reign of Henry VIII. That it was still in use in that of Edward VI is demonstrated by Chudleigh Church, where churchwardens' accounts still extant in the nineteenth century but since lost showed that the south aisle and porch (fig. 22) were built in 1552. Owing apparently to a misprint, this date appears as 1582 in Mary Jones's *History of Chudleigh*, published in 1852, but in her source, a manuscript history of Chudleigh by her brother, the Revd J.P. Jones, the date is given as 1552, and as the accounts for 1582, which are still extant, show no evidence of building activity in that year, 1552 is evidently the correct date.[39] The long, narrow aisle (fig. 23) is separated from the nave by an arcade of standard Devonshire granite piers whose mid-sixteenth-century date is betrayed only by the slightly unusual chamfered blocks on which they stand. The provision for a rood-loft stair reminds us that in Devon the rood and its loft were generally taken down with the greatest reluctance and almost invariably set up again immediately after Mary's accession.[40] Although roods were everywhere removed early in Elizabeth's reign in obedience to the royal injunctions of 1559, some rood-lofts survived much longer. This was evidently the case at Chudleigh, where, despite the expenditure of 1s. 4d. in 1562 'For taking downe the Roode lofte and making a new Deske', the operation was repeated in 1577, when the rood-loft was pulled down and a cresting put up in its place.[41] In Lancashire, another county whose people were obstinately devoted to the old religion, a church (Standish) could be rebuilt complete with rood-loft stairs as late as 1582,[42] so the provision of stairs at Chudleigh in 1552 need cause no surprise.

A feature of the new south aisle at Chudleigh to which attention should be drawn is the way the south porch was economically integrated into its west end, entrance to the church being gained through a doorway in the east wall of the internal porch. Porches so situated are a Devonshire peculiarity, occurring, or formerly occurring, at Bulkworthy, Cockington, Cullompton (fig. 9), Dawlish and Feniton.[43] Besides Chudleigh, there are four other churches in South Devon where this feature forms part of an aisle lit by South Hams windows: Dodbrooke (fig. 24), Highweek, East Allington and Loddiswell. As we have seen, the aisle at East Allington can perhaps be dated to the 1540s by its screen, that at Chudleigh more definitely to 1552 by the lost churchwardens' accounts. At Highweek it was stated in 1904 by a competent local historian that the aisle was 'supposed' to have been 'built in the time of Queen Mary'.[44] Although he did not say why or by whom, the dating is so unusual that it must presumably have had some basis in record or tradition. Evidence of a different kind may suggest a similar Marian dating for the aisle at Dodbrooke. Two reliable antiquaries of the eighteenth and early nineteenth centuries – Dean Milles and Samuel Lysons – both testify to the former existence in the South Hams windows of stained glass representing saints with triple crowns over their heads.[45] If (as is likely) these were papal saints, they could hardly date from the latter part of the reign of Henry VIII, but they could well have been Marian, which might in turn suggest that the aisle was built as well as glazed some time between 1553 and 1558.[46] Expressions of religious or political loyalty in stained glass were not unknown in Tudor Devon, for in 1566/7 the churchwardens of Tavistock spent 15s. 6d. on having the queen's arms and those of their lord, the Earl

24. Dodbrooke Church, Devon: the south aisle and internal porch, probably built in the mid-sixteenth century.

25. Loddiswell Church, Devon: the south aisle and internal porch, probably built in the mid-sixteenth century.

26. (*above*) St Budeaux Church, Devon, from the south-east.

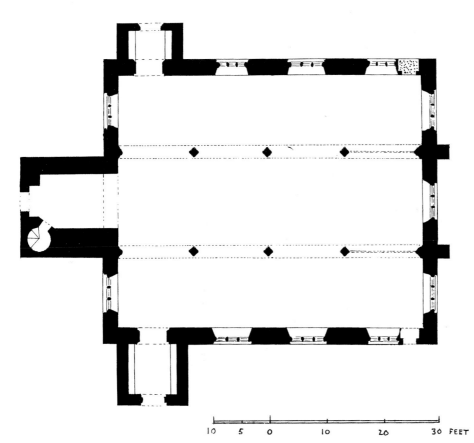

10 5 0 10 20 30 FEET

27. St Budeaux Church, Devon, built in 1563–4: ground-plan.

of Bedford, set into one of the windows in their church.[47] As for the fourth church, Loddiswell, there is nothing to date the aisle, but the crudity of the tracery (fig. 25) would fit in well with a mid-sixteenth-century date.

My next exhibit is the church of St Budeaux, a village now on the northern outskirts of Plymouth. The fact that this church was rebuilt in the reign of Elizabeth I was noted by Tristram Risdon in his *Survey of Devon*, written early in the seventeenth century. He says that the former church stood 'in a remote and unhealthy place by the sea side' and that the new one was built in a better situation by Robert Budshead (or Budockshead), the lord of the manor, at his own expense.[48] A note in the parish register records the first baptism 'in the new church' on 30 July 1564, and the date of erection is given as 1563 by Lysons and others.[49]

St Budeaux Church is a simple building, consisting of an aisled nave and chancel of the usual Devon type (fig. 27), that is to say, without a chancel arch or other structural division between the two, and without a clerestory; the piers conform to one of the two types (the one labelled A by Pevsner) that were standard in pre-Reformation Devon. At the east end there are three three-light windows with normal Perpendicular tracery, but at the west end both aisles are lit by windows with South Hams tracery, and there is another South Hams window symmetrically placed in the middle of the south wall, between two three-light square-headed windows (fig. 26). This symmetrical grouping of the windows is the chief architectural indication that this is an Elizabethan and not a medieval church. Inside, as a former incumbent noted, there is 'no trace of screen or roodloft, stoups, piscinae, sedilia, or other vestiges of Romanist worship'.[50] A square-headed Tudor doorway at the east end of the south aisle and a similar one, now blocked, on the north side, probably indicate that the east ends of both aisles were intended for use as family chapels, and slots in the eastern piers and responds suggest that there were screens of some sort between them and the chancel. The northern chapel does in fact contain monuments to members of the Budshead family.

More doubtful examples of Elizabethan church-building are to be found at Dean Prior near Ashburton and at Kilkhampton in north-east Cornwall. At Dean Prior the surviving churchwardens' accounts, starting in 1567, record in the first year the writing of the Ten Commandments, the 'makyng of the Table', and the sale of three altar-stones and of a considerable quantity of lime (it fetched £24).[51] This looks like the aftermath of a building campaign or at least of the belated adaptation of the church to Protestant worship. Unfortunately Dean Prior Church was largely reconstructed in 1853, and although both aisles are lighted by South Hams windows it would be rash to claim that they or any other part of the existing fabric date from the 1560s.

At Kilkhampton there is a large church all of one build with the exception of the porch and tower, and originally lit entirely by windows of the South Hams type. The three eastern ones were mischievously replaced by Scott in 1858–60, but fortunately there is an excellent record of the previous appearance of the church made by Buckler in 1827 (fig. 28). Note the absence of buttresses, often an indication of late date. The rebuilding may have been due to the Grenvilles, who

28. Kilkhampton Church, Cornwall, as drawn by John Buckler in 1827 (British Library, Add. MS 36360, f. 155).

lived at Stowe House in the parish. Their arms appear, or formerly appeared, on the font and its cover, and in scutcheons over the arcades as well as over the door of their burial vault at the east end of the south aisle (now resited over the adjoining priest's door in the south wall). On the porch is the date 1567 and the initials of John Grenville, presented to the rectory in 1524 by his father, Sir John Grenville, who retained his benefice through all the changes of the reigns of Henry VIII, Edward VI, Mary and Elizabeth, until his death 'at a patriarchal age' in 1580.[52] It was largely on the strength of this dated porch that J.C. Cox considered that the whole church was Elizabethan.[53] Unfortunately the porch is not of one build with the wall of the aisle, and the existence of rood-loft stairs and of an aumbry or piscina in the Grenville Chapel make it more likely that the church was built before the Reformation than under the patronage of the Protestant Grenvilles in the reign of Elizabeth.

Then there is Northam Church near Barnstaple, where an inscription on one of the piers of the north aisle records its building in 1593 or 1595 ('This yele was made anno 1593'). The building contract was still extant in the 1830s, and the raising of the money among the parishioners is recorded in a manuscript in the Bodleian Library.[54] The arcade survives with large clumsy cubical capitals, but the outer wall and windows were rebuilt in 1849–65, so their original form remains unknown. Finally there is Walkhampton Church, whose south aisle, built of large blocks of coursed granite with South Hams windows (fig. 29), must be Elizabethan if not

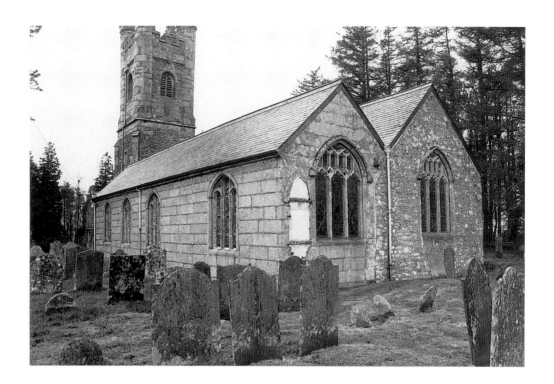

29. (*above*) Walkhampton Church, Devon, showing the south aisle, probably built *circa* 1600.

30. Kelly Church, Devon: one of the two 'South Hams' windows in the south wall of the chancel, dated 1710.

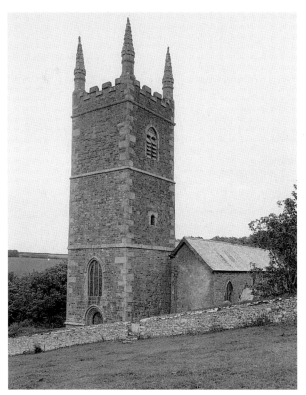

31. Morwenstow Church, Cornwall, showing the west tower, built *circa* 1540.

32. Witheridge Church, Devon: the west tower, begun in or soon after 1568.

Jacobean. There appears to be no documentary evidence, but Hoskins' dating to *c.*1600 cannot be far wrong.[55]

It would be tedious to describe all the other churches with South Hams windows somewhere in their fabric. Those so far noted total thirty-seven in Devon and three in Cornwall.* There may be a few more that have escaped my notice or whose windows were replaced in the nineteenth century. About half the total represents the building or rebuilding or at least the refenestration of one or both aisles, the remainder the partial refenestration of existing naves, aisles or chancels. In the absence of churchwardens' accounts or other documentary evidence reliable dates are difficult to establish, and only a detailed structural analysis of each church might make it clear precisely what place the South Hams windows have in its architectural history. But if the indications of date given above for Marldon, East Allington and Chudleigh are accepted, this type of window was clearly a common feature of Devonshire church architecture in the sixteenth century, and particularly in the reign of Henry VIII. Its persistence into the seventeenth century is illustrated by windows dated 1641–2 at St Petrox, Dartmouth, and 1685 at Thurlestone. Positively its last appearance is at Kelly in 1710 (fig. 30).

A Tudor date is also likely for a number of church towers in Devon and Cornwall: the one at Morwenstow (fig. 31), which was under construction in 1540, has already been mentioned. A much grander tower, that at Cullompton, was begun in 1545 and completed four years later, in the reign of Edward VI (fig. 33).

* See Appendix, p. 48.

33. Cullompton Church, Devon: the west tower, built in 1545–9 in a Somerset style.

34. Lydford Church, Devon: the west tower, probably built early in the seventeenth century.

Typologically, however, it belongs to Somerset rather than to Devon, and was not influential in its own county.[56] There are a good many relatively simple towers similar to the one at Morwenstow which may likewise be sixteenth-century but are mostly impossible to date with any confidence, though one at Witheridge (fig. 32) is known to have been begun in or soon after 1568, when there was a bequest 'to the beginning of the building of the Tower of the church at Witheridge'.[57] Only a systematic typological study might achieve some results. Meanwhile it may be pointed out that at Morwenstow the west window of the tower is of a modified South Hams type, and that as similar windows are to be found in several Devon-shire towers, such as Highweek, Cockington, Modbury and Lydford, they too may be sixteenth-century in date. This is probably true of Highweek and Cockington, but not of Modbury, where the window is clearly an insertion into an older tower, presumably contemporary with other South Hams windows in this church. At Lydford, however, it is an original feature of the tower. This tower (fig. 34) is neither dated nor documented, but its large granite ashlar masonry, its round-headed belfry windows and structural indications of an earlier tower, all suggest that

45

it is post-Reformation. It is, in fact, a slightly reduced version of the tower at Christow, about seven miles west of Exeter, which is clearly dated 1630 on its doorway, and is itself a fine version of one of the standard types of late medieval tower in Devon, with clasping buttresses and the staircase not expressed externally (fig. 11). A third tower of this type at Exbourne is built of the same large granite ashlar and exhibits some curious detailing that is very likely early seventeenth-century. Other seventeenth-century church towers in Devon, all obstinately conservative, are Stokenham (1636), Burlescombe (1638?) (fig. 35), Charles Church, Plymouth (1657), Clyst Hydon (1665) and Pilton (1696).[58] On such tower, at Goodleigh near Barnstaple, is said to have been built in the reign of Charles II.[59] It has a west window with simple intersecting tracery of a type which is found in several other west towers, some of which may perhaps be seventeenth-century too.

There is, therefore, considerable evidence of church-building in Devon in the sixteenth century, particularly in the reign of Henry VIII, of some further activity here and there in the second half of the century, and of a revival of tower-building in the early seventeenth century. Architecturally, it is conservative, rustic, even (if a pun may be permitted) somewhat ham-fisted. But survivals deserve attention as well as innovations and revivals, and these churches are of more than merely antiquarian interest, for the volume of church-building in the south-west in the Reformation period has been called in evidence in the historical debate about the strength of popular religion in the face of Protestant attack. In his book on the subject, published in 1989, Robert Whiting listed thirty-two 'church-building projects' (towers, aisles, porches, etc.), datable between the years 1520 and 1570.[60] If the reader is persuaded that South Hams windows are characteristic of church architecture in Devon during that period, then Whiting's total needs to be roughly doubled. If, in addition, some undated aisles with square-headed windows are included, the total, though indeterminate, becomes substantial.

How is this localised church-building activity, possibly greater than in any part of England at that time, to be explained? The answer is probably as much economic and demographic as religious. By the mid-sixteenth century Devon had become one of England's wealthier counties, a producer of wool of increasingly good quality and a major manufacturer and exporter of woollen cloth of various kinds.[61] This was the time of 'high farming', which lasted well into the eighteenth century and brought prosperity to Devon gentry and yeomen farmers, especially in the fertile South Hams, with their rich soil and favourable climate. As John Aubrey tells us, the Devonshire men had the reputation of being 'the earliest Improvers', and he reported a saying of Oliver Cromwell that 'he had been in all the Counties of England, and that the Devonshire husbandry was the best.'[62] Fishing was also profitable, and tin and other metals were mined on Dartmoor. As a result, Devonshire was one of the most heavily populated counties in Tudor England.[63] Between 1524 and 1570 the number of able-bodied men liable to be mustered rose from 11,720 to some 17,000.[64] No parochial figures are available before the institution of parish registers in 1538, but in one South Hams parish (Thurlestone) whose registers have been studied statistically, there was between 1559 and 1599 an excess of 114 baptisms over burials, and that in a population of only 300 plus.[65] At Plymtree,

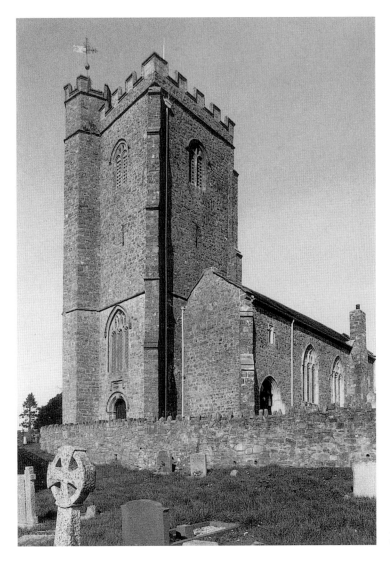

35. Burlescombe Church, Devon: the west tower, built in the 1630s.

another South Devon parish, the number of births recorded between 1538 and 1600 was nearly double the number of deaths, 405 to 209.[66]

The need for enlarged churches is therefore not surprising. It was felt in the city of Exeter as well as in the villages. Exeter's minuscule churches were quite inadequate for the large Protestant congregations of the late sixteenth century. In 1581 and again in 1601 the city tried to obtain an Act of Parliament authorising the suppression of several small parishes and their amalgamation into a single large one with a big church capable of holding 2,000 people. The scheme was defeated by the Bishop, who feared to lose his patronage in the city.[67] But had that church been built, it would obviously have been a major example of Elizabethan church-building – probably the largest and most important of its date in England. It would also have been the most striking demonstration both of the need for bigger churches in Tudor Devon, of which I have tried to set out the considerable architectural as well as the somewhat exiguous documentary evidence, and of the extent to which the men of Devon were still active in maintaining and sometimes in enlarging their places of worship both during and after the period of the Reformation.

APPENDIX

List of churches in Devon and Cornwall with 'South Hams' windows presumed to be of sixteenth-century date:

DEVON
Bere Ferrers
Blackawton
Brixton (windows altered in nineteenth century)
Buckfastleigh
Buckland Monachorum
Bulkworthy
Chudleigh
Churchstow
Cockington
Dean Prior (largely rebuilt 1853, presumably following original design of tracery).
Denbury
Dodbrooke (N aisle added 1887 copies original South Hams windows in S aisle).
East Allington
Ermington
Exeter, All Hallows (demolished 1906)
Halwell
Heanton Punchardon
High Bickington
Highweek
Hittisleigh

Kingsbridge
Kingston (N wall rebuilt to original design 1892–3)
Loddiswell
Lydford
Malborough
Marldon
Modbury
Pyworthy
Revelstoke
St Budeaux
South Pool
Sutcombe
Throwleigh
Thurlestone
Ugborough
Walkhampton
Woodleigh

CORNWALL
Kilkhampton
Lewannick
Morwenstow
? Stratton (in N aisle, rebuilt in nineteenth century, perhaps following original design)

Notes

1 *Cornwall* (The Buildings of England), 1951, p. 18; cf. *Devon* (2nd ed. by Bridget Cherry, 1989), pp. 42–4.

2 On this subject see particularly Eamon Duffy, *The Stripping of the Altars. Traditional Religion in England 1400–1580* (Yale, 1992).

3 For Burntisland see the *Fife* volume of the Buildings of Scotland, for the Paradis at Lyon, David Thompson, 'Protestant Temples in France *c.*1566–1623' in *L'Église dans l'architecture de la Renaissance*, ed. J. Guillaume (De Architectura series, Paris, 1995).

4 *Trans. Leicestershire Archaeological Soc.*, xxxv, 1959.

5 For Standish see *Trans. Historic Society of Lancs. and Cheshire*, NS xix, xx and xxii, 1903–4 and 1906, and Malcolm Airs, 'Lawrence Shipway, Freemason', *Architectural History*, 27, 1984. For Leicester's church at Denbigh see the article by Lawrence Butler in *Jrnl. British Archaeological Assn.*, 3rd ser. xxxvii, 1974.

6 At Calstock in Cornwall the Edgecombe Chapel at the east end of the north aisle (fig. 5) was built in 1588 by Richard Edgecombe of Cothele, whose memorial slab records the fact. For another example at St Budeaux (1563) see below, p. 40. In the eighteenth century the incumbent of Northleigh told Dean Milles that 'the N. Isle seems to have been added by the Haydons about Q. Elizabeth's time' (Bodleian Library, MS Top. Devon b. 2, f. 5), but it has since been too drastically altered to retain any obviously Elizabethan work.

7 W.G. Hoskins, *Devon* (A New Survey of England), 1954, p. 272.

8 See *Churchwardens' Accounts of Ashburton 1479–1580*, ed. A. Harnham, Devon & Cornwall Record Soc., NS xv, 1970; J.R. Chanter, *Memorials of St Peter's Church, Barnstaple*, 1882, pp. 77–85; *The Churchwardens' Accounts of St Michael's Church, Chagford 1480–1600*, ed. F.M. Osborne, Chagford, 1979; *Kilmington Churchwardens' Accounts*, ed. R. Cornish, Exeter, 1901; a Milton Abbot account for 1588 printed in *Monthly Mag.* 29, 1810, pp. 458–62; 'Molland Accounts', ed. J.B. Phear in *Trans. Devonshire Association*, xxxv, 1903, pp. 211–38; South Tawton, ibid. xxxviii–xli, 1906–9; Stratton (Cornwall) in *Archaeologia*, xlvi, 1881, pp. 195–236, and *The Records of Blanchminster's Charity*, ed. R.W. Goulding, Louth 1898; R.N. Worth, *Calendar of Tavistock Parish Records*, Tavistock, 1887.

9 Pevsner and Cherry, *Devon*, 1989, p. 49; Joanna Mattingly, 'The Dating of Bench-ends in Cornish Churches', *Jrnl. Royal Institution of Cornwall*, NS ii (1), 1991.

10 Robert Whiting, *The Blind Devotion of the People, Popular Religion and the English Reformation*, Cambridge, 1989, pp. 94, 264.

11 At Kentisbeare the arms are those of John Whyting (d. 1529), who is buried in the chapel. For Ugborough see below.

12 Whiting, *The Blind Devotion of the People*, pp. 30–1.

13 Bodleian Library, MSS Top. Devon c. 8–12.

14 *Risdon's Survey of Devon* (1811), p. 243. For the Risdon family see J.L. Vivian, *Visitations of the County of Devon*, 1890–5, p. 648. Unfortunately all the windows in Parkham Church were replaced in the nineteenth century.

15 Evan's effigy is on the north side of the chapel, and his name as *factor istius operis ann. regni Regis Henrici octavi secundo* is carved on the desk of a pew.

16 These dates are determined by the coat of arms carved over the doorway of the chapel. An earl's coronet dates it after Bourchier's succession to the title in 1539, and the impaled arms of his first wife Eleanor, who died in 1547, make it earlier than his second marriage in 1548.

17 D.H. Pill in *Trans. Devonshire Assn.*, 98, 1966, p. 267.

18 The ultimate source of this date, given by Pevsner and E.R. Delderfield, *Exmouth Milestones*, Exmouth, 1948, has not been traced.

19 The consecration is recorded in Bishop Vesey's Register, vol. 11, f. 82.

20 'RYCHARD. WATERMAN EMMA. HYS. WYF' and 'THE. YERE. OF. OURE. LORDE. GOD. MDXLVII'.

21 At Lustleigh a figure of the Virgin Mary still survived in one of these windows in the eighteenth century (Bodleian Library, MS Top. Devon c. 10, f. 97).

22 According to the 'Historical Notes' sold in Atherington Church, the north aisle was built in 1579. Although the aisle is clearly earlier, this may well be the date of the windows.

23 The only other examples known to me are a window in the brick transept or funerary chapel added

to Little Hadham Church, Herts., in *c.*1600, and two in the tower of St Bartholomew's Church, Smithfield, London, built in 1628.

24 Notes on Devonshire churches by Sir Stephen Glynn, printed in *Notes & Queries*, 164, 1933, p. 169.

25 Charles Worthy, *Ashburton and its Neighbourhood*, Ashburton, 1875, p. 139.

26 Stratton may provide a fourth example in Cornwall, but the windows in question (in the north aisle) were rebuilt in the nineteenth century, though presumably to their original design.

27 PRO, PROB 11/10, f. 11.

28 *Calendar of Patent Rolls 1476–85*, p. 522.

29 PRO, PROB 11/27, f. 29.

30 Illustrated by B. Cresswell, *The Churches of Exeter*, 1908, p. 7.

31 Bodleian Library, MS Top. Devon c. 10, f. 143.

32 For legal evasion see Kreider, *English Chantries*, 1979, pp. 75 et seq.

33 For help in identifying the arms I am indebted to Dr J.M. Robinson. For the Fountain family see J.L. Vivian, *The Visitations of the County of Devon*, 1895, p. 369.

34 John Harvey, *English Mediaeval Architects*, rev. ed. 1984. p. 295.

35 Whiting, *The Blind Devotion of the People*, p. 93, citing P.R.O., E 117/1/48.

36 F. Bligh Bond and Dom Bede Camm, *Roodscreens and Roodlofts*, 1909, ii, 287; Pevsner and Cherry, *Devon*, p. 346.

37 Bond and Camm, *Roodscreens and Roodlofts*, p. 294.

38 The entry in the churchwardens' accounts for 1547/8 (Devon Record Office, 269A PW 5) is as follows: 'unto Rogger Palmer for hys comyng to make the bargayne of the wyndowe by the processyon dore viijd. Item payd the masons for makyng of the same wyndowe xxvjs. viijd. Item payd unto Stephyn Skynner for takyng down of the old wyndowe xijd.' It seems unlikely that the door in question was the main south doorway, and the one at the west end is called the 'steeple door' elsewhere in the accounts.

39 See Jones's MS in the Bodleian Library, MS Top. Devon e. 3, f. 16ᵛ. The surviving churchwardens' accounts are in the Devon Record Office, Chudleigh PW 1.

40 E. Duffy, *The Stripping of the Altars*, especially pp. 497–502.

41 Bond & Camm, *Roodscreens and Roodlofts*, p. 305.

42 See note 5 above.

43 Plans of those at Cockington and Feniton will be found in *Exeter Diocesan Architectural Soc.'s Trans.*, I (2), 1843, p. 181. At Dawlish (destroyed in 1824) the same arrangement was noted by Dean Milles in the 18th century (Bodleian Library, MS Top. Devon c. 9, f. 78). South Huish (now in ruins) appears to have been another example.

44 A.J. Rhodes, *Newton Abbot: Its History and Development*, Newton Abbot, 1904, p. 105.

45 Bodleian Library, MS Top. Devon c. 9, f. 94; BL, Add. MS 9694, f. 28.

46 I am grateful to Dr Hilary Wayment for his comments.

47 R.N. Worth, *Calendar of the Tavistock Parish Records*, 1887, p. 29.

48 T. Risdon, *Survey of the County of Devon*, 1811, p. 209.

49 S. Lysons, *Magna Britannia: Devonshire*, 1822, p. 89.

50 *South Devon Monthly Magazine*, iv, 1834, p. 141.

51 Devon Record Office, Dean Prior PW 1.

52 A.L. Rowse, *Tudor Cornwall*, 1941, p. 155.

53 J.C. Cox, *The Churches of Cornwall*, 1912, p. 134.

54 In 1831 the incumbent informed John Dunkin that the N aisle was built in 1595 at a cost of £75, 'as appears from the contract . . . lodged in the parish chest' (Dunkin's notes on Devonshire churches in National Art Library, 86 FF 66, f. 80). For the raising of the money see Bodleian Library, MS Top. Devon b. 2, f. 75 and the churchwardens' accounts in the County Record Office, which confirm the date 1595.

55 *Devon*, p. 511.

56 G. Oliver, *Ecclesiastical Antiquities in Devon*, i, 1840, p. 109. An inscription, now illegible, recorded that work on the tower began in 1545. Another Devon tower of Somerset type, that at Chittlehampton, has been dated to the 1520s on typological grounds (P.P. Wright, *The Parish Church Towers of Somerset*, 1981, p. 193).

57 *Devon & Cornwall Notes & Queries*, 19, 1936, p. 163. This tower was for long only two storeys high, the present upper stage and pinnacles being added during the incumbency of the Revd W.P. Thomas (1832–43).

58 Stokenham tower is dated 1636 by large iron figures on the door (now inside the church). At Charles Church, Plymouth, the dates 1657 and 1708 recorded the building of the tower and of the spire respectively. The masons' contract for the tower at Clyst Hydon, dated 15 Jan. 1664/5, is in the Cathedral Library, episcopal MS 765. The rebuilding in 1696 of the tower at Pilton (destroyed in the Civil War) is recorded by an inscription.

59 F.J. Snell, *Devonshire* (Mate's County Series, 1907), p. 79. The fact that there had been a former tower in a different position was remembered in the eighteenth century (Bodleian Library, MS Top. Devon b. 1, f. 234).

60 R. Whiting, *The Blind Devotion of the People*, pp. 87, 281.

61 Hoskins, *Devon*, pp. 62–3, 94–5; G.E. Fussell, 'Four Centuries of Farming Systems in Devon 1500–1900', *Trans. Devonshire Assn.*, 83, 1951; P.J. Bowden, *The Wool Trade in Tudor and Stuart England*, 1971, p. 33.

62 Bodleian Library, MS Aubrey 2, f. 83; Robert Fraser, *General View of the County of Devon*, 1794, p. 17.

63 Hoskins, *Devon*, p. 170.

64 Whiting, *The Blind Devotion of the People*, p. 8.

65 N.C. Oswald, 'Thurlestone Families', *Trans. Devonshire Assn.*, 110, 1978, p. 54.

66 The *Registers of Plymtree*, ed. Etty, Devon & Cornwall Record Soc., 1970.

67 W. MacCaffrey, *Exeter 1540–1640*, Harvard, 1958, pp. 196–7.

IV

RECYCLING THE MONASTERIES: DEMOLITION AND REUSE BY THE TUDOR GOVERNMENT, 1536–47

THE DISSOLUTION OF the monasteries was arguably the greatest single act of architectural vandalism in English, perhaps even in European history. Though far more grievous, the destruction of ancient Rome was effected over many centuries and by many agencies. The damage done by warfare, from the sieges and sackings of the Middle Ages to the bombings and shellings of the twentieth century, never resulted in the general destruction of any given category of monument throughout an entire country. The French Revolution did indeed leave its mark on almost every church in France, but even there it was the symbols of the *ancien régime* rather than the buildings as such that were sought out for destruction, which varied in its thoroughness from one place to another.

But in England between 1536 and 1540 every monastery was dissolved in a country whose culture had for five hundred years been largely embodied in its churches and religious houses, and the great majority of their buildings were (to use the contemporary expressions) 'plucked down' or 'defaced'. This was done by the authority of a grasping and tyrannical king, and effected by his minister, Thomas Cromwell, through subordinates who were for the most part ruthless, cynical and philistine men. That the monasteries, as institutions, deserved their fate, is of course a debatable question which it is not my purpose to discuss here. But the government that, rightly or wrongly, decided to extirpate what their detractors called those 'caterpillars', the monks and friars, felt no obligation whatever to preserve the garden that they had inhabited – or should one say infested? – for so long. In all the mass of letters and papers relating to the dissolution it is hard to find any hint that either Thomas Cromwell or his agents recognised that there was any force in the rebel Aske's claim that 'the said Abbeys was one of the beauties of this realm to all men and to strangers passing through the same.'[1] The king's chaplain, Thomas Starkey, did indeed protest that it was a shame to destroy 'so much fair housing and goodly building', as a result of which 'our country might appear to be defaced as [if] it had been lately overrun in time of war', but it was of no avail.[2] Even to Starkey the problem was as much social as aesthetic, and to others the architectural loss was naturally secondary to the religious one. What outraged them was sacrilege rather than vandalism, the destruction of the tombs of their ancestors rather than the loss of outstanding works of sculpture, the disappearance of a source of employment and hospitality rather than of the complex of buildings on which it had been based. Too often it is not until it is already too late that men begin to appreciate the work of previous generations, and it needed the shock of the 'bare ruin'd choirs' to arouse in antiquaries such as Dugdale, Dodsworth, Erdeswicke and Aubrey that sense of the past that has been with us ever since. With the monasteries there perished many funerary monuments, and in 1560 a royal proclamation against 'defacers of monuments in churches' showed that Queen Elizabeth herself was concerned at the loss of these memorials of family history. An even more precocious expression of interest in the visual relics of the past occurred in 1562, when, following a general survey of the castles of the Duchy of Lancaster, a high-powered committee headed by the Lord Treasurer (William St John, Marquess of Winchester) decided that nearly all of them should be preserved for one reason or another, one (Tutbury) because it was 'old and statly', another (Pontefract) because it was 'an honourable castle' and a third (Tickhill) because it was deemed to be 'an ancient monument'.[3]

But to Henry VIII and his ministers the buildings of the monasteries they were dissolving were something to be disposed of to the best advantage, without sentiment or regret. They might be seen either as premises to be converted to other purposes, as properties to be sold, or as quarries of building materials to be reused or otherwise disposed of. The first category (conversion) included the eight cathedral priories that were to continue as secular cathedrals under the management of deans and chapters,* and the six great Benedictine or Augustinian houses that were to be 'altered' (as the phrase went) by transformation into the cathedral churches of newly established sees. These latter were Bristol, Chester, Gloucester, Oxford (Osney), Peterborough and Westminster. They were the modest outcome of what was originally a much more ambitious scheme that would have anticipated the ecclesiastical reorganisation of the nineteenth century by setting up a new episcopal see in every major county or pair of counties. Had this been implemented, Bodmin, Bury, Dunstable, Fountains, St Albans, Shrewsbury, Waltham and Welbeck would have been among the ex-monastic churches earmarked for cathedral status.[4] Some of these did survive, in whole or in part, as parish churches, and St Albans eventually became a cathedral church in 1877, but Bury was one of the major architectural losses, together with Abingdon, St Augustine's Canterbury, Evesham, Faversham, Glastonbury, Reading and Winchcombe. Two more major monasteries, Burton (Staffs.) and Thornton (Lincs.), were converted into short-lived collegiate churches,[5] and a number became parish churches, occasionally by free gift from the Crown (as at Christchurch, Hants.),[6] more often by purchase, either directly from the Crown by the parishioners (as at Tewkesbury, fig. 36)[7] or by someone who later gave, sold or bequeathed the building to the parish (as at Dorchester, Malmesbury and Sherborne).[8]

In statements whose character resembles that of modern 'press releases', it was

---

* Canterbury, Carlisle, Durham, Ely, Norwich, Rochester, Winchester and Worcester.

36. Tewkesbury Abbey, Gloucestershire: the east end of the church saved from demolition by the inhabitants, who purchased it from the Crown after the dissolution of the monastery in 1540. The nave was already in parochial use (from *Building News*, 12 April 1881).

37. Wymondham Abbey, Norfolk: the east end of the monastic church demolished because the inhabitants did not want (or could not afford) to save it by purchase. As at Tewkesbury, the nave was already in use as the parish church (from a drawing by G.E. Chambers in M.R. James, *Suffolk and Norfolk*, 1930).

implied that the whole operation represented an enlightened redeployment of ecclesiastical resources in which education and charity would also benefit by the establishment of new schools and almshouses.[9] In 1538 the University of Cambridge, in congratulating Henry VIII on his 'reformation of religion', expressed the hope that the monasteries, formerly given over to superstition, might be made into colleges to promote good letters and true doctrine,[10] but the king's response was ultimately to endow Regius professorships at the university rather than to convert any former religious house into an academic institution. In 1540 he consulted certain bishops about choosing twelve monasteries where boys might be brought up in learning,[11] but although a number of cathedral schools were continued and some others established in various places under royal patronage,[12] no dissolved monastery appears to have been converted into a school by royal direction, though one or two private benefactors were to acquire ex-monastic buildings for this purpose, notably at Repton and the London Charterhouse.

For the vast majority of dissolved monasteries, however, the outcome was total or partial demolition. Was this a deliberate, even a vindictive, act of policy, designed to prevent any restoration of monasticism in the future, or was it just the inevitable result of the abolition of the way of life that they had been designed to serve? How many abbeys or priories were pulled down for the sake of the materials, and how many were adapted for new purposes?

Of deliberate demolition as an act of policy there is some evidence. There is a well-known story of the man who, alarmed at the news that Queen Mary was restoring some of the monasteries, immediately got together a demolition squad and in the course of a single day pulled down Repton Priory church, 'saying he would destroy the nest for fear the birds should build there again'.[13] Cromwell himself set an example by promptly having the great Romanesque priory church of Lewes, of which he was the grantee, expertly demolished under the direction of the Italian military engineer Portinari.[14] In the instructions given to the commissioners for the suppression of the lesser monasteries in 1536, they were asked to value the lead and bells and such buildings as might be sold, but nothing was said about demolition.[15] However, in some later commissions the demolition of what was termed 'superfluous buildings' was clearly envisaged. Thus in the 'certificate' returned by the commissioners appointed in 1539 to take the surrender of the monasteries in Hampshire, Wiltshire and Gloucestershire, they specify which buildings were 'deemed to be superfluous' and which were 'assigned to remain'. In virtually every case the superfluous buildings comprised church, chapter house, dormitory, frater and infirmary, while the abbot's lodging was 'to remain undefaced', obviously because it was likely to be an eligible dwelling for a gentleman.[16] Here we have no evidence that the superfluous buildings were forthwith demolished by the commissioners. That was usually left to their purchasers: indeed, when ex-monastic buildings were sold it was sometimes specified that they should be demolished and the site cleared within a stated period, such as three years.[17] But at Furness in Lancashire a man called Holcroft was 'put in trust' to pull down the abbey church immediately after the surrender in June 1537,[18] and many friars' churches were demolished by the commissioners in 1537–8. A list survives of East Anglian friaries which the

38. Kirkstead Abbey, Lincolnshire: all that remained of one Lincolnshire monastery after the systematic demolition of its buildings by the Tudor government (from an engraving in B. Howlett's *Selection of Views in the County of Lincoln*, 1800).

commissioners had 'not as yet defaced nor razed', carefully specifying the reason in each case.[19] The commissioner charged with dissolving the Midland friaries, Dr John London, told Cromwell that although he had not completely demolished any friary, he had nevertheless 'so defaced them as they should not lightly be made friaries again'. In doing so he had apparently exceeded his instructions, since he promised Cromwell that henceforth he would 'deface no house unless I have your or the King's Grace's special commandment'.[20] This indeed is what some draft instructions, probably of 1539, lay down: nothing was to be 'plucked down' without orders from the king or the Chancellor of the Court of Augmentations.[21] At least one commissioner certainly did have general orders for demolition. This was John Freeman, the Lincolnshire representative of the Court of Augmentations, who wrote to Cromwell in August 1539 to say that 'the King's Commission commandeth me to pull down to the ground all the walls of the churches, steeples, cloisters, fraters, dorters, chapter houses, with all other houses, saving them that be necessary for a farmer.' However, he pointed out that there were many large monasteries in the county, with thick walls and few purchasers for the materials. To demolish them all would be a slow and expensive business which would cost the king at least £1,000. He suggested that it would be better just to pull down the roofs, battlements and stairs and let the walls stand, selling the stones if and when there was a demand for them.[22] As Lincolnshire was a county where some of the religious houses had been centres of disaffection in 1536, it is possible that here the government was motivated by the determination to extirpate all traces of monasticism. At any rate Freeman was evidently told to carry out his instructions, for in a later statement he reports that he has 'defaced and pulled down to the ground five houses', and that the sale of the materials has exceeded the cost by a small margin.[23] It is a measure of the thoroughness with which he performed his task that so little remains above ground of Lincolnshire's substantial quota of religious houses (fig. 38).

The universal cause of ruin was not so much deliberate demolition as the stripping of lead from the roofs. In every commission great emphasis is laid on the reservation to the king of lead, bells and any precious metals in the form of church ornaments. Then as now, lead was a valuable commodity, and almost every monastery had some on its roofs and in its gutters and downpipes. To realise this metallic wealth was one of the commissioners' first duties, and their letters are full of estimates of the quantity and value of lead at every house they dealt with. In May 1537 the Duke of Norfolk gleefully wrote to Henry to tell him that 'Jervaulx is well covered with lead and as for Bridlington there is none like it. It has a barn all covered with lead, the longest, widest and deepest roofed that ever I saw. The whole [of the] lead cannot be worth less than £3,000 or £4,000, and standing near the sea it can be easily carried away.'[24] In Lincolnshire the value of the bells and lead was reckoned to be £8,227, more than the annual value of all the monastic estates in the county, and four times the value of the plate.[25] In 1540 there were said to be 6,867 fothers★ of lead on the buildings of northern abbeys not yet prostrated.[26] At the current rate of about £4 the fother this would be worth over £27,000. Some of this harvest of lead was used in the king's works, on the roof of Westminster Hall and at the royal houses at Greenwich, Woodstock and elsewhere, and on the new coastal artillery forts.[27] Some of it was sold to private individuals, and to churchwardens and others who needed it for building or repairs. But in order to preserve the royal monopoly and thus keep up the price, relatively little was released onto the open market until 1544, when the king's financial needs induced his Council to try to realise its value, then estimated at £50,000. The idea was to export it to the Low Countries, where some of it could be sold outright and some deposited as security for the repayment of loans to be obtained from Antwerp merchants. Stephen Vaughan, the English financial agent at Antwerp, reckoned that up to 3,000 fothers a year could profitably be disposed of in this way, but the King's Council unwisely flooded the market with an initial shipment of 12,000 fothers. The result was that the price fell, much of the lead remained unsold on Vaughan's hands and was ultimately exchanged for Spanish alum. Alum was another valuable commodity, of which the Spaniards had a monopoly. Gradually released over a period of years it would have sold well, but in bulk it was subject to the same disadvantage as lead, and in the end the transaction resulted in a loss to the Crown of over £8,000.[28] Lord Lisle, the governor of Calais, probably did better in a private deal with a French nobleman who offered him good-quality wine in exchange for four fothers of lead which he wanted for a house he was building at Compiègne.[29] After 1544 some substantial sales of lead were made to merchants like Sir Thomas Gresham or noblemen like John Dudley, who hoped to sell it at a profit either at home or abroad,[30] and in Queen Mary's reign there was a careful round-up of what remained and an audit of all the sales of lead, bell-metal, plate, jewels and other items that had been disposed of since the death of Henry VIII. The commissioners brought to light several cases of lead that had been misappropriated, for instance by Sir Richard Cromwell (evidently for his new house at Hinchingbrooke) and

★ A fother was a measure of lead weighing a little less than a modern ton.

39. Tintern Abbey, Monmouthshire: a Victorian photograph of the shell of a great Cistercian church abandoned to decay after the sale of its lead and timber-work at the time of its dissolution in 1539 (British Architectural Library, Photographic Collection).

demanded authority for the use of 1,497 fothers by the surveyors of various of the king's works both civil and military.[31]

Although lead did not prove to be quite as easily realisable an asset as was at first anticipated, the importance attached to it is very clear. Whatever the ultimate fate of the former monastic buildings, the lead was reserved to the Crown, and one of the commissioners' earliest actions was almost invariably to set about having it stripped off and cast into blocks for ease of transport. The destruction that this caused is easy to imagine (fig. 39). A Yorkshireman who was a boy at the time of the dissolution recalled 'what tearing up of the lead there was and plucking up of boards, and throwing down of the spars, and when the lead was torn off and cast down into the church . . . the tombs [were] all broken' and 'the persons that cast the lead into fodders, pluck'd up all the seats in the choir . . . and burned them and melted the lead withall.'[32] If the church was to be kept for parochial or other use the lead might be either sold or given to the new owners,[33] but then as now officials and workmen were sometimes not over-careful. At York even the buildings reserved for the king's own use were defaced by predatory officials of the Augmen-

59

tations[34] and it is likely that some buildings were irreparably damaged before anyone could be found to purchase them. Undoubtedly the stripping of the lead was the prime cause of destruction: once the lead was off the weather would get in, the roofs would collapse, walls would begin to decay and the whole building would be open to progressive disintegration accelerated by the depredations of local people.

Whenever possible the commissioners aimed to sell as much of the materials of the 'superfluous' buildings as they could on the spot. Inventories were made for this purpose, and they include everything from roofs (minus the lead), glass, iron window bars, pavements and gravestones to alabaster reredoses, images of saints, lecterns and candlesticks. In general such useful materials as wood, iron and paving-stones proved saleable, and to the damage done by the stripping of the lead was added that of tearing out iron bars from windows and taking up the paving. If one looks at the records of these sales it is not always easy to understand the motives of the buyers. At Merevale, for instance, Walter Devereux, Lord Ferrers, was the new owner of the site, and may well have had a good use for the iron, glass and pavements, but what did he do with the choir-stalls, a pair of organs and six old altars with images?[35] At Repton Thomas Thacker (he whose son was to pull down the church in Mary's reign) acquired the site and thought it worth while to lay out 50 shillings on a similar miscellany of religious bric-à-brac, yet declined to buy the roof, glass, iron or paving-stones, which remained unsold.[36] Any suspicion that either of these men was a crypto-Catholic piously salvaging something from the wreckage is quickly dispelled when we recall that Devereux was a staunch upholder of the Tudor regime and that Thacker was actually Cromwell's steward and right-hand man. It is much easier to understand a note in the inventory of Upholland Priory in Lancashire that in the church there were twenty-one images of wood and stone 'which are not yet valued because it is doubted whether any one will buy any of the stone images or not'.[37] The wooden ones, presumably, were saleable as firewood. If the fate of parochial church fittings twenty years later is any guide, most of the images on altars or rood-lofts were simply burned, while wood from dismantled rood-lofts was sometimes converted into seats, communion-tables or panelling in private houses, and Easter Sepulchres and pyxes, though often burned, occasionally found new uses as meat-safes, clothes presses or chicken-coops. These details come from the systematic survey of church goods made in Lincolnshire in 1566.[38]

As might be expected, building materials were much more easily disposed of in towns than elsewhere: and what was not promptly sold was apt to be pilfered. Writing from Warwick in 1538, Dr London told Cromwell that poor people were everywhere so greedy for the spoils from the friars' houses that they fell on them both night and day as long as any door, window, iron, glass or loose lead remained.[39] There were similar complaints from Bristol, Bridlington, Coventry, Norwich and Oxford.[40] As already noted, the purchasers of monastic buildings were sometimes required to pull them down within a specified period.[41] But in remote country areas like the Yorkshire dales there were few purchasers, and it is no accident that some of our finest monastic ruins are those of Cistercian abbeys in characteristically remote situations.

In a few selected cases the Crown itself demolished or dismantled in order to reuse the materials elsewhere. The monasteries in question were nearly all in the Thames valley, where most of the king's houses lay, and where water transport facilitated the operation. Rewley on the outskirts of Oxford, Abingdon, Bisham, Chertsey and Barking were the principal Thames-side abbeys that were systematically demolished under the direction of the royal works and accounted for by James Nedeham as the King's Surveyor. From Rewley came clerestory windows which were re-erected at Hampton Court to form a bowling-alley.[42] Bisham and Chertsey both provided materials for Oatlands, where part of the old moat was filled in with rubble from those houses,[43] and so probably did Abingdon,[44] while Barking was pulled down mainly for the benefit of the king's new house at Dartford. Here it was not rubble that was sought but freestone. The business of the ten miners, twenty-four common labourers and three carpenters employed by Nedeham for some eighteen months in 1541–2 was 'undermining and casting down the late abbey church of Barking for the providing of the best and fairest coin stones and other Caen stone'. These were carried to Barking Creek and thence by water to Dartford, some ten miles downstream on the other side of the Thames.[45] It was, of course, the relative ease of transport by water that allowed stone from the dissolved monasteries of Faversham and St Augustine's at Canterbury to be used in the great refortification of Calais in 1539–40, itself largely financed by the revenues of the suppressed monasteries now flowing through the Court of Augmentations.[46] Elsewhere materials from dissolved monasteries were occasionally used for the repair of other royal buildings. In 1538, for instance, the President of the Council in the Marches of Wales made a note to ask Cromwell for a warrant to have the stones, iron, lead and glass from Wigmore Abbey for the repair of the royal castles for which he was responsible.[47] He also got hold of lead from Basingwerk Abbey and timber from an 'old frerehouse' in Ludlow for the same purpose.[48] In 1539 one of the commissioners, Dr London, sent Cromwell a memorandum about building materials in various Midland friaries that he thought might be useful for the royal works and suggested that the king's Master Carpenter might be sent to inspect them. He particularly mentioned a 'fair lodging' at Warwick that might be 'translated' into the king's castle there, a roof on the Austin friars at Northampton that was 'meet for Grafton', and two other roofs at the Black and White Friars that would also be suitable for reuse at Grafton, a royal country house in Northamptonshire.[49] These, being of timber, could be dismantled and carried to their destinations much more easily than masses of heavy masonry. Whether any of London's suggestions were followed up is not recorded, and certainly nothing came of his inquiry whether the king wanted him to preserve the gilt bronze effigy of the latter's ancestor Blanche, Duchess of Lancaster, in the Grey Friars' church at Stamford.[50] In this church there was another royal tomb, that of Princess Joan (d. 1385), erected by Richard II. Both these were destroyed, like the tombs of Henry, Earl of Lancaster (d. 1345), Henry, 1st Duke of Lancaster (d. 1361), Constance, Duchess of Lancaster and wife of John of Gaunt, and Mary Bohun, mother of King Henry V, in the collegiate church of the Newarke at Leicester, when that was dissolved in 1548.[51] The Newarke had been founded by Henry, Earl of Lancaster, in the reign of Edward II and was therefore in the king's own patronage, like the

Yorkist foundation at Fotheringhay in Northamptonshire, St Stephen's Chapel at Westminster and St George's Chapel at Windsor. For this particular act of destruction Henry VIII was not responsible: in 1545 he had declared that he 'would not deface any of his great colleges':[52] and it was not until after his death that St Stephen's Chapel became the House of Commons, Fotheringhay (minus its choir) a parish church, and what Leland described as the 'exceeding fair' church at Leicester was lamentably demolished, together with all the monuments of its Lancastrian founders.

Finally there are the religious houses which were converted into royal residences. It must be remembered that in the past the itinerant royal court had often stayed in the great Benedictine abbeys. By dissolving the monasteries Henry VIII destroyed a source of hospitality that had been regularly made use of by his predecessors. One obvious way of filling this gap was for the king to take over some of the former monastic buildings himself, and this he did at Dartford, Dunstable, Guildford, Reading, Rochester, St Albans, Syon and St Augustines's, Canterbury. When the college of Bonhommes at Ashridge in Hertfordshire was dissolved in 1539 its buildings were retained, chiefly, it seems, as a country residence for the royal children, and in the north St Mary's Abbey at York and the house of the Austin friars at Newcastle were reserved in order to provide accommodation for the King's Council in the North. Dunstable, Reading and St Albans were major religious houses on main roads out of London, so their selection as royal houses is easy to understand. Guildford had long been the site of a royal dwelling associated with the castle, and only a few years before the dissolution a new royal lodging had been built within the precinct of the Dominican friary in the town. What happened in 1538 was that the whole of this friary was taken over by the Crown. Dartford and Rochester were on the king's route to the south coast, which he was engaged in fortifying, while Canterbury was specifically designed to accommodate Anne of Cleves on her arrival in England as Henry's fourth wife. Except at York, very little remains of any of these royal conversions, and only for Dartford, Rochester and Canterbury do detailed accounts of the works survive. At Canterbury and York and probably also at Dunstable, Reading and St Albans it was the abbot's or prior's lodging that formed the nucleus of the new royal house. At Canterbury the great church that had been the cradle of English Christianity was demolished, together with the tombs of St Augustine and the early Saxon kings of Kent. At Reading the same fate befell the great Romanesque church built by Henry I. At St Mary's, York, the church was unroofed, but the abbot's house was preserved for royal use and later in the sixteenth century the aisles were converted into galleries which faced one another across the open space previously occupied by the nave. At Dunstable and St Albans the churches survived in parochial use. But at Rochester, where the priory church continued to serve as the cathedral church of the diocese, the entire cloister quadrangle was taken over and converted into a house containing the usual separate apartments for king and queen. The result must have been rather like Holyroodhouse at Edinburgh, with church and palace standing side by side. After Henry's death the house was granted to Lord Cobham, who sold it to the Dean and Chapter of Rochester. As they already had their own residences in the

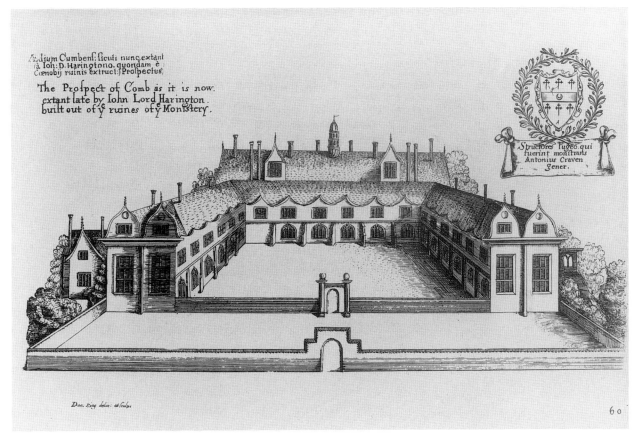

40. Combe Abbey, Warwickshire: a dissolved monastery converted into a country house. The church, which stood in the foreground, was completely demolished, leaving the remaining three sides of the cloister court to form the nucleus of the house (from an engraving in Daniel King's *The Cathedrall and Conventuall Churches of England and Wales Orthographically Delineated,* 1656).

vicinity of the cathedral they had no use for the former royal house and proceeded to have it pulled down for the value of the materials. Today the only memento of Henry VIII's occupation of Rochester Cathedral Priory is the large number of its books which he appropriated and which now form part of the King's Library in the British Library.[53]

The dissolution of the monasteries was a remarkable demonstration of the power of the Tudor state. Having (in modern terms) nationalised the property of over 800 religious corporations, Henry VIII's government proceeded first to systematic asset-stripping in the form of lead, and then to privatisation by selling many of the properties to courtiers, local magnates and newly established gentry.[54] By the end of Henry's reign the recycling of the monasteries was largely accomplished. Throughout the country, ex-monastic buildings were either in ruins or in process of conversion to other purposes. At first the Crown itself reserved several for its own use, but, with the exception of the King's Manor at York, which had an institutional function as the seat of government in the north, few of them were permanently retained as royal residences.[55] In the private sector, on the other hand,

63

former abbeys and priories had an after-life as country seats which in many cases has lasted to the present day (fig. 40). 'Abbey' joined 'Hall', 'House', 'Court' or 'Place' as the typical designation of an English country house. For Jane Austen and her readers the title of *Northanger Abbey* was an obvious complement to that of *Mansfield Park*. In the nineteenth century the Gothic Revival gave an especial cachet to a country house that had once been a medieval monastery. A rich man like William Beckford might even build a supposititious 'abbey' where none had existed before. But living in a Gothic house and calling it an abbey implied no rejection of the English Reformation on the part of its owners. However much antiquaries might sigh over the 'bare ruin'd choirs' (fig. 41), there were few who seriously regretted the Tudor revolution that had overthrown the monks and set the gentry and aristocracy in their place as the secular landowners of so much of Protestant England.

41. Dale (or Stanley Park) Abbey, Derbyshire: the east end of the choir depicted as a romantic ruin in John Ward's *Dale and its Abbey*, 1891.

Notes

1 *Letters and Papers of Henry VIII* [hereafter *L & P*], xii(1), 901, pp. 405–6.

2 *Early English Text Society*, extra series 32, 1878, p. lviii.

3 For the proclamation of 1560 see E. Cardwell, *Documentary Annals of the Reformation in England*, i, 1839, pp. 257–60. For the Duchy of Lancaster castles see my article on 'Castles and Government in Tudor England', *English Historical Review*, lxxxiii, 1968, pp. 231–2. See also Margaret Aston, 'English Ruins and English History: the Dissolution and the sense of the Past', *Journal of the Warburg and Courtauld Institutes*, xxxvi, 1973.

4 *L & P*, xiv(2), 429, *Addenda*, 1457; *Letters relating to the Suppression of the Monasteries*, ed. T. Wright (Camden Soc., 1843), pp. 263–4.

5 These two collegiate churches, each staffed by a dean and four prebendaries, were dissolved in 1545 and 1546 respectively. At Burton the buildings passed into the possession of the 1st Lord Paget of Beaudesert (d. 1563), who converted some part of them into a house, which he had license to fortify (*L & P*, xxi(1), 149 (39)). That he regarded this as more than just an old-fashioned 'license to crenellate' is suggested by a contemporary plan of the abbey from the Paget papers (deposited in the RIBA Drawings Collection) on which Tudor artillery bastions have been sketched.

6 *VCH Hants.*, v, p. 108.

7 H.J.L.J. Massé, *The Abbey Church of Tewkesbury*, 1900, p. 15. Goring (Oxon.) is a little-known case of purchase from the Crown by the parish, documented in PRO, E117/14/183. Royston (Herts.) is another (*VCH Herts.*, iii, p. 264).

8 *VCH Oxon.*, vii, p. 59; *Wiltshire Archaeological Mag.* i, 1854, p. 249; *VCH Dorset*, ii. p. 68.

9 *L & P*, xv, 248 (p. 90), 954.

10 *L & P*, xiii(2), 593, 677. One they had specifically in mind was the Franciscan friary at Cambridge (ibid., 760).

11 *L & P*, xv, 269. See also 383 for an echo of this scheme.

12 See N. Orme, *English Schools in the Middle Ages*, 1973, ch. 9 ('The Schools under Henry VIII').

13 W. Dugdale, *Monasticon Anglicanum*, vi(1), 1849, p. 429.

14 *L & P*, xiii(1), no. 590.

15 *L & P*, x, nos. 721, 1191: E 111/57.

16 PRO, E 315/494.

17 *Letters relating to the Suppression of the Monasteries*, ed. T. Wright (Camden Soc. 1843), pp. 273, 277; cf. the contract to demolish Dunkeswell Abbey printed in *Trans. Devonshire Assn.*, 46, 1914, pp. 148–9.

18 *L & P*, xii(2), no. 205.

19 PRO, SP 5/4/152.

20 *L & P*, xiii(2), no. 719, printed in full in Ellis, *Original Letters*, 3rd ser., iii, 1846, pp. 130–4.

21 *L & P*, xiv(1), no. 1190.

22 *L & P*, xi, no. 242, printed in full in Ellis, *Original Letters*, 3rd ser., iii, 1846, pp. 268–9.

23 *L & P Addenda*, no. 1094 (SP 1/44, f. 47).

24 *L & P*, xii(1), no. 1172. For a list of friaries 'which have any substance of lead' see *L & P*, xiii(2), no. 489.

25 *L & P*, xiii(2), no. 459; cf. *L & P*, x, no. 1026.

26 *L & P*, xv, no. 139 (2), See also *L & P*, xii(2), nos. 432, 1083.

27 Bodleian Library, MS Rawlinson D. 809, ff. 1–9, is a general declaration by James Nedeham as Surveyor of the King's Works, of monastic lead used on various royal buildings. See also *L & P*, xii(2), no. 545, xiii(2), nos. 313, 1021.

28 W.C. Richardson, 'Some Financial Expedients of Henry VIII', *Economic History Review*, 2nd ser., vii, 1954–5, pp. 36–48; I. Blanchard, 'English Lead and the international Bullion Crisis of the 1550s', in *Trade, Government and Economy in Pre-Industrial England*, ed. D.C. Coleman and A.H. John, 1976.

29 *L & P*, xiv(2), no. 233.

30 E 117/14/179, item 6; E 117/14/201, and Sotheby's, 24 Oct. 1972, lot 380.

31 For the commission see *Cal. Pat. Rolls Philip & Mary 1555–7*, pp. 25–6, 116, and for its operations E 117/14/173 and E 163/24/20 and 21. For a transcript of the latter document I am indebted to Dr A.J. Taylor. See also W.C. Richardson, *History of the Court of Augmentations*, Louisiana UP, 1961, pp. 238–40.

32 Michael Sherbrook, 'The Fall of Religious Houses' in *Tudor Treatises*, ed. A.G. Dickens, Yorks. Arch. Soc. Record Series, cxxv, 1959, p. 124.

33 A number of instances are recorded in E117/13/1, a book of recognisances for the sale of monastic woods, lead and bells sold in the years 1536–40.

34 *History of the King's Works*, ed. Colvin, iv, 1982, p. 356.

35 PRO, E315/172, a book of sales at Midland monasteries.

36 Ibid. (printed in full in R. Bigsby, *Description of Repton*, 1854, pp. 86–9).

37 PRO, DL 41/11/47.

38 *English Church Furniture in the Period of the Reformation*, ed. E. Peacock, 1866.

39 *L & P*, xiii(2), no. 757.

40 *L & P*, xii(2), no. 92, xiii(2), nos. 325, 934, xiv(1), no. 3; E 36/116, ff. 32–33.

41 Above, p. 56.

42 *History of the King's Works*, iv, 1982, pp. 132, 137.

43 Ibid., pp. 208–9.

44 The accounts for pulling down Abingdon (E101/458/1) show that some members of the demolition team were also employed at Chertsey.

45 Bodleian, MS Rawlinson D. 782.

46 *History of the King's Works*, iii, 1975, p. 353: *L & P*, xvi, no. 852.

47 *L & P*, xiii(2), no. 736; E117/13/112.

48 *History of the King's Works*, iii, p. 175.

49 *L & P*, xiii(2), no. 757; xiv(1), no. 3.

50 *L & P*, xiv(1), no. 3.

51 *History of the King's Works*, i, 1963, pp. 267–8, 487; Leland's *Itinerary*, ed. Toulmin Smith, 1907, i, pp. 15–16.

52 *L & P*, xx(1), no. 1222.

53 *History of the King's Works*, iv, p. 3 and under the individual buildings in question.

54 For the conversion of monastic buildings into private houses see Maurice Howard, *The Early Tudor Country House*, 1987, ch. 7.

55 *History of the King's Works*, iv, 1982, pp. 7–8 and under the names of the respective houses.

V

POMPOUS ENTRIES AND ENGLISH ARCHITECTURE

THE DAYS OF public pomp and circumstance are largely over. In the twentieth century the great agents of political advertisement and persuasion have been the press, the radio, the television and the aerosol. Our ancestors believed in the sermon, the oath, the pageant and the procession. In war the victory parade is not yet quite obsolete, but European union has been achieved without anything more symbolically expressive than a row of flags outside the EU offices in Brussels. Even church ceremonial is, in the West at least, sadly reduced from its former splendour. When both Church and State have lost interest in something that was once a major preoccupation of both, it is time for the historian to give it his attention.

Much has indeed been written about the symbolism of the pageant and the triumph by the historians of art and drama.[1] But so far they have received rather less attention from the historian of architecture, partly because he may well be daunted by the weight of literary and art-historical scholarship, and partly because this was after all ephemeral architecture and as such perhaps only of passing interest.

But the importance in the nineteenth and twentieth centuries of the exhibition – an equally ephemeral display of art, architecture or manufactured goods – in the dissemination of new ideas in design is universally recognised. Think of the Great Exhibition of 1851, the Paris Exhibition of 1855, or the Festival of Britain (1951). In fact, of course, it was precisely the ephemeral character of the festive displays of the sixteenth, seventeenth and eighteenth centuries that made them important vehicles for new architectural ideas. Being constructed only of insubstantial materials such as timber and canvas, these temporary structures could represent accurately sophisticated architectural designs that could not easily be got through to an unlettered and untravelled mason or bricklayer. It is a commonplace that in both France and England it was easier in the sixteenth and early seventeenth centuries to decorate basically Gothic architecture with classical ornament than it was to impose the discipline of the Orders on native workmen. But a timber or canvas arch was merely a drawing blown up: for once the artist or the architect who designed it was in full control. Compare, for instance, the arch built by the Florentine merchants in Antwerp in 1549 (fig. 42) with the normal products of Flemish mannerism, or with the half-hearted approximation to a classical gateway that was being built in Whitehall Palace in England at about the same time (fig. 43).

TRIVMPHALIS FLORENTI-
norum porticus, in via Coriaria,
& intus & foris ſpectandus.

Tota altitud. pe. lx.
Latitud. ped. L.
Profund. pe.C.xxx.

42. Triumphal Arch erected by the Florentine merchants in Antwerp for the entry of Philip, Prince of Spain, in 1549 (from Cornelius Graphaeus, *Spectaculorum in susceptione Philippi Hisp. Principis*, . . . , Antwerp, 1550, Bodleian Library).

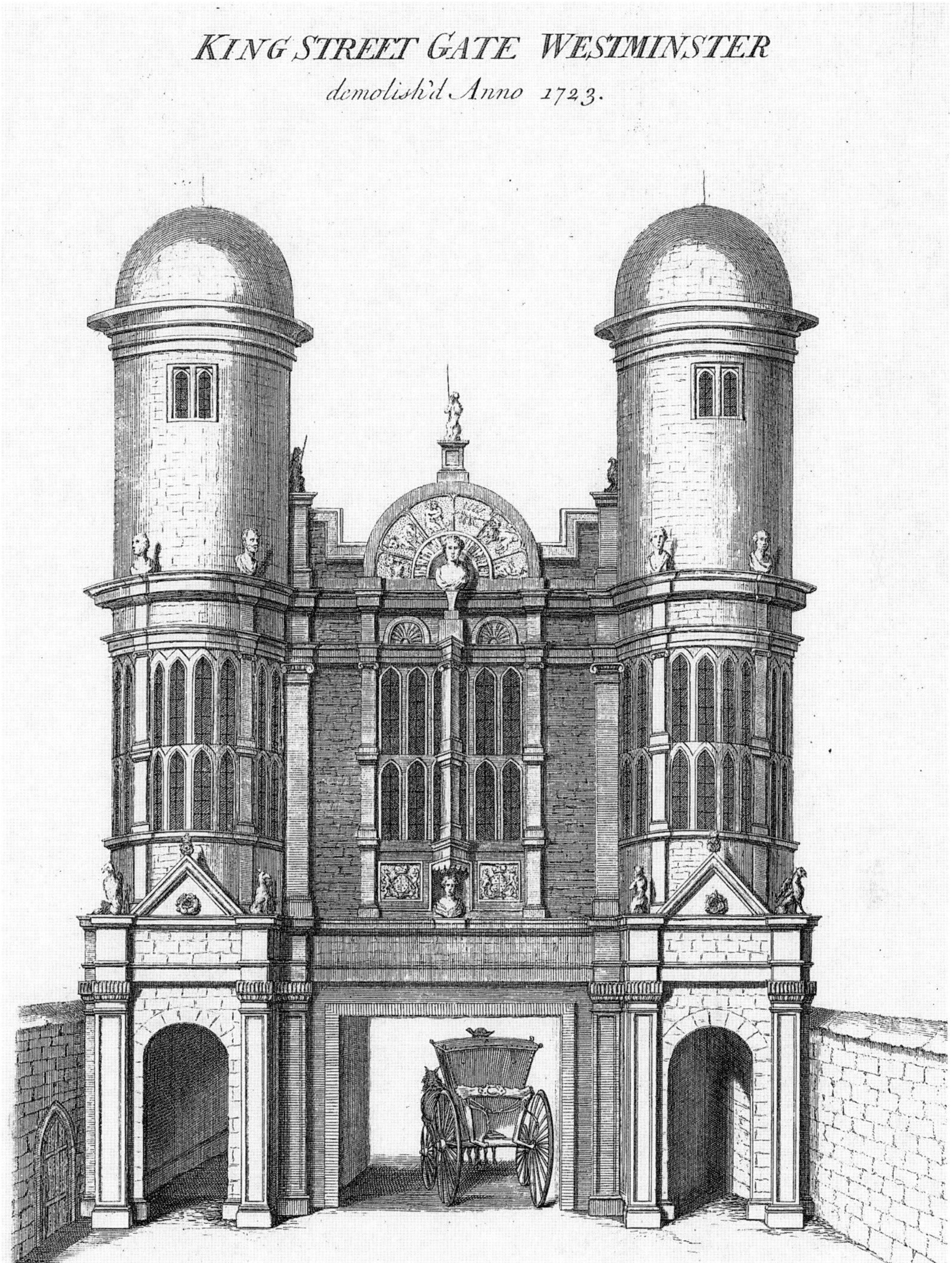
KING STREET GATE WESTMINSTER
demolish'd Anno 1723.
Sumptibus Societatis Antiquariæ Lond: 1725.

43. The King Street Gate of Whitehall Palace, built *circa* 1548 (from an engraving by George Vertue published by the Society of Antiquaries, 1725).

Moreover, these displays were, at least in the sixteenth century, often of an international character. So we find the principal foreign communities of merchants – Florentine, Genoese and English – paying for the erection of arches to celebrate the entry of the Prince of Spain into Antwerp in 1549, German merchants making themselves responsible for one of the pageants to celebrate Anne Boleyn's coronation as Henry VIII's queen in 1533, and both German and Italian ones building arches in London streets for the coronation of Queen Mary in 1553.

It was these displays by foreign merchants that, with the exception of the Duke of Somerset's unfinished palace in the Strand, almost certainly provided the first sight of authentic classical architecture that most Englishmen had ever had. This would not necessarily be true of courtiers, some of whom may have witnessed foreign state entries or have been present at Greenwich in 1527, when, for the receipt of a French embassy, a temporary banqueting hall was built with features designed by Giovanni da Maiano and other Italian artists. At one end there was a triumphal arch 'fatto a l'anticha'.[2] As it had a wide central arch flanked by two smaller ones, designed for service purposes, it was evidently a true classical triumphal arch, almost certainly the first ever constructed in England. Others, like Charles Brandon, Duke of Suffolk, may have made inquiries about the mode of Italian festivities,[3] and a good deal of Italianate design (though no triumphal arch) was incorporated in the English pavilions at the Field of Cloth of Gold in 1520. For Anne Boleyn's coronation procession in 1533 the Hanseatic merchants showed a 'marvellous cunning pageant' of Apollo and the Muses on Mount Parnassus, with the Fountain of Helicon running with Rhenish wine. It was probably for this tableau that Holbein made a surviving design which shows Apollo and the Muses seated above a triumphal arch, but whether any such three-dimensional arch actually formed part of the pageant is very doubtful.[4] For Edward VI's coronation there was, as the Imperial ambasssador noted, 'no very memorable show of triumph or magnificence'.[5] Neither the written nor the pictorial record indicates that anything in the nature of triumphal arches marked the route of the royal procession from the Tower through the City of London to Westminster. What was offered was merely a series of 'pageants' or tableaux.[6]

But in 1553 the principal presentations along the ceremonial route were, as one chronicler tells us, 'made with gates to pass through', and they were considered to be 'very high [and] stately'.[7] Just how many arches were erected is not clear, but all commentators were agreed that the finest were those for which the communities of foreign merchants were responsible. The Genoese provided one in Fenchurch Street, the Hanse another at St Benet Gracechurch and the Florentines a third outside the Leadenhall at the north end of Gracechurch Street. Of these the Genoese arch was deemed to be 'the most beautiful and the best made and the largest of all', exceeding all the rest in novelty and elegance of design. The Florentine arch was also remarked upon, but as for the rest, 'all erected by the English, except one by the German Hanse Towns...they were not of the beauty and rare quality of the two abovementioned.'[8] That the outstanding arches should have been erected by these particular foreign communities is not surprising. French diplomacy had favoured the Duke of Northumberland and Lady Jane Grey rather than Mary, and in any case the French merchants did not have the strong sense of corporate identity that distinguished their Florentine and Genoese counterparts.[9] Neither did the Netherlandish merchants who, as subjects of the Emperor Charles V, would no doubt have favoured Mary's succession. But for all the foreign communities the return of a Catholic monarch to the English throne after twenty years of breach with Rome would have been a cause of rejoicing, and it was this, no doubt, that inspired the Genoese and Florentines to celebrate the occasion by a particularly splendid architectural display.

Unfortunately there is no known representation of the arches in question in drawing or woodcut, but a hitherto unnoticed printed description of them by an Italian diplomat makes it clear that they were sophisticated architectural compositions.[10] The writer was Giulio Raviglio Rosso of Ferrara, who had been sent to England in 1554 to congratulate Philip and Mary on their marriage. By then, ten months after the coronation, the arches had presumably been dismantled, but Rosso was well informed about recent events in England and, besides acknowledging the help of the Venetian ambassador, would no doubt have met members of the Italian communities who had been responsible for setting them up. His account may be translated as follows:

In the streets there were many triumphal arches, but two of these were much more impressive than the others, one erected by the Genoese merchants, the other by the Florentines. The former was of the Corinthian order, such as the Ancients were accustomed to dedicate to Virgins, a Corinthian maiden having given the name to this style of building. It was very beautiful to behold, being, both by its proportions and by its ornament, so pleasing to the eye that in truth it could, by imitation [of Antiquity], be compared with those that the ancient Romans made with so much cost, so well were Sacrifices, Battles, Histories and Architecture represented as if in marble, and in painting festoons of foliage, fruit and flowers, besides many figures which displayed profound design, accomplished perspective, marvellous invention, judgement in composition and care in execution. On one side of the arch was inscribed MARIAE REGINAE INCLYTAE, CONSTANTI, PIAE, CORONAM BRITANNICI IMPERII, ET PALMAM VIRTVTIS ACCIPIENTI, GENVENSES PVBLICA SALVTE LAETANTES CVLTVM OPTATVM TRIBVVNT. [To Queen Mary, glorious, constant, pious, receiving the crown of British government and the palm of virtue, the Genoese, rejoicing in the public weal, offer their long-desired reverence.]

And on the other,

VIRTVS SVPERAVIT, IVSTITIA DOMINATVR, VERITAS TRIVMPHAT, PIETAS CORONATVR, SALVS REIPVBLICAE RESTITVTVR. [Virtue has overcome, Justice has prevailed, Truth has triumphed, Piety is crowned, the public weal is restored.]

The Florentines' arch was composed without keeping to one order, yet with great judgement and much beauty. The column was Corinthian, but fluted like the Ionic Order, the capital was composed of Doric, Ionic and Corinthian, the abacus and cymatium were Doric, the volutes[s] and the fillets Ionic, the astragals and the leaves Corinthian. Its base on the two towers was Doric, but the two scotias and the astragal and the ornamental details showed as Corinthian. The architrave, frieze and cornices were Ionic, and altogether [it was] so well composed that it demonstrated how able the Architect was in the knowledge of design, having left nothing without measure, and much care, nor any part without much consideration. Being then decorated with painting of divers foliage, of birds of many sorts, of various groups of little figures and of animals mingled together, in various well judged compartments: there were seen on one side, in their niches four statues of the Cardinal Virtues, and above a [figure of] Fame to which the following verse alluded:

VIRTVTES FAMA REGINAM [*sic*] AD SIDERA TOLLVNT. [The Virtues raise the fame of the Queen to the heavens.]

And then lower down it read:

MARIAE BRITANNORVM REGINAE VICTRICI, PIAE, AVGVSTAE, FLORENTINI GLORIAE INSIGNIA EREXERVNT. [To Mary, Queen of Britain, victorious, pious, august, the Florentines have set up these marks of her glory.]

On the other side beneath the image of the Queen in triumph [were various inscriptions, printed below, p. 91].

In view of Rosso's emphasis on the Ancient Roman character of the Genoese arch it may be conjectured that it was a conventional tripartite arch of the kind best known from the Arch of Constantine in Rome. An arch of this sort had been erected by the English merchants for the entry of Philip Prince of Spain into Antwerp in 1549 (fig. 44). Designed for them by Lambert Van Noort, it was also of the Corinthian order and likewise had only one inscription on each side.[11] By 1553 the Genoese had had considerable experience in the designing and erection of triumphal arches in their own city, which had welcomed Louis XI of France in 1507, the Emperor Charles V in 1529 and again (after the crushing of a *coup d'état*) in 1533, and then his son Philip in 1548. Perino del Vaga's designs for the arches erected in 1529 and 1533 survive. They were competent classical compositions which were intended to recall the arches of Imperial Rome. In fact it is particularly in Genoa that the transformation of the late medieval *joyeuse entrée* with its succession of acted tableaux, into the revived *trionfo romano* can be observed.[12] The Antique character of the arch erected by the Genoese in London in 1553 is therefore not unexpected.

The Florentine arch is more difficult to envisage. Rosso refers to 'la colonna' as if a single column was its principal feature. It is possible that by 'la colonna' he merely meant 'the order employed', but in 1594 a triumphal arch surmounted by a single column was among those erected in Antwerp for the entry of Prince Ernest, Archduke of Austria, and the Florentine arch erected in London in 1553 may have been essentially the same. The Antwerp arch was a single one, with two minor columns of the Doric order on each side of the arch, and a great Doric column

PRIVATVS ANGLORVM ARCVS,

Tota alt.pe.
lxxiij. Lati.
ped.lviij.
profun.xxx

DIVO CAROLO
MAX. IMP. CÆS·
AVG. AC MAG·
NO PHILIPPO
ILLIVS F. HIS-
PANIARVM.&c.

44. Triumphal Arch erected by the English merchants in Antwerp for the entry of Philip, Prince of Spain, in 1549 (from Cornelius Graphaeus, *Spectaculorum in susceptione Philippi Hisp. Principis . . .*, Antwerp, 1550, Bodleian Library).

ARCVS PVBLICVS AD FORVM LINARIVM.

45. Triumphal Arch erected in Antwerp in 1594 for the entry of the Archduke of Austria (from J. Bochius, *Descriptio publicae gratulationis etc. in adventu sereniss. principis Ernesti Archiducis Austriae,* Antwerp, 1595, Bodleian Library).

(symbolising 'Constancy') standing on top of it (fig. 45). The mixture of Doric, Ionic and Corinthian features described by Rosso points to a Composite order such as the one illustrated in Palladio's *Quattro Libri* of 1570 (Book I, Cap. xviii), which exhibits most of the features he mentions. The Composite order might have been suggested by its use on the Arch of Titus in Rome. This is of one arch only and Rosso's reference to the 'two towers' ('due Torri') on which the base of the column stood, suggests the two piers flanking a central arch, each presumably decorated with paired columns, between which would be the four niches he mentions, two on either side of the arch, one above the other. The hypothesis that the Florentine arch was of one opening only is consistent with a Spanish account in which it is stated to have been 'not so large as that of the Genoese'.[13] As Gracechurch Street narrowed considerably towards its northern end, a single arch would probably have been better suited to the site than a triple one.

Rosso refers to the designer of the Florentine arch as an 'architect' and presumably an Italian, but does not name him. In Antwerp in 1549 the Genoese arch was designed by an otherwise unknown Italian called Stefano Ambrosio Schiappalari. It is tempting (but idle) to speculate that he might have been employed to design the Genoese arch in London four years later.[14] Whoever designed them, the Genoese and Florentine arches set up in the streets of London in 1553 must have provided thousands of Englishmen with their first sight of the classical orders properly handled in the Italian manner.[15] It was an architectural education that was not to be repeated for the coronation of Queen Elizabeth five years later. For the Catholic mercantile communities in London the accession of a Protestant queen was not an occasion for special rejoicing, and as for the City, it prided itself on having 'beautified it selfe . . . without any forayne person'.[16] Although at least one of the three principal pageants was displayed on a triumphal arch with one large opening and two smaller ones, decorated with columns, capitals and bases,[17] what attracted attention was not the architecture but the groups of children personifying such themes as the 'Union of the Houses of Lancaster and York', 'the Seat of Worthy Governance' and 'the Eight Beatitudes'.[18]

For James I in 1603 the City of London set up a series of arches, designed chiefly by a master joiner called Stephen Harrison, in which the traditional tableaux were presented in an architectural setting.[19] The result was a particularly riotous display of Anglo-Flemish mannerism (fig. 46), only one arch presenting a degree of classical decorum. This, in Gracechurch Street, was once more 'erected by the Italians; the cost theirs; the Invention their own' (fig. 47).[20] The dimensions given by Stephen Harrison for his own arches show that in designing them he did attempt to conform to some simple modular proportions, but his engravings demonstrate how little adherence to such proportions could actually mean in visual terms. 'Teeming farragos of infelicitous detail',[21] they no doubt appealed to an uneducated populace in much the same way as the architecture of Disneyland does today. But, unlike the arches of 1553, they can have done little to further the education of English architects and craftsmen in classical design.

Of the triumphal arch set up in the Inns of Court in 1616 to celebrate the creation of the future Charles I as Prince of Wales we know nothing,[22] and the

46. One of the Triumphal Arches erected in London in March 1603/4 for the coronation of King James I (Stephen Harrison, *The Arch's of Triumph erected in honor of . . . James . . . King of England . . . at his Majesties entrance and passage through his Honourable Citty . . . of London,* 1604, Bodleian Library).

47. Triumphal Arch erected in London in March 1603/4 by the Italian merchants (Stephen Harrison, *The Arch's of Triumph*, as in fig. 46).

48. Design for a Triumphal Arch at Temple Bar drawn by John Webb in 1636 (British Architectural Library, Drawings Collection).

king's coronation in 1626 was a fiasco from the point of view both of the City of London and of the architectural historian. Five 'most superb' arches had been erected, two by the citizens and three by foreign merchants, at a cost of several thousand pounds, when Charles cancelled the procession, ostensibly because of an outbreak of the plague, but really (so it was believed) to save himself the expense. 'The murmurings of the people and the disgust of those who had spent the money' laid the foundations of Charles I's unpopularity in the City of London.[23]

Who had been employed to design the arches we do not know. All that the City records disclose is that the carver Gerard Christmas (d. 1633) was responsible for three 'pageants', which were presumably associated with arches.[24] If they were, then it is likely that the arches were mannerist confections rather than manifestations of Jonesian classicism. However, a claim against the Exchequer by the German artist Francis Cleyn for work done 'by his Majesty's Special Command' in 1625, including '11 daies in Mr. Survaier his howse where I made all maner of drawings for the Arch Triumphall', shows that Inigo Jones did design an arch at this time, probably the one in Westminster Hall traditionally associated with the Coronation Banquet.[25] The banquet, like the procession, was abandoned, so the arch was never built.

Ten years later Inigo Jones was involved in a project for the rebuilding of Temple Bar, then in a decayed state, in which the king took a personal interest. We have not only entries in the records of both Privy Council and City in 1636–7, but also several original drawings showing, as we would expect, an orthodox version of a Roman triumphal arch – the Arch of Constantine, in fact, though with its proportions modified to fit the width of the street.[26] In this, as in some other respects, it resembled the triumphal arch designed by Palladio for the entry of King Henri III of France into Venice in 1574, which Jones would presumably have known from engravings.[27] Two versions of the design are preserved, one drawn by

49. Temple Bar as it might have appeared in the early nineteenth century had the design made by Inigo Jones and John Webb in 1636/7 been carried out: drawing by Paul Draper.

Jones himself, the other by his disciple John Webb (fig. 48). The former is surmounted by a coat of arms (whether of the king or the city is not clear), the latter by an equestrian statue of the king similar to the one by Le Sueur now at Charing Cross. Jones's arch was to have been of the Corinthian order, Webb's of the Composite, and detailed notes in Webb's hand of the dimensions of 'the Designe of the Composite Order' are preserved.[28] In the end nothing came of the project, but Paul Draper's drawing (fig. 49) shows it as it might have appeared to a person entering the City from the west early in the nineteenth century.

50. One of the Triumphal Arches erected in London for the coronation of King Charles II in 1661 (W. Ogilby, *The Relation of His Majesties Entertainment . . . with a Description of the Triumphal Arches*, 1661, Bodleian Library).

Charles II's coronation was the occasion for a great demonstration of loyalty which included a series of triumphal arches designed by Peter Mills, a leading city artisan-architect, in collaboration with 'another person, who desired to have his name conceal'd'. There is reason to think that this was Sir Balthazar Gerbier, miniature-painter, art-dealer and occasional architect, then some seventy years old, whose more than dubious loyalty to the Stuarts had recently led to his dismissal from the office of Master of Ceremonies at Charles II's court. Gerbier had been a friend of Rubens, and echoes of the arches designed by the latter for the reception of the Cardinal Infante Ferdinand at Antwerp in 1635 (published in 1641–2 as *Pompa Introitus Serenissimi Principis Ferdinandi Austriaci Hispaniarum Infantis*, etc.) can by detected in the baroque designs made by Mills and Gerbier (fig. 50).[29]

It would be possible to continue the story of the 'pompous entry' and the triumphal arch in England on into the eighteenth and even the nineteenth century. But the taste for these displays was ebbing. Royalty showed less appetite for such occasions, and as symbols of submission to royal authority they were no doubt felt to be less appropriate after 1688. The tendency for kings and queens to go about in coaches rather than on horseback made it less easy for them to read elevated inscriptions and to respond to speeches made from the tops of triumphal arches. In London the Lord Mayor's Show took over from the royal entry as the great processional event.[30] Temporary arches were still dutifully set up in Westminster Hall for the coronations of James II, George II, George III and George IV, in Green Park to celebrate the Treaty of Aix-la-Chapelle in 1748, and on various other occasions, public and private.[31] With the Napoleonic Wars the triumphal arch reverted to its original function, the celebration of victory in war, and all over Europe suitably neo-classical arches were erected to celebrate deliverance from Bonaparte's empire. In London the Marble Arch of 1828 and the Constitution Hill arch of 1846 (originally surmounted by a statue of the Duke of Wellington) were permanent, if belated, examples.

It remains to consider the significance of the earlier triumphal arches for the architectural historian – something quite different from the message of loyalty and apotheosis that they were intended to have for those they honoured, and different also from the significance that they have assumed for the historians of iconography and drama.

As we have seen, triumphal decorations were often engraved in order to perpetuate the memory of these great but transitory occasions. Those who designed them naturally wanted their work to be remembered after its brief exposure to public gaze, and those who paid for them were anxious that the object of their expenditure should not be forgotten. In 1604 it was at the City's behest that Stephen Harrison's arches were 'put in print in a book to bee kept by Mr Chamberlen to the Citty's use'.[32] There are in fact hundreds of engravings of European state pageants of the sixteenth and seventeenth centuries.[33] As a result the triumphal arch took on an existence of its own independent of actual state occasions. Books appeared like Francini's *Livre d'Architecture* of 1631, reissued in English by Robert Pricke in 1669 as *A New Book of Architecture wherein is represented fourty figures of Gates and Arches Triumphal*, which consists exclusively of ornamental classical arches detached from their surroundings. Another mutation of the triumphal arch was the architectural title-page. It was, no doubt, natural that the first engraved title-page printed in Rome should be architectural in character, for the book it prefaced was Labacco's *l'Architettura* of 1552 (fig. 51). But many other examples could be given, from Pierre Vallet's *Le Jardin du Roy Henry IV* (Paris, 1608) (fig. 52) to an atlas of 1655 with its Vignolesque gateway opening to reveal a prospect of the oriental world (fig. 53). Title-pages of this kind were sometimes designed by professional architects. In England we have a notable example in John Webb's design for the *Polyglot Bible* of 1657 (fig. 54), probably for many of his contemporaries his best-known work, and another in James Gibbs's very baroque title-page for Flamsteed's *Historia Coelestis* of 1713. The close connection between the triumphal arch and the title-page is neatly illustrated by a design for an arch celebrating the victories of William III which Francis St John obtained from the collection of John Talman and used as the title-page of a volume of architectural designs collected by himself (fig. 55).[34]

What we see, both in a book such as Francini's, in the title-pages and in the

51. Title-page of Antonio Labacco, *Libro appartenente a l'architettura*, Rome, 1552 (Bodleian Library).

52. Title-page of Pierre Vallet, *Le Jardin du Roy Henry IV*, Paris, 1608 (Bodleian Library, Douce Prints W. 21 (200)).

53. Title-page of J. Blaeu's *Atlas Major*, Amsterdam, 1665, Part VI.

54. Title-page of the *Polyglot Bible* published in London in 1657, designed by the architect John Webb (St John's College Library, Oxford).

Willielmo 3. Aur: Principi confederatae Belgiae Provin: Gubern

Designes
of
Architecture
Sacred and Civil.
drawn
by severall hands
collected
by
Francis St John

55. Title-page to Francis St John's collection of architectural drawings, utilising a design for a Triumphal Arch in honour of William III from the collection of John Talman (Victoria and Albert Museum).

56. Merton College, Oxford: frontispiece in Fellows' Quadrangle, 1610.

triumphal arches, is the isolation of the orders from the architecture of which they properly formed part. Again and again the arch and its framework of columns is taken out of any normal architectural context and exhibited as a feature on its own. Instead of giving meaning and proportion to a whole elevation, as it should, it stands in a void dictated by the width of a street or the breadth of a page. The effect of this aesthetic isolation on an unsophisticated viewer can easily be imagined. Just as for the modern builder and his clients the half-timbered gable stands for 'Tudor', the plastic pediment for 'Georgian', the raking rubble chimney-stack for 'Prairie-style Modern', so in the sixteenth and seventeenth centuries the gateway with its superimposed orders was apt to stand for the classical architecture of Italy. Never mind if the windows were mullioned and transomed, the parapets battlemented, and the mouldings medieval: the gateway was a sufficient affirmation of classical

57. Wadham College, Oxford: frontispiece of Front Quadrangle, *circa* 1613.

taste to satisfy most building owners and their friends. So eventually the architecture of the triumphal arch was assimilated into the show-fronts of such grand houses as Kirby Hall, Northamptonshire (1572), Burghley House, Stamford (1583), Cobham Hall, Kent (1591–4), or Stonyhurst, Lancashire (*c*.1595), and even into the porches of some humbler manor-houses (e.g. Waterston House, Dorset, 1586, Studley Priory, Oxfordshire, 1587). The same phenomenon can be observed in Oxford, where, then as now, architecture formed no part of the academic curriculum, and most dons were little more learned in architecture than country gentlemen. At Merton College (1608–10) the tower in the Fellows' Quadrangle climbs up order by order, quite oblivious to its sub-Gothic setting (fig. 56); at Wadham (1610–13) there is at any rate one string-course that ranges with one of the cornices of the frontispiece (fig. 57). As for the 'Tower of the Five Orders' in the Schools

58. Bodleian Library, Oxford: the Tower of the Five Orders in the Schools Quadrangle, *circa* 1615–20.

Quadrangle (*c*.1615–20), it is no better handled architecturally, but exhibits just such a tableau in stone (of King James I presenting copies of his written works, one to Fame, the other to the University) as contemporaries saw acted in the flesh against the upper stage of some triumphal arch in Cheapside or Fleet Street (fig. 58). At Cambridge, on the other hand, the Porta Honoris at Caius College (1575), though rather naively detailed, is a three-dimensional structure, and no mere assemblage of columns stuck up against a wall (fig. 59). Perhaps it falls into place best if one thinks

59. Gonville and Caius College, Cambridge: the Porta Honoris of 1575.

of it as a permanent version of the sort of ceremonial archway that was (as we have seen) so common in the capital cities of Europe at that time, here symbolising academic rather than military or political achievement.

The influence of the triumphal arch in English architecture must not be over-stated. However much the two Italian arches of 1553 were admired at the time, the fact that (so far as we know) they were not engraved, meant that they could never have been given to a master mason to copy in the way that Sambin's terms were

60. One of the Triumphal Arches erected in London in March 1603/4 for the coronation of King James I (Stephen Harrison, *The Arch's of Triumph erected in honor of . . . James . . . King of England . . . at his Majesties entrance and passage through his Honourable Citty of London*, 1604, Bodleian Library).

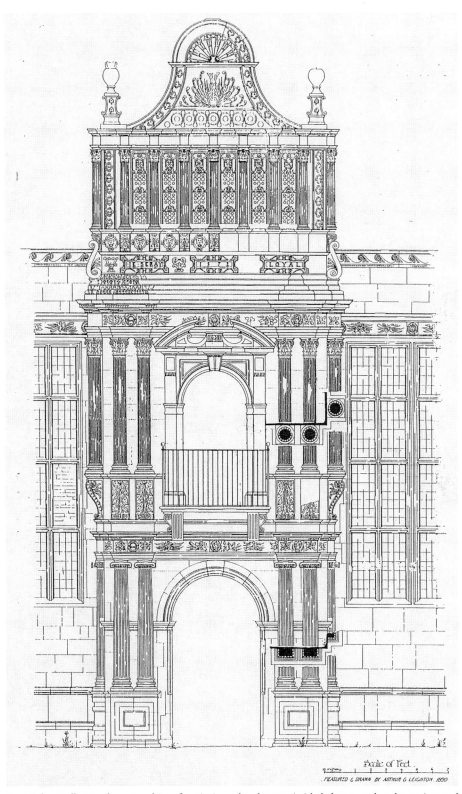

61. Kirby Hall, Northamptonshire, frontispiece dated 1572 (with balcony and archway inserted 1635): measured drawing from J.A. Gotch, *Early Renaissance Architecture in England*, 1901.

at Raglan Castle in the 1570s (below, p. 116). No sudden crop of gateways adorned with classical trappings can be detected after Queen Mary's coronation. Indeed, it is not until the last quarter of the sixteenth century that such gateways begin to become a characteristic feature of English domestic architecture. But even if the one is not directly dependent on the other, the affinity between two such towering confections of columns as those illustrated in figures 60 and 61 is obvious. They were both the products of a society in which architecture was expected to emphasise rank and status by appropriate display, especially at points of entry which could be the focus of social ceremonial. Triumphal arches were a prominent feature of court culture throughout Europe in the sixteenth and seventeenth centuries, and the advertisement they gave to classical architecture in the streets of London must (along with foreign travel, foreign craftsmen and foreign textbooks) be accounted as one element in the architectural education of Elizabethan and Stuart England.

APPENDIX

Description of the Triumphal Arches Erected for Queen Mary's Coronation, 1553

The description printed below is taken from Giulio Raviglio Rosso, *I Successi d'Inghilterra dopo la Morte di Odoardo Sesto fino alla giunta in quel regno del Sereniss. Don Filippo d'Austria Principe di Spagna*, Ferrara, 1560, pp. 35–37.

Although so similar to Rosso's as to suggest a common source, the manuscript account of the accession of Queen Mary by Monsignor (later Cardinal) Commendone, published by C.V. Malfatti as *The Accession, Coronation and Marriage of Mary Tudor as related in four manuscripts of the Escorial* (Barcelona, 1956), fails to describe the arches but does give the inscriptions on them, though with some minor variations (see notes below).

Nelle strade si trouarono piu Archi trionfali, ma però dui ve ne furono di molta piu consideratione de gli altri. L'uno de Mercatanti Genouesi, l'altro de Firentini. Il primo era opera Corinthia come cosa da gli antichi solita a dedicarsi alle Vergini, hauendo dato il nome di questa maniera di edificare vna giovine Corinthia, porgendo molta belleza a riguardanti, essendo & per la proportione, & per l'ornamento che n' appariua cosi vago agli occhi, che veramente per imitatione, si poteua agguagliare a quelli, che gia con tanta spesa fecero gli antichi Romani, tanto erano ben finti di marmo Sacrifici, Battaglie, Historie & Architetture, & di pittura Festoni di frondi, di frutti & di fiori, oltre a molte figure nelle quali si vedeua profondità di dissegno, prospettiua artificiosa, inuentione mirabile, discretione nel comporre, & diligenza nel finire: da vna parte del qual Arco si leggeua.
MARIAE REGINAE INCLYTAE, CONSTANTI, PIAE, CORONAM BRITANNICI IMPERII, ET PALMAM VIRTVTIS ACCIPIENTI, GENVENSES PVBLICA SALVTE LAETANTES CVLTVM OPTATVM TRIBVVNT.
Et nell' altra parte,
VIRTVS SVPERAVIT, IVSTITIA DOMINATVR, VERITAS TRIVMPHAT, PIETAS CORONATVR, SALVS REIPVBLICAE RESTITVITVR.
Quello de Firentini era opera composta senza ordine seruato, però con gran giudicio & con molta vaghezza. La colonna era Corinthia, ma cannellata come la Ionica, il capitello era

90

composto di Dorico, di Ionico, & di Corinthio, l'abaco & il cimatio era Dorico, il vuouolo & le strie Ioniche, gli astragali & le foglie Corinthie, la sua base per li due Torri era Dorica, ma per le due scotie & lo astragalo & i lauori delicati si mostraua Corinthia. L'architraue, fregio & cornice, era opere Ionica, & tutto insieme cosi ben composto che faceua conoscere quanto era stato prudente l'Architetto in saperlo ordinare, non gli hauendo lasciato cosa senza misura, & molta auertenza, ne parte alcune senza molta consideratione. Essendo poi di pittura ornato di fogliami diuersi, di chiocciole di piu maniere, di variati groppi, di figurette & d'animali mescolati insieme, con diuersi compartimenti di gran giudicio: Vi si vedeuano da vna parte, ne suoi nicchi quattro Statue per le prime virtù, & di sopra vna Fama alle quali alludeua il seguente verso.

VIRTVTES FAMA REGINAM AD SIDERA TOLLVNT.★

Et poi piu a basso si leggeua.

MARIAE BRITANNORVM REGINAE VICTRICI, PIAE, AVGVSTAE, FLORENTINI GLORIAE INSIGNIA EREXERVNT.

Nell'altra parte sotto la imagine della Reina trionfante, era scritto.

SALVS PVBLICA. [The public weal.]

Sotto la imagine di Pallade.[†]

INVICTA VIRTVS. [Virtue unconquered.]

Sotto la Historia di Tomiri.[‡]

LIBERTATIS ALTRICI. [To her who nurtures Liberty.]

Sotto Giudith.[§].

PATRIAE LIBERATRICI. [To the liberator of her country.]

Et poi piu a basso in vn panno d'argento i sequenti versi.

MAGNANIMIS PER TE QVOD PAX SIT PARTA BRITANNIS
EXILIO AC REDEANT IVSTITIA, ET PIETAS,
ET VIRGO PRAESTES, QVOD VIX EFFECERIT VLLVS,
VIR SVMMVM QVI SIT VECTVS[¶] AD IMPERIVM:
DVM RECIPIT VIRTVS AVGVSTAM RITE CORONAM,
ET REDDVNT OMNES PVBLICA VOTA DEAE:
LAETA TIBI TALEM TRIBVIT FLORENTIA CVLTVM
QVI TAMEN ARCANO PECTORE MAIOR INEST.

[Because, through you, peace has been secured for the brave Britons
And Justice and Piety return from exile,
And you, as a virgin, are achieving what scarcely any
Man who has been raised to the highest power has accomplished:
While the Goddess Virtue duly receives the august crown,
And all make their votive offerings to her:
Florence gladly pays such reverence to you
Which is none the less felt even more in the breast.]

★ Commendone's version: *Virtutes famam Reginae ad sydera tollunt*, is clearly preferable. As Professor D.A.F.M. Russell has kindly pointed out, the last three words echo Virgil, *Aeneid*, xi, 37.

† Pallas Athene, the goddess of war and wisdom.

‡ Tomyris, a redoubtable oriental queen who defeated and killed the Persian king Cyrus the Great in 529 BC.

§ Judith, a Jewish heroine who saved her native town by cutting off the head of Holofernes, the general of a besieging Assyrian army, as related in the Biblical 'Book of Judith'.

¶ Commendone reads *natus* for *vectus*.

1   See especially *Les Fêtes de la Renaissance*, ed. J. Jacquot, 3 vols, Paris, 1956, 1960 and 1975, B. Wisch and S.S. Munschower, *Art and Pageantry in the Renaissance and Baroque*, 2 vols, Pennsylvania 1990, and M. Fagiolo dell' Arco and S. Carandini, *L'Effimero Barocco, strutture della festa nella Roma del '600*, Rome, 1977; and for England, S. Anglo, *Spectacle, Pageantry and Early Tudor Policy*, 2nd ed., 1997, David M. Bergeron, *English Civic Pageantry 1558–1642*, 1971, and Graham Parry, *The Golden Age Restor'd, The Culture of the Stuart Court, 1603–42*, Manchester, 1981.

2   S. Anglo, *Spectacle*, pp. 212–14.

3   John Shearman, 'The Florentine *Entrata* of Leo X, 1515', *Jnl. Warburg and Courtauld Institutes*, xxxviii, 1975, p. 136.

4   A.B. Chamberlain, *Hans Holbein the Younger*, 1913, ii, pp. 30–3; Anglo, *Spectacle*, p. 250; O. Bätschmann and P. Griener, *Hans Holbein*, 1997, fig. 109.

5   *Calendar of State Papers Spanish*, ix, p. 47.

6   Anglo, *Spectacle*, pp. 283–4. An eighteenth-century copy of a lost contemporary wall-painting depicting the procession, formerly at Cowdray Place, Sussex, is reproduced in Derek Keene, *Cheapside before the Great Fire*, Economic and Social Research Council, 1985.

7   'Two London Chronicles', ed. C.L. Kingsford, *Camden Miscellany*, xii, 1910, p. 30.

8   *The Accession of Queen Mary* (contemporary narrative of Antonio de Guaras), ed. R. Garnett, 1893, p. 119; cf. *The Accession, Coronation and Marriage of Mary Tudor*, ed. C.V. Malfatti, Barcelona, 1956, pp. 31–2, 153.

9   M.E. Bratchel, 'Alien merchant colonies in sixteenth-century England; community organisation and social mores', *Jnl. of Medieval and Renaissance Studies*, 14 (1), 1984, p. 55.

10 Giulio Raviglio Rosso, *I Successi d'Inghilterra dopo la morte di Odoardo sesto . . .* Ferrara, 1560, pp. 35–9. The Italian text is printed below, pp. 90–1.

11 Cornelius Graphaeus, *Spectaculorum in Susceptione Philippi Hisp. Prin. Divi. Caroli V . . . An. MDXLIX Antwerpiae . . . Mirificus Apparatus*, Antwerp, 1550; *Les Fêtes de la Renaissance*, ed. Jacquot, ii, p. 309.

12 G.L. Gorse, 'Triumphal Entries into Genoa during the sixteenth century', in B. Wisch and S.S. Munschower, *Art and Pageantry in the Renaissance and Baroque*, part 1. See also Yona Pinson, 'L'évolution du style renaissant, dans les entrées de Charles Quint à Valenciennes (1540–1549)', *Gazette des Beaux-Arts* cxiii, 1989, pp. 201–13.

13 *The Accession, Coronation and Marriage of Mary Tudor*, ed. Malfatti, p. 153.

14 The only person in England capable designing such arches would probably have been Nicholas of Modena (below, p. 103). He died in Westminster in 1569, but was still active in the 1550s (see Biddle, op. cit. on p. 133).

15 In 1553 the outstanding classical building in London was the unfinished Somerset House in the Strand, built in 1547–52. It is difficult to decide whether the degree of architectural naïveté evident in John Thorpe's well-known drawing of the Strand front was due to the draughtsman or inherent in the design, but, as Summerson points out, its architectural antecedents were, in any case, French rather than Italian. Other early classical buildings were the open-air pulpit in the 'Preaching Place' in Whitehall Palace (*History of the King's Works*, ed. Colvin, iv, 1982, p. 313, pl. 23) and probably the SW tower of Nonsuch Palace (see Martin Biddle in *Burlington Mag.*, July 1984, fig. 21), both dating from the 1540s.

16 *The Royall Passage of her Majesty from the Tower of London, to her Palace of White-hall* (1604), D2v.

17 *Calendar of State Papers Venetian*, vii, p. 13.

18 *The Royall Passage* (see n. 16), A4, Bv, B3.

19 See the plates in Stephen Harrison, *The Arch's of Triumph*, 1604.

20 Ibid.

21 John Peacock, *The Stage Designs of Inigo Jones*, Cambridge, 1995, p. 63.

22 D.S. Bland, 'The Barriers', *Guildhall Miscellany*, I, no. 16, 1956, p. 10.

23 D.M. Bergeron, *English Civic Pageantry 1558–1642*, pp. 107–9; cf. Robert Ashton, *The City and the Court 1603–1643*, Cambridge, 1979, pp. 172–6.

24 D.M. Bergeron, 'The Christmas Family. Artificers in English Civic Pageantry', *Jrnl. English Literary History*, 35, 1968, p. 358.

25 PRO, E 404/153, pt. 1, f. 10; cf. E. Croft-Murray, *Decorative Painting in England 1537–1837*, 1970, p. 196.

26 PRO, Privy Council Register PC2/46, p. 111, 27 April 1636; City of London Records, Repertories 50, f. 199 (5 May 1636), 51, f. 172 (9 May 1637), all referring to conferences between representatives of the City and Inigo Jones as Surveyor of the King's Works 'touching a convenient gate' to be built at Temple Bar.

27 L. Puppi, *Andrea Palladio*, 1975, pp. 406–8.

28 British Library, Harleian MS 6839, f. 146: 'Notes of Practise upon the Gate at Temple Barr: 1638. The Designe of the Composite Order'.

29 J. Ogilby, *Relation of His Majestie's entertainment passing through the City of London to his coronation with a description of the triumphal arches*, 1661, 2nd ed., 1662. For the drawings see *RIBA Drawings Catalogue; G–K*, pp. 18–19.

30 D.M. Bergeron, *English Civic Pageantry 1558–1642*, 1971, p. 121. See also R.M. Smuts, 'Public ceremony and royal charisma: the English royal entry in London, 1485–1642', in *The First Modern Society. Essays in Honour of Lawrence Stone*, ed. A.L. Beier et al., Cambridge, 1989.

31 For the arches in Westminster Hall see *History of the King's Works*, ed. Colvin, v, 1976, p. 454, vi, 1973, p. 647, with illustrations, and below, figs. 106–7.

32 City of London Records, Repertory 26, Part 2, f. 370b, 22 May 1604.

33 In addition to the works referred to in n. 1 above, see John Landwehr, *Splendid Ceremonies, State Entries and Royal Funerals in the Low Countries, 1515–1791: A Bibliography*, Leiden, 1971, with numerous illustrations, and *La Festa a Roma dal Rinascimento al 1870*, ed. Marcello Fagiolo, Turin, 1997.

34 On triumphal arches and title-pages, see H.F. Bouchery, 'Des Arcs Triomphaux aux frontispices de livres', in *Les Fêtes de la Renaissance*, ed. Jacquot, i, 1956, and Margery Corbett and R.W. Lightbown, *The Comely Frontispiece: The Emblematic Title-page in England 1550–1660*, 1979, pp. 6–9.

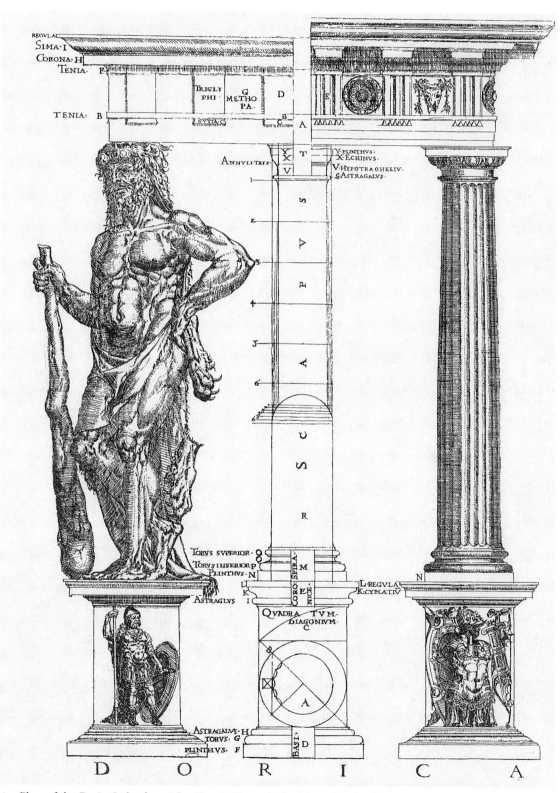

REGVLA
SIMA·I
CORONA·H
TENIA·F

TENIA·B

TRIGLY
PHI   G   METHO   D
PA.

GVTAE·C

B   C   A

E

ANNVLITRIS

YX   T
V

Y·PLINTHVS·
X·ECHINVS·
V·HYPOTRACHELIV·
S·ASTRAGALVS·

S
C
A
P
V
S

R

TORVS SVPERIOR·
TORVS INFERIOR·P
PLINTHVS·N

ASTRAGLVS·I

TORVS SVPERIOR
COROSPIRA
NICE

M
E
C

L·REGVLA
K·CYMATIV

N

QVADRA   TVM·
DIAGONIVM·
C

A

BASI·D

ASTRAGALVS·H
TORVS·G

PLINTHVS·F

D   O   R   I   C   A

62. Plate of the Doric Order from John Shute's *First and Chief Groundes of Architecture*, 1563.

VI

HERMS, TERMS
AND CARYATIDS IN ENGLISH ARCHITECTURE

THE IDEA THAT the classical orders of architecture were related to the human figure goes back to Antiquity and is enshrined in the pages of Vitruvius.[1] John Shute, the author of the first English architectural treatise (*The First and Chief Groundes of Architecture*, 1563), leaves the reader in no doubt as to the anthropomorphic nature of the orders: every one of his five plates shows an appropriate human figure posing beside a column (fig. 62). Vitruvius tells the legendary story of how the Greeks took vengeance on the Caryans for allying with their enemies the Persians. First they killed the men and enslaved the women, and then they commemorated the latter's shame architecturally by using statues of them as load-bearing columns: hence the 'caryatid' order. A similar story, also recounted by Vitruvius, associates the male equivalent, or 'persian' order, with a portico or stoa commemorating a victory of the Spartans over the Persians in 479 BC. A famous exemplar, also dating from the fifth century BC, was the south portico of the building on the Acropolis at Athens known as the Erechtheum, whose entablature is supported by six female figures instead of columns (fig. 63).

Neither of the legends recounted by Vitruvius tells the whole story, for it is difficult to see such statuesque figures as those of the Erechtheum as the humiliated representatives of a defeated state, while the male ones of the Spartan stoa apparently stood in front of (or possibly above) the columns and so did not themselves act as structural supports. Even if they did, they would have been examples, rather than prototypes, of an architectural feature otherwise known in its male form as *atlantes* (after Atlas, the Titan who supported the World on his shoulders) or *telamones* (derived from a Greek word meaning 'supporters').[2] Whatever their real history, for the Romans such figures had strong associations with the idea of imperial authority over conquered peoples,[3] and as 'caryatids' and 'persians' the two anthropomorphic orders would form part of the established vocabulary of revived classical architecture from the Renaissance onwards. If an engraving of 1602 is to be trusted, they both figured on the exterior of a Roman tower which stood in Pavia until its collapse in 1584 (fig. 64),[4] and in a well-known design the Italian artist Raimondi (*c*.1470–*c*.1530) shows them combined into a single façade (fig. 65). Both in Italy and in France caryatid figures began to appear in sculpture in the second quarter of the sixteenth century, notably in the Strozzi tomb in Sant'Andrea in Mantua (by Giulio Romano, *c*.1530), and in the 'tribune des

63. Portico of the Erechtheum, Athens (British Architectural Library, Photographic Collection).

64. Roman tower at Pavia, with figures of caryatids above 'persians': an engraving of 1602 showing the tower (perhaps not quite accurately) before its collapse in 1584 (see note 4 on p. 133).

65. Engraving of a façade with caryatids and persians, by Marcantonio Raimondi (*c.*1470–*c.*1530).

caryatides' in the great ballroom of the Louvre palace in Paris (by the sculptor Jean Goujon, 1550–1).[5] Before long, however, both caryatids and persians would be confused with two other anthropomorphic forms derived from classical antiquity: herms and terms.

A herm was a stone shaft surmounted by a head or bust, particularly of the Greek god Hermes. No other part of the body was represented except the male genital

97

66. Herms represented on a Greek vase of the fifth century BC in the Louvre, Paris. Note the projecting lugs for hanging garlands on the central herm and sockets for them on the other two.

organs, which were carved on the front. A herm was therefore a reminder that Hermes was (among other things) a fertility god whose body was, as it were, imprisoned in the stone, only the head and the genitals being exposed. Precisely what significance these archaically grinning, ostentatiously phallic objects (fig. 66) had for the Greeks remains unclear, but that they were regarded as sacred is shown by the furore that followed the malicious mutilation of some of them at Athens in 415 BC.[6] Herms were generally placed out of doors, and as Hermes was the protector of travellers they sometimes served as road-markers, notably on the roads round Athens. They could also serve as memorials to celebrated individuals, such as philosophers, poets and rulers. When fulfilling the latter function, they might carry portrait busts and inscriptions identifying the persons commemorated. At shoulder level there were often two projections like vestigial arms for the hanging of votive garlands. In surviving herms these have usually disappeared, but the sockets sometimes remain.[7]

The use of herms was continued by the Romans, whose boundary deity, Terminus, was represented by a stone of similar character: hence *termini*, boundary markers resembling herms, and regarded as identical with them by early writers on classical antiquities such as Montfaucon (1655–1741).[8] By the eighteenth century the word 'term' was generally used for both, especially in France, where 'herme' was avoided 'par une crainte servile pour les aspirations'.[9] Some writers went so far as to conflate the two words as 'therme'.[10]

Herms and terms survived in considerable numbers to be rediscovered by Renaissance antiquaries and published in collections of engravings such as Statius'

Illustrium Virorum . . . Vultus (Rome, 1569) and Boissard's *Antiquitatum Romanarum* (Frankfurt, 1597–1602) (fig. 67). But, however fascinated artists might be by these rediscovered relics of Antiquity, their assimilation into the Christian civilisation of Western Europe presented obvious difficulties. Although such openly pagan symbols might be flaunted in the pages of an esoteric work like Francesco Colonna's *Hypnerotomachia Poliphili*, published in 1499 (fig. 68), they could hardly be resurrected as familiar objects of town or countryside. Suitably emasculated, however, they were seized on as alternatives to caryatids for the decoration of tombs, chimney-pieces, doorways and title-pages. When, as in some Hellenistic examples, the upper part of the body was fully modelled down to the hips, only the legs and feet being replaced by a tapering shaft, the difference between a caryatid and a term was in fact small, but the latter could more easily be lengthened or shortened or otherwise distorted, and lent itself to all manner of geometrical elaboration with strapwork decoration by those who did not share Jean Goujon's mastery of the human figure. Already in France in the 1540s there were chimney-pieces in the royal Château de Madrid (in the Bois de Boulogne near Paris), which figured

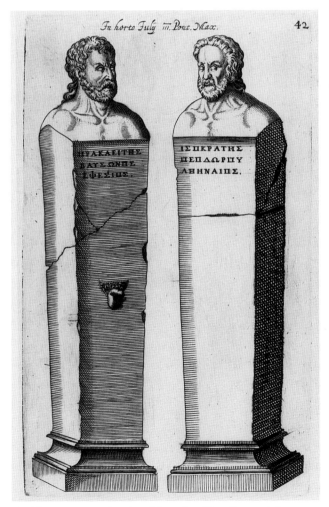

67. Herms representing the philosopher Heraclitus and the orator Isocrates (J.J. Boissard, *Antiquitatum Romanarum*, Frankfurt, 1597–8, pl. 36, Bodleian Library).

68. Nymphs sacrificing to Priapus in the form of a herm: an engraving from the Renaissance romance entitled *Hypnerotomachia Polyphili*, published in Venice in 1499.

69. Two chimney-pieces of the 1540s in the Château de Madrid near Paris, flanked by mannerist caryatid-terms: from Jacques Androuet du Cerceau, *Le Premier Volume des plus excellents Bastiments de France*, Paris, 1576.

caryatids or terms of markedly mannerist form, very different from the elegantly draped females of the Louvre: some transmuted into consoles or balusters, others ending in coiled tails (fig. 69).[11] Thus, by the second half of the sixteenth century, herms, terms, persians and caryatids had for practical purposes been amalgamated into a new decorative form which proved immensely popular with mannerist architects and sculptors like the Italian Galeazzo Alessi (1512–72), the Flemish Cornelis Floris (?1514–75), the Spanish Jerónimo del Corral (fl. 1550–80) and innumerable English and Scottish masons and wood-carvers. Prominently displayed on the title-pages of several of the five books into which Serlio's great treatise on architecture (1537–75) was divided, the caryatid-term in various forms was seen by everyone who consulted this leading architectural textbook of the day (fig. 70). Caryatid-terms figured in a number of suites of engraved designs by artists such as Agostino Veneziano, Jean Mignon and Crispin de Passe the younger, and in 1565 a collection of designs devoted entirely to 'caryatids (commonly called terms) or atlantes' (*Caryatidum* (*Vulgus Termas Vocat'*) *sive Athlantidum . . .*) was published in Antwerp. This was the work of Hans (Johan) Vredeman de Vries (1527–1606), a prolific author of mannerist designs, and offered a large selection of more or less fantastic figures for the benefit of 'masons, cabinet-makers, glass painters and other craftsmen'. Both male and female, they lent themselves to pairing on either side of a doorway or fireplace. Holding hands but locked in strapwork, or eyeing one another from their fixed pedestals, they could be in their way as sexually suggestive as their pagan prototypes (fig. 71). Endlessly repeated on screens and galleries or carved onto the brackets supporting the overhanging front of a timber-framed building, they ministered to the same taste for the grotesque that had produced the

SEBASTIANI SERLII,
COMMVNIA PRAECEPTA
ARCHITECTVRAE

Ad quinque ædificiorum genera,

Tuscanum, Doricum, Ionicum, Corin-
thium , atque Compositum
mirificè conducentia:

A IOANNE CAROLO
Saraceno ex Italico in Latinum
sermonem elegantissimè nunc
conuersa, fidelissimeque
translata.

LIBER QVARTVS.

Antiquitatum exemplis insuper, quæ pleraque
à Vitruuiana doctrina haud abhorrere ui-
dentur, aptissimè insertis appositisq;

VENETIIS,
Apud Franciscum de Franciscis Senensem, & Ioannem Chriger.
M D LXVIII.

70. Title-page of the fourth Book of Sebastiano Serlio's *Opere d'
Architettura*, in the *Latin* edition of 1568, featuring caryatid-terms.

71. (*below*) Caryatid-terms from Hans Vredeman de Vries' engraved
designs, published in Antwerp in 1565 (Victoria and Albert
Museum).

72. (*right*) A pair of caryatid-terms on either side of a chimney-piece at Aston Hall, Birmingham, *circa* 1630.

73. (*far right*) Detail of a caryatid-term decorating a chimney-piece at Aston Hall, Birmingham (cf. figure 72).

74. (*below*) Tablet in the church of St Dunstan-in-the-West, London, to Gerard Legh (d. 1563), the author of a book on heraldry. The flanking figures represent Mercury (symbolising Heraldry) and Friendship.

medieval corbel and the Gothic gargoyle. In figures of this sort, the rules of anatomy and of architecture are alike suspended. Human bodies tail off into tree-trunks or basket-work, or grasp the tops of the tapering containers out of which their bodies emerge (figs. 72, 73). Some support the architrave, some the cornice, some nothing at all. Those with cushions on their heads to mitigate their burden (cf. fig. 70) are visibly acting an architectural part, but others, standing free on either side of tomb or overmantel (fig. 74), have renounced it in order to personify the civil or military attributes of those who commissioned them.

It was at Henry VIII's court that terms first made an appearance in English decorative art and architecture. They were part of the apparatus of mannerist motifs that Henry derived from the palaces (particularly Fontainebleau) of his rival Francis I, and that Francis had introduced from Italy by employing accomplished artists and craftsmen such as Rosso and Primaticcio. Although Henry himself had never seen any of the French palaces, in 1540 his ambassador, Sir John Wallop, had been conducted round the celebrated gallery at Fontainebleau by Francis himself,[12] and others had no doubt reported on its elegant and highly sophisticated stucco-work, in which terms and caryatids of various forms abounded.[13] One of the Italian artists working for Francis fled to England to avoid the consequences of a fraud in which he was involved. This was Nicholas of Modena, a pupil of Giulio Romano, and it is to Nicholas that a surviving design for the decoration of one of Henry VIII's palaces is attributed.[14] Datable to between 1543 and 1546 by the badge of Queen Katherine Parr, it shows an elaborately modelled wall in which two

75. Design for the decoration of a wall in a Tudor royal palace attributed to Nicholas of Modena and datable to the years 1543–6 (Musée du Louvre, Paris, Département des Arts Graphiques, inv. 19215, photo R.M.N.).

76. Nonsuch Palace, Surrey. Detail from Joris Hoefnagel's coloured drawing of 1568, showing the centre of the south front, ornamented with stucco panels. Two terms can be seen, one on either side of the window in the projecting bow (private collection, by kind permission of the owners).

caryatid-terms flank a doorway (fig. 75). Soon figures of this sort were to be seen in woodwork in one of the new galleries in Whitehall Palace, where sixty 'termes of waynscot' were carved to 'garnish' its panelling,[15] and in stucco decorating the celebrated garden front of Nonsuch Palace (completed by 1546), where two terms can be discerned, one on either side of the central window as represented in Joris Hoefnagel's drawing of 1568 (fig. 76).[16] In 1544 an elongated term formed part of Hans Holbein's design for a clock-cum-hourglass intended as a New Year's gift to Henry VIII by the paymaster of his works at Whitehall, Sir Anthony Denny, and in 1546 the English ratification of the Anglo-French Treaty of Camp, written in fine italic script, took the form of a bound volume whose first page was decorated by a correctly drawn classical entablature supported by two elegant caryatid-terms.[17]

It was for the tombs of great Tudor courtiers that what are probably the earliest surviving examples in England of sculptured terms were made. Pagan though they were in origin, terms, caryatids, persians and their derivatives found their way into churches both Catholic and Protestant in the course of the sixteenth century. For the tomb of Pope Julius II (1503–13) in St Peter's itself, Michelangelo envisaged bound captives (originally, it seems, intended to symbolise the Italian provinces subjected to the papacy) standing, like those of the Persian stoa, in front of pilasters, themselves in the form of caryatid-terms.[18] In the 1540s a painting of the 'Deposition' in the church of Trinità dei Monti in Rome was flanked by stucco caryatid-terms which were wittily represented as supporting an entablature with their heads while holding a capital in one hand and trying with the other to manoeuvre a column into place beneath it.[19] At Oosterend in the Spanish Netherlands, inscriptions 'FIGUR DER CARIATIDES' and 'FIGUR DER PERSEN' proudly draw attention to the male and female figures decorating elegant classical galleries or tribunes built in the parish church in 1554.[20] In England even so strict a cleric as Archbishop Cranmer had himself painted (in 1545) with a female term in the background (what it signified is an iconographical puzzle that has yet to be solved).[21] But in a country where there was so little church-building in the century after the Reformation, almost all the terms or caryatids in English churches formed part of funerary monuments.

Herms and terms had a special place in the iconography of death. Their memorial function in Antiquity has already been mentioned, and although they were not normally used in cemeteries, they are occasionally found carved on Greek tombstones. Renaissance scholars were well aware of this association. As early as 1519 the Dutch humanist Erasmus had a medal struck with the head and shoulders of a term, and the motto 'TERMINUS CONCEDO NULLI'. 'Death,' he explained, was 'the end (*terminus*) that yields to none,' the fate that none can escape. In due course this emblem was carved on his tombstone in Basle Cathedral. In France Claude Gouffier (d. 1570), master of the horse to Francis I, adopted as his motto a phrase with a similar play on the word 'term': HIC TERMINUS HAERET, meaning 'this end is fixed', or 'this is the [inescapable] end,' and decorated his château at Oiron in Poitou with finely moulded terracotta terms, one of which can be seen in the Louvre.[22] In England small caryatid-terms form part of the decoration of one of the tombs set up by the Howard Dukes of Norfolk in Framlingham Church, Suffolk, in the middle of the sixteenth century (fig. 77). The tomb in question was that of Henry Fitzroy, Duke of Richmond, Henry VIII's illegitimate son, whose wife was a Howard. He had died in 1536, but the tomb, originally intended to

77. (*above*) The tomb of Henry Fitzroy, Duke of Richmond (d. 1536) in Framlingham Church, Suffolk, begun before 1547, but not completed until 1555 (Professor Lawrence Stone).

78. Old Basing Church, Hampshire: the southern of the two Paulet chapels.

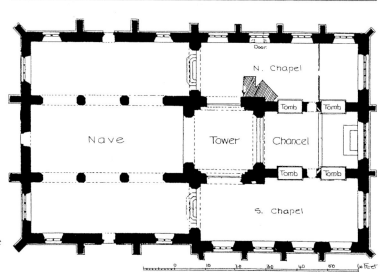

79. Plan of Old Basing Church, Hampshire (RIBA *Transactions*, NS V, 1889).

80. 'The quick and the dead' as represented by pairs of terms above the tomb of William Paulet, 1st Marquess of Winchester (d. 1572) (Dr John Crook).

stand in Thetford Priory, was not completed until 1555.[23] Much more remarkable is the frieze of terms that decorates the southern of the two funerary chapels built by the Paulet family on either side of the chancel of Old Basing Church, Hampshire (fig. 78). The northern chapel was built by Sir John Paulet (d. *c.*1525), and contains the tombs of himself and his father John (d. 1488), set in arched recesses in a new ashlar wall which replaced the former north wall of the chancel. The similar southern chapel (fig. 79) was evidently built by Sir John's son, William, 1st Marquess of Winchester, who had been a leading figure in the household of Henry VIII and was Queen Elizabeth's Lord Treasurer from 1550 until his death in 1572. Its northern wall similarly replaced the southern wall of the chancel and contains two matching tombs, without effigies or inscriptions. However, heraldic badges carved in the spandrels of the eastern arch and incorporating the garter and a marquess's coronet make it clear that the tomb beneath was that of the first marquess and his first wife Elizabeth, who died in December 1558 and was interred at Basing with great ceremony.[24] As Lord Winchester was given the garter in 1543 and elevated to the marquessate in 1551, the tomb (and therefore the chapel of which it forms an integral part) was evidently constructed after 1551, and presumably before his second marriage in 1566. A date in the 1550s seems most likely. Along both sides of the wall above the tomb recess there runs a frieze or cresting consisting of terms separated by conventional foliage.[25] Topped alternately by bearded heads and skulls (fig. 80), the terms gaze poignantly at one another in a

81. Turvey Church, Bedfordshire: tomb of the 1st Lord
Mordaunt (d. 1562).

form of *memento mori* apparently unique in Renaissance art, English or European.
The carving is less remarkable than the conception, but bearing in mind Paulet's
eminent place at the Tudor court, some connection – direct or indirect – with one
of the French or Italian artists attracted by the patronage of Henry VIII seems
possible.

The terms and caryatids that decorated many Elizabethan and Jacobean tombs
were more conventional, if sometimes more elegantly carved. As flanking features
of a classically detailed tablet or aedicule they begin to appear in the 1560s (1st Lord
Mordaunt, d. 1562, at Turvey, Beds., fig. 81; Gerard Legh, d. 1563, at St Dunstan-
in-the-West, London, fig. 74) and 1570s (Anthony Cave at Chicheley, Bucks,
erected 1576; Elizabeth Darcy at Hornby, Yorks., erected 1578; Richard Harford,
d. 1579, at Bosbury, Herefs.), a little later than in France, and were quite common
by the early seventeenth century (fig. 82). Though often without any obvious
symbolical significance, caryatids lent themselves readily to the representation of
Virtues, as in Le Sueur's monument to the Duke of Richmond and Lennox
(d. 1624) in Westminster Abbey, where they symbolise Faith, Hope, Charity and
Prudence, or of attributes peculiar to the person commemorated, heraldic in the
case of Gerard Legh, already mentioned, who was the author of a book on *Armoury*,
military in that of Lieutenant Colonel William Prude (d. 1632) in Canterbury

82. (*above*) Burford Church, Oxfordshire: the monument to John Osbaldeston (d. 1614). Cf. figure 83.

83. (*above right*) Engraving by Hans Vredeman de Vries (1568) used by the sculptor of the Osbaldeston monument illustrated in figure 82 (Victoria and Albert Museum).

84. Bishop's Tawton Church, Devon: the monument to Francis Chichester (d. 1698). The employment of caryatids alongside columns was a solecism condemned by Sir William Chambers because the bulky human figure makes the columns 'appear very trifling' (*Treatise on the Decorative Part of Civil Architecture*, 1791).

85. Harlton Church, Cambridgeshire: the Fryer monument of 1632, with its canopy supported by caryatid terms.

Cathedral. At Harlton in Cambridgeshire, a pair of mourning caryatid-terms on the Fryer monument of 1632 perform the same function as medieval weepers (fig. 85). The male one appears to be a friar (a common type of weeper) and if so an allusion to the family name must be intended.[26] At Bockleton, Worcestershire, eight small caryatid-terms stand sentinel between the shields decorating the sides of the tomb chest (dated 1594) of Richard Barneby (d. 1597) (fig. 86), much as traditional men in armour do round that of the Earl of Huntingdon (d. 1561) at Ashby-de-la-Zouche, Leicestershire, while two larger ones support the inscription tablet on the wall behind.

Even more common were caryatid-terms as a decoration for screens and chimney-pieces in the houses of the aristocracy and gentry. On hall screens in particular, they often proliferate in a manner that shows the promiscuous and untutored taste of the artisan rather than of the architect. On the screen in Middle

86. Bockleton Church, Worcestershire: tomb of Richard Barneby (d. 1597), erected in 1594.

87. The screen in the hall at Knole, Kent, showing some of the forty-one terms with which it is decorated (National Trust).

Temple Hall in London (*c.*1570), seventeen terms or caryatids are deployed at different levels, with four more flanking the two doorways, at Audley End in Essex (*c.*1610) fifteen, at Knole in Kent (*c.*1605) no fewer than forty-one (fig. 87). Caryatid-terms were also liberally displayed on most of the temporary arches erected in the streets of London for the coronation procession of King James I in 1603 (fig. 46). 'French terms' is what these rather gross figures were called in two contemporary descriptions (one by the 'joiner and architect' responsible),[27] as were

88. Aston Hall, Birmingham: tapering pilasters over a side doorway, *circa* 1630 (*British Architect*, 9 February 1879).

also the terms decorating two chimney-pieces made for Hatfield House in 1611.[28] That terms of this sort should be described as 'French' is not surprising in view of earlier examples in the French royal châteaux, particularly those in the Château de Madrid, engravings of which had been published by Du Cerceau in 1576 (fig. 69). Another important chimneypiece here featured consoles in the form of caryatids below, and above, tapering pilasters of a kind first used by Michelangelo in the vestibule of the Laurentian Library in Florence. Pilasters of this form had obvious affinities with terms, and examples such as those at Aston Hall, near Birmingham (fig. 88), can perhaps be read as terms in which the bust has been eliminated and a capital takes the place of the head.

As Mr Anthony Wells-Cole has shown,[29] many Elizabethan and Jacobean caryatid-terms were copied from the engravings of Cornelis Bos (*c.*1510–*c.*1565), Jan Vredeman de Vries and other Netherlandish artists, whose fertile invention provided a great variety of models to choose from (cf. figs. 71, 83). Few of these engraved terms or caryatids bore much relation to their ancient prototypes, but one

113

89. Design for a chimney-piece with caryatid-terms, late sixteenth-century, from the Smythson Collection (British Architectural Library, Drawings Collection).

90. Raglan Castle, Monmouthshire: the two surviving caryatids supporting one end of a chimney-piece in the ruined Long Gallery built by William, Earl of Worcester, in the 1570s (Mr Richard Avent).

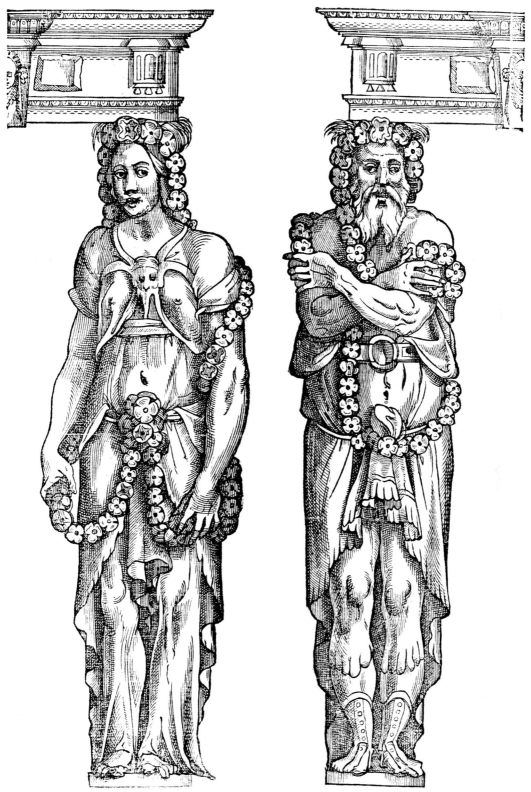

91. Two designs for caryatids in the Earl of Worcester's own copy of Hugues Sambin's *La Diversité des Termes* (Dijon, 1572). These were the source for the two caryatids shown in figure 90. Note that the positions of their arms were reversed in execution.

of De Vries's designs does show the projecting lugs (on which garlands were hung), and this authentic detail is also found in a design for a chimney-piece in the collection of architectural drawings made by the Smythson family of mason-architects in the sixteenth and early seventeenth centuries (fig. 89). So far no English chimney-piece has been found that follows this design, but in the cloisters of Liège Cathedral the exquisite monument to Dean Jean Stouten (d. 1557) is flanked by classical terms of this sort.[30]

Although the prints of De Vries and others must have circulated in considerable numbers, they are very rare today. In Britain only one complete set of De Vries' designs for caryatids is recorded – in the Bodleian Library at Oxford. The originals must have been bought by workshops rather than for libraries, and were either worn out by repeated use or discarded when they became unfashionable. The rough handling they received is illustrated by a tattered copy of Hugues Sambin's *La Diversité des Termes* in the writer's possession. Although described on the title-page as 'Architecte', Sambin was primarily a joiner, and in France most of his identified works are elaborately decorated cabinets rather than buildings.[31] His book was published at Dijon in 1572, and the copy in question bears on its title-page the signature 'Worcester', that is William Somerset, Earl of Worcester, who no doubt acquired it in 1573, when he was sent to Paris by Queen Elizabeth as a special envoy (see frontispiece).[32] Inside, several of Sambin's designs for caryatids are marked with large crosses, and on a blank page the earl's motto ('mutare vel timere sperno') has been written out in a sixteenth-century hand, perhaps for a carver to copy it. At the time Worcester was engaged in remodelling his family seat at Raglan Castle in Monmouthshire: in particular, he constructed a long gallery at first-floor level immediately to the south of the great hall.[33] Ruined in the Civil War, Raglan today retains few decorative features of the Elizabethan earl's work, but in what remains of the long gallery, one half of a chimney-piece survives, with two caryatids taken direct from the fifth pair of engravings in Sambin's book (figs. 90, 91). Here the patron was himself responsible for obtaining and prescribing the published source, but most engravings of this sort were probably imported by printsellers and shown to clients by workmen as possible models.

In another French publication, Du Cerceau's *Seconde Livre d'Architecture* of 1561, designs for chimney-pieces are offered complete with a variety of caryatids. Early in the seventeenth century two of Du Cerceau's plates were imitated at Careston in Forfarshire, the seat of Sir Harry Lindsay, afterwards 13th Earl of Crawford (d. 1623) (figs. 92, 93). What Du Cerceau's strange design of entwined snakes emerging from urns grasped by nude atlantes meant to this Scottish laird is difficult to guess.

The indiscriminate profusion of caryatid-terms must have been one of the features of Elizabethan and Jacobean architecture that Inigo Jones found least to his taste, and he made relatively little use of them.[34] A grand display of caryatids was, however, envisaged in the unexecuted designs for a new royal palace in Whitehall for which his pupil John Webb made many drawings from his directions.[35] Super-imposed persian and caryatid figures were to surround a square or circular court, various combinations of orders being considered, e.g. Tuscan and Doric, or Ionic and Corinthian (fig. 94). Other figures of the caryatid family appear from time to

92. The source of the chimney-pieces at Careston: two engravings in J. Androuet du Cerceau's *Seconde Livre d'Architecture* (Paris, 1561) (Victoria and Albert Museum).

93. Careston, Forfarshire: two early seventeenth-century chimney-pieces derived from plates in J. Androuet du Cerceau's *Seconde Livre d'Architecture* (Paris, 1561) (*Country Life*).

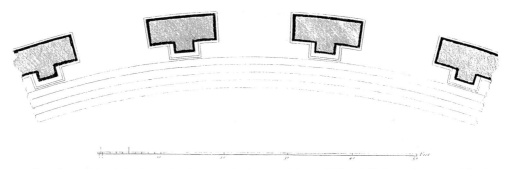

94. Three bays of the design for a circular court in the new Palace of Whitehall planned for King Charles I by Inigo Jones and John Webb, redrawn by Henry Flitcroft for publication in William Kent's *Designs of Inigo Jones* (1727), i, pls. 48–9. Here the persians support Tuscan capitals, the caryatids Corinthian ones, but other possible combinations of orders were envisaged in Webb's drawings.

95. Norgrove Court, Worcestershire: a plaster overmantel in a house built in 1649. For the source of the caryatids see figure 83.

time in Jones's designs for masques and other ephemeral occasions. In one of these, 'the House of Oceanus' (1624), a grotto-like structure was to be supported by tiers of straining atlantes. In another, the fallen 'House of Chivalry' (1610), he has introduced a Roman building called Les Tutelles which he had recently seen in France, complete with atlantes or telamones in its upper story.[36]

The plaster overmantels of 1649 at Norgrove Court in Worcestershire (fig. 95) must represent one of the last appearances of caryatid-terms of Netherlandish origin in English architecture, but terms of a more authentically classical character were to reappear in one of Sir Christopher Wren's earliest works, the Sheldonian Theatre at Oxford (figs. 96, 97). 'True Latin' was his avowed objective in the designing of St Paul's Cathedral, and in the memoir written by his son we read that the assembly-hall which he designed for Archbishop Sheldon was designed 'with a view to the ancient Roman grandeur discernible in the Theatre of Marcellus at Rome'.[37] Characteristically, Wren treated his model with considerable freedom, and the full display of classical architecture that the Roman source implied could not be realised for lack of funds. Still, the classical pretensions of the Sheldonian Theatre were obvious, and Wren was evidently anxious that they should extend to the railings that separated it from the street. For an appropriate design the illustrated textbooks (Vitruvius, Serlio, Palladio, etc.) offered no help. Almost certainly this matter was still unresolved when the foundations of the Theatre were laid in July 1664. Then, in the summer of 1665, Wren went abroad to France and did not return until early in the following year. It was in Paris that he saw the domed churches that so powerfully influenced his designs for St Paul's Cathedral. But he also visited a number of châteaux, including Vaux-le-Vicomte, then only just finished to the designs of Louis Le Vau.[38] As he approached this magnificent house the first thing he would have seen was the screen (fig. 98). Treated as double-headed terms, the piers with their iron railings offered an attractive model for the Sheldonian screen,

96. The Sheldonian Theatre, Oxford (1664–9), with its screen of 'termains'.

97. The two 'termains' on either side of the entrance to the Sheldonian Theatre, a detail from David Loggan's *Oxonia Illustrata* (1675).

98. Vaux-le-Vicomte, France: the screen of double-headed terms designed by Louis Le Vau and seen by Wren in 1665. Double-headed terms were common in Antiquity and were appropriate where, as here, they were approached from both sides.

100. (*right*) Engraving (reversed) of a herm (of Thucydides) with a square hole in its shoulder (from J.J. Boissard, *Antiquitatum Romanarum*, Frankfurt, 1597–8, Bodleian Library).

99. Perge, Pamphylia (now Turkey): a balustrade of terms erected in the theatre in about 250 AD to separate spectators from gladiatorial and other games. They have all lost their heads.

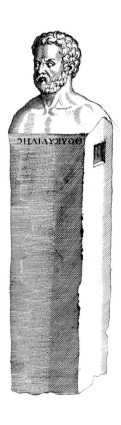

101. Istanbul: a relief on the base of the obelisk in the Hippodrome, showing the Emperor Theodosius (379–395 AD) and his entourage in an enclosure whose railings were supported by terms.

for which Wren must have given directions immediately he got back. Work on it started in May 1666, two or three months after his return. Originally there were fourteen piers, and in the accounts the mason-sculptor William Byrd was paid for twelve 'termains' at £3 10s. apiece and two at £5 10s. apiece.[39]

For terms as upright supports for stone or marble balustrades there was good classical precedent. Modern archaeology has revealed their use for this purpose in several places, notably in front of an early third-century nymphaeum at Lepcis Magna in North Africa, and round a rectangular pool attached to a fourth-century Roman villa near Trier in Germany.[40] When a theatre at Perge in Pamphylia was converted into an arena for gladiatorial and other games in about AD 250, a balustrade punctuated by herms was erected to separate the spectators from the participants[41] (fig. 99). None of these examples could have been known to Wren or Le Vau. What a seventeenth-century architect could have observed were the representations of privileged enclosures on carved reliefs in Rome and Constantinople. The former, on the north face of the Arch of Constantine in Rome (built in AD 312–315), shows the Emperor making a formal address (*allocutio*) from a platform in

122

the Forum; the latter, carved on the base of an obelisk still standing in Istanbul, shows the Emperor Theodosius (379–395) and his entourage watching the horses racing in the Hippodrome from the imperial box (fig. 101). In both, the balustrades are supported by terms. But neither Le Vau nor Wren had been to Rome, still less to Constantinople, and no detailed engravings of either of these reliefs appear to have been available at the time. What Le Vau or Wren would have seen were engravings of herms and terms with square holes cut in their shoulders (fig. 100), from which they could have deduced that they had served as supports for railings.[42] Wren, moreover, would certainly have been familiar with Cicero's well-known letters to Atticus, in one of which he asked for some terms to decorate his library or 'academy'.[43] Here then was Ancient authority for the use of terms in an academic environment. Impeccably Antique, vouched for by Cicero, and recently used by the French royal architect, they provided just that combination of classical authority and architectural scholarship that would appeal to a don like Wren, brought up on the Latin authors, and determined to give the University a building of suitable character for its formal occasions (all, of course, then conducted in Latin).

For illustrations of ancient terms to copy, Wren had only to turn to books by authors such as Boissard and Ursinus, which we know were in his library.[44] The personages represented (and identified by inscriptions) were celebrated poets, philosophers, historians and statesmen – men like Aristotle, Seneca, Herodotus, Thucydides and Themistocles (figs. 67, 100), and Wren's fourteen unnamed 'termains' were presumably intended to suggest worthies of this sort. Unfortunately the early guide-books to Oxford, which devote a great deal of attention to the interior of the Theatre, and especially to the ceiling painting by Robert Streeter, with its elaborate allegory of Learning repelling the attacks of Ignorance, unanimously ignore the row of terms outside. More recent commentators are equally uninformative. One facetiously suggests that they represent 'Heads of Houses in the Dark Ages'.[45] By American visitors, Max Beerbohm tells us, they 'are frequently mistaken for the twelve Apostles'.[46] By nearly everyone else, including Beerbohm himself, they have traditionally been supposed to represent the Emperors of Rome. In fact, the Caesars were normally represented as a set of twelve (not fourteen) busts, nor were any of the twelve bearded or moustached.[47]

Indirect confirmation that Wren's 'termains' were indeed intended to represent learned worthies such as philosophers comes from a description of the once famous garden at Bretby in Derbyshire, the seat of the Earls of Chesterfield, wantonly destroyed in 1780. It was laid out during the last sixteen years of the seventeenth century, from 1684 onwards, and William Talman, Wren's colleague at the Office of Works, was very likely involved.[48] Here there was 'an Iron Palisade supported at equal distances by the Busts of 13 of the most eminent Grecian and other ancient Philosophers: behind which . . . was formed a very deep and spacious Piece of water called the Philosopher's Pond'.[49] An engraving shows a curved screen similar to the one at Oxford, with the rectangular pool beyond it (fig. 102). At Dyrham Park in Gloucestershire, a house definitely designed by Talman, there was formerly another screen of this sort: 'the end of [the] Parterre is fenc'd in from the Park with curious Iron Work, on Dwarf Walls; and on Pillars between the Spikes are fix'd Variety of

102. Bretby Hall, Derbyshire: the 'Philosophers' Pond', separated from the smaller pool by a screen of piers or terms representing philosophers, as at Oxford (J. Kip and L. Knyff, *Britannia Illustrata*, i, 1714, pl. 26).

Heads carv'd out of fine Stone.'[50] No representation of this screen is known, but in Dr Plot's *Natural History of Staffordshire* (1686) there is an engraving of a third example formerly at Aqualate Hall in that county (fig. 103).

By the end of the seventeenth century the idea that the orders were related to the human figure was going out of fashion. In one of his writings on architecture (*Tract* I) Wren made it clear that he found it unconvincing, and the Sheldonian Theatre was the only building of his to feature terms or caryatids. They were in fact rarely used in English architecture of his time. At Hampton Court Vanbrugh wittily

103. (*above*) Aqualate Hall, Staffordshire: the screen of piers surmounted by busts in a manner recalling the screen of terms at the Sheldonian Theatre (engraving by Michael Burghers in Robert Plot, *The Natural History of Staffordshire*, Oxford, 1686).

104. Hampton Court Palace: chimney-piece in the Queen's Guard Chamber designed by Sir John Vanbrugh, 1716–18 (Historic Royal Palaces).

105. Imaginary reconstruction of a Roman circus building showing terms incorporated in a Venetian window: from O. Panvinio, *De Ludis Circensibus*, Venice, 1600, p. 62 (the Provost and Fellows of Worcester College, Oxford).

made figures of yeomen of the guard serve as atlantes at either end of the chimney-piece in the Queen's Guard Chamber (fig. 104), and at Blenheim Palace a group of six caryatids adorns the west bow. In one of his designs for the Clarendon Building at Oxford, Hawksmoor shows caryatid figures facing one another on either side of the entrance, much as they do at Sansovino's Library in Venice, but this characteristically striking feature was not executed.[51]

Herms, terms and caryatids were equally rare in the conventional Palladian architecture of Georgian England, except in state rooms, where elegantly draped caryatids (often of the console variety) flank many a marble chimney-piece. Despite the popularity of the 'Venetian window', no English architect followed a hint in a book on Roman circuses and circus architecture, published in Venice in 1600, by substituting terms for the uprights (fig. 105). William Kent, whose years in Italy had given him a certain taste for the mannerist and the baroque, did use giant caryatids as the main order of the triumphal arch which he designed for the coronation banquet of King George II in Westminster Hall in 1727. In his original design these figures, representing Charity(?), Fortitude, Justice and Prudence, were to be caryatid terms (fig. 106), but as executed (in painted wood and canvas) they took the more classically correct form of complete female figures (fig. 107).[52] Kent also liked to station terms about his gardens, notably at Chiswick House, and the practice continued through the eighteenth century. Thus, in his *Compleat Body of Architecture* (1756), Isaac Ware observes that terms are 'a frequent ornament in gardens' and are also sometimes placed 'in decorated rooms to support vases, or other elegant works'. But their 'proper situation is as the boundary of lands', and he offers a design for a quadruple term 'placed as a mark of the boundaries of four counties'.[53] Sir William Chambers considered that terms 'are proper ornaments in gardens' and offered some judicious observations on the use of 'Persians and Caryatides' (cf. fig. 84), but himself made little use of the latter except in chimney-pieces, tripods, etc.[54]

The caryatid and the herm naturally formed part of the repertoire of the Greek Revival. The caryatid-term was generally shunned as a mannerist hybrid (though under Nash's characteristically less fastidious direction it was used at Cornwall Terrace in Regent's Park by the young Decimus Burton), and elegantly draped female figures were again employed as substitutes for columns by architects such as Soane, Inwood and Wilkins. All the caryatids used by Soane at the Bank of England and elsewhere were made of Mrs Coade's artificial stone, as were those supporting the figure of Britannia that crowned the Nelson Monument at Yar-

106. Design by William Kent for the Triumphal Arch in Westminster Hall for the coronation banquet of King George II in 1727 (Public Record Office, WORK 36/68/46).

107. The Triumphal Arch in Westminster Hall as executed to William Kent's designs in 1727 (British Library, King's Maps XXIV, 24 m). The figures represent Temperance, Fortitude, Justice and Prudence.

108. St Pancras Church, London, built 1819–22, showing one of the two caryatid porticos, serving as vestries, etc. The caryatids are of terracotta and hold ewers and inverted torches, symbolising life and death.

mouth, designed by Wilkins.[55] The near replicas of the Erechtheum, complete with terracotta caryatids, that project on either side of Inwood's St Pancras Church in London illustrate both the elegance and refinement of the Greek Revival and the scholarly pedantry of which its practitioners were capable (fig. 108). Atlantes in the cupola of the Fitzwilliam Museum at Cambridge and caryatids supporting a gallery in St George's Hall at Liverpool show how a greater architect (C.R. Cockerell) could give renewed life to ancient forms. Despite their commemorative function in Antiquity, herms failed to find favour with neo-classical sculptors like Flaxman and Westmacott, though in the former's monument to Dr Joseph Warton in Winchester Cathedral, herms of Homer and Aristotle are appropriately intro-

duced in the background to symbolise the classical learning of an eighteenth-century headmaster.[56]

Besides once more appearing in their ancient forms, caryatids and herms were sometimes used with unexpected freedom by early nineteenth-century architects, though less so in England than in Revolutionary France, where one architect (Lequeu) proposed to revive the original vindictive character of the caryatid in the form of chained aristocrats supporting the entablature of a national hall of assembly, while another (Durand) envisaged a 'Temple of Equality' whose twin porticos were to be sustained by gigantic herms representing the public virtues.[57] For the use of herms, which (unlike caryatids) were originally free-standing objects, as architectural components, there was in fact ancient precedent. In the Odeion of Agrippa at Athens, built *circa* 15 BC, the front of the stage was supported by a row of marble herms,[58] and on the end of a sarcophagus of about AD 200 in the Towneley Collection in the British Museum, a pair of herms is represented as supporting a canopy over a figure of Bacchus (fig. 109). Even the use of herms as legs of marble furniture is known from excavated fragments, and from surviving examples in the Vatican Museum.[59] It was therefore with Ancient authority that the wealthy amateur Thomas Hope (1769–1831) used herms to support a shelf of Greek vases in his London house (fig. 110), and that in 1829 the architect A.H. Wilds incorporated several of them into an archway at the entrance to an urban development at Worthing (fig. 111). More esoteric were the Egyptianising herms or caryatids with which 'Greek' Thomson enlivened the tall tower of St Vincent's Church in Glasgow (1857–9).

As the century progressed, the neo-classical gave way to a more eclectic revivalism, which embraced not only the Middle Ages but the Renaissance as well. Gothic Revivalists naturally had no use for herms or caryatids, but by the 1860s there was a demand for neo-Jacobean rooms, which architects such as E.M. Barry and Harold Peto were prepared to provide complete with appropriate caryatid-terms in marble or plaster.[60] So far as caryatids are concerned, by far the most

110. Greek Revival herms supporting a shelf of ancient Greek vases in Thomas Hope's house in London (Thomas Hope, *Household Furniture and Interior Decoration*, 1807).

111. Archway at Worthing, Sussex, designed by A.H. Wilds, 1829.

113. A term overlooking the water garden at Buscot Park (formerly Berkshire, now Oxfordshire), designed by Harold Peto in 1904.

112. (*left*) Michelangelesque caryatids decorating the façade of a house in Mortimer Street, London, designed by A. Beresford Pite in 1896.

114. Bronze herms by Dame Elisabeth Frink adorning a multi-storey car park in Worthing, Sussex, *circa* 1990.

remarkable products of this historicism were the white marble caryatids designed and executed by Alfred Stevens for the dining-room of Dorchester House in London and now in the Victoria and Albert Museum. Though these crouching Michelangelesque figures might seem more suitable for a funerary monument than for a dining-room, they were undoubted masterpieces of their kind. Another striking pair in the same mannerist genre can be seen in the façade of number 82 Mortimer Street, London, a house designed in 1896 by the architect A. Beresford Pite (fig. 112). For caryatids on funerary monuments and for herms and terms in gardens, the Victorians had little use. As symbolical figures in cemeteries they preferred angels, and as garden ornaments, vases. In that great repository of nineteenth-century architectural taste, Loudon's *Encyclopaedia of Cottage, Farm and Villa Architecture* (first edition 1833, second 1846), on a page full of specimen garden vases, the author makes only passing reference to 'therms', while, in his *Art and Craft of Garden Making* (3rd ed., 1912), the well-known 'landscape architect' Thomas Mawson considers what he calls 'acroliths' to be 'only suitable for use in gardens laid out on formal lines and usually in conjunction with clipped hedges'.[61] Lutyens, rather surprisingly, seems never to have used herms or terms in his formal garden layouts, but Harold Peto did, e.g. at Buscot (formerly in Berkshire, now Oxfordshire) in 1904 (fig. 113).[62] By the beginning of the twentieth century they were obsolescent, if not yet quite forgotten. When, in 1936–8, perhaps in a dubious attempt to demonstrate the classical affinities of the 'Modern Movement', Lubetkin paradoxically introduced two Erechtheum caryatids into the porch of his Highpoint flats in London, it was to be the last appearance of such figures in English architecture for many years. With the revival of classical architecture in the last years of the twentieth century they are, however, bound to reappear: indeed, herm-like bronze figures by Dame Elisabeth Frink are already to be seen adorning the blank exterior of a multi-storey car park in Worthing (fig. 114).

NOTES

1 Vitruvius, *De Architectura*, Book I, ch. 1, IV, ch. 1.

2 See Théophile Homolle, 'L'origine des Caryatides', *Revue Archéologique*, 5th ser. v, 1917; Charles Picard, 'Vitruve, le portique des Perses à Sparte, et les origines de l'ordre persan', *Comptes rendus de l'Académie des Inscriptions et Belles Lettres*, 1935; J.J. Coulton, *The Architectural Development of the Greek Stoa*, Oxford, 1976, p. 39; Hugh Plommer, 'Vitruvius and the Origin of Caryatids', *Journal of Hellenic Studies*, 99, 1979, pp. 97–102; also Andreas Schmidt-Colinet, *Antike Stützfiguren*, Frankfurt, 1977, and Evamaria Schmidt, *Geschichte der Karyatide*, Würzburg, 1982. According to W.H. Leeds (*The Orders and their Aesthetic Principles*, 1874, pp. 87–8), persians were properly represented clothed in 'loose attire or imaginary Persian costume', atlantes as supporting the weight of the architrave on their shoulders, and telamones with raised or bended arms.

3 Notably in the Forum of Trajan at Rome, where the 'persians' represented defeated Dacians (James Packer, 'Trajan's Forum in 1989', *American Journal of Archaeology*, 96, 1992, pp. 158–9 and figs. 1–2) and at Corinth (see American School of Classical Studies at Athens, *Corinth* I(ii), 1941, figs. 40, 50, 51, and IX, 1931, pp. 101–27).

4   According to the engraving this tower was decorated with an order of caryatids over another of persians. A drawing by Giuliano da Sangallo, probably made in 1494, shows the latter as captives bound with their backs to the tower rather than as conventional 'persians', but in either case they were evidently intended to represent defeated enemies; see Stefano Borsi, *Giuliano da Sangallo, I Disegni di Architettura e dell' Antico*, Rome, 1985, pp. 97–100.

5   For the Strozzi monument and other designs by Giulio Romano incorporating caryatids see E. Gombrich et al., *Giulio Romano*, Milan, 1989, pp. 561–2. At the Louvre Goujon was following a plaster model made by the architect Pierre Lescot (David Thomson, *Renaissance Paris*, 1984, p. 90).

6   For this episode see Robin Osborne, 'The Erection and Mutilation of the Herms', *Proceedings of the Cambridge Philological Society*, 1985.

7   For herms in general, see the useful discussion by Evelyn B. Harrison in *The Athenian Agora*, xi (American School of Classical Studies at Athens, Princeton, 1965), pp. 108–41.

8   B. de Montfaucon, *Antiquity Explained* (London, 1722–4) i, p. 53: 'These Hermes's are what the Latins called Termini.'

9   *Encyclopédie ou Dictionnaire raisonné des sciences, des arts, etc.*, 1751–65, viii, pp. 168–9.

10   S. Le Clerc, *Traité d'Architecture*, Paris, 1714, pp. 113–14. Cf. A.C. Daviller, *Cours d'Architecture*, Paris, 1720, pp. 873–4 and *The Builder's Dictionary*, London, 1734, ii, s.v. TERM.

11   Monique Châtenet, *Le Château de Madrid*, Paris, 1987, especially pp. 117–18.

12   *State Papers of Henry VIII* (Record Commission, 1849) viii, pp. 482–4.

13   See S. Béguin et al., *La Galerie François Ier au Château de Fontainebleau, Revue de l'Art* (special number), 1972, and *L'Art de Fontainebleau*, ed. A. Chastel, CNRS, Paris, 1975.

14   Martin Biddle, 'Nicholas Bellin of Modena. An Italian artificer at the Courts of Francis I and Henry VIII', *Jrnl. British Archaeological Assn.*, 3rd ser. xxix, 1966, and Sylvie Béguin, 'A propos d'un dessin de Nicolas da Modena', *La Revue du Louvre*, 1970, no. 1, pp. 9–14.

15   Bodleian Library, MS Eng. hist. b. 192, f. 49ᵛ (a fragment of the Whitehall building accounts dating from the 1540s): a payment of £7 10s. to 'John Mannyng of Westminster carver for ye carving and full finisshing of the seelinge of lx termes of waynscot for the garnishing of the seeling of the foresaid gallerie'.

16   For this drawing see Martin Biddle, 'The stuccoes of Nonsuch', *Burlington Mag.*, 126, July 1984, pp. 411–16. I am indebted to Professor Biddle for drawing my attention to the representation of terms in this drawing.

17   For both these examples, see *Henry VIII: A European Court in England*, ed. D. Starkey, 1991, pp. 86, 135.

18   G. Vasari, *Le Vite de' piu eccellenti pittori, scultori, ed architetti*, ed. Milanesi, Florence, 1875–85, vii, p. 164; George Hersey, *The Lost Meaning of Classical Architecture*, Cambridge, Mass., 1988, pp. 90–103; and cf. fig. 64 above.

19   Bernice Davidson, 'Daniele da Volterra and the Orsini Chapel', *Burlington Mag.*, 109, Oct. 1967, p. 554, fig. 3.

20   W. Kuyper, *The Triumphant Entry of Renaissance Architecture into the Netherlands*, Leyden, 1994, i, pp. 145–8, ii, pls. 159–60.

21   The portrait, by Gerlach Flicke, is in the National Portrait Gallery. It is discussed by D. MacCulloch, *Thomas Cranmer*, Yale, 1996, p. 541, and by A. Wells-Cole, *Art and Decoration in Elizabethan and Jacobean England*, Yale, 1997, p. 34.

22   For Erasmus and Gouffier see Jean Guillaume, 'Hic Terminus Haeret', *Jrnl. Warburg and Courtauld Institutes*, 44, 1981, pp. 186–92.

23   For the Howard tombs see L. Stone and H. Colvin in *Archaeological Jrnl.*, 122, 1965, pp. 159–71, and R. Marks, ibid., 141, 1984, pp. 252–68.

24   For the inscriptions and heraldry see R.A. Cayley and J.A. Salter, *An Architectural Memoir of Old Basing Church, Hants.*, Basingstoke, 1891. For Elizabeth Paulet's funeral see *The Diary of Henry Machyn*, ed. J.G. Nichols, Camden Soc. 1847, pp. 187–8.

25   The four achievements of the Paulet arms which interrupt the frieze are later insertions, probably of the time of the second marquess (1572–6).

26   For the Fryer monument see Marcus Whiffen, 'A Note on the Fryer Monument at Harlton, Cambridgeshire', *Burlington Mag.*, lxxxi, 1942, pp. 281–2 and RCHM, *West Cambridgeshire*, 1968, p. 132.

27   Stephen Harrison, *The Arch's of Triumph erected in Honor . . . of James . . . King of England*, 1604, pl. 5; Thomas Dekker, 'The Magnificent Entertainment given to King James', in *The Dramatic Works of Thomas Dekker*, ed. F. Bowers, ii, Cambridge, 1964, p. 260: 'a great French Terme, of stone, advanced upon wodden Pedestalls'.

28 Hatfield House Bills 58/43. For this information I am indebted to Mr R. Harcourt Williams, Archivist at Hatfield House.

29 A. Wells-Cole, *Art and Decoration in Elizabethan and Jacobean England: The Influence of Continental Prints 1558–1625*, Yale UP, 1997.

30 G. Denhaene, *Lambert Lombard*, Antwerp, 1990, fig. 323.

31 Jacques Thirion, 'Les termes de Sambin, mythe at réalité', in *Art, Objets d'art, collections, Hommage à Hubert Landais*, Paris, 1987, pp. 151–9; *Le Dessin en France au XVIᵉ siècle* (Exhibition Catalogue, École Nationale Supérieure des Beaux Arts, 1995), no. 75.

32 *Dictionary of National Biography*.

33 See the guidebook published by CADW.

34 Chiefly in designs for chimney-pieces, such as the one at Oatlands Palace in 1636, for which two designs, both with caryatid-terms, are illustrated by Harris and Higgott, *Inigo Jones. Complete Architectural Drawings*, 1989, pp. 221–3. The source for these was French rather than Palladian.

35 Margaret Whinney, 'John Webb's Designs for Whitehall Palace', *Walpole Society*, xxxi, 1942–3.

36 John Peacock, *The Stage Designs of Inigo Jones*, Cambridge, 1995, p. 283 and pl. 169.

37 Stephen Wren, *Parentalia*, 1750, p. 335.

38 Margaret Whinney, 'Sir Christopher Wren's Visit to Paris', *Gazette des Beaux Arts*, 6th ser., 51, 1958, pp. 229–42.

39 *Wren Society*, xix, pp. 91–9.

40 See H. Wrede, *Die Spätantike Hermengalerie von Welschbillig*, Berlin, 1972, pp. 121–33 for these and other examples.

41 A.C. Rossetto et al., *Theatri Greci e Romani*, Turin, 1995, sect. 3, p. 357.

42 Whether any of the sockets were made for this purpose (rather than for the lugs mentioned above) is another matter. In most of the ancient examples stone or marble panels fitted into vertical slots on either side of the terms, so that no sockets were required. However, as late as 1890 the *Dictionary of Greek and Latin Antiquities*, by William Smith et al, refers, s.v. 'Hermae', to 'the square holes in their shoulders into which the transverse rail was inserted'.

43 Cicero, *Letters to Atticus*, ed. Shackleton Bailey, Cambridge, i, 1965, p. 115.

44 See the catalogue of Wren's library, sold (with that of his son), 24 Oct. 1748, and reprinted in *Sale Catalogues of Libraries of Eminent Persons*, vol. iv (Architects), ed. D.J. Watkin, 1972, pp. 1–43; I. Boissard, *Antiquitatum Romanarum*, Frankfurt, 1627; F. Ursinus, *Imagines Illustrium . . . Vultus*, Antwerp, 1606. The prints in Wren's sale included 'Eleven heads of philosophers, &c. in mezzotinto'.

45 *Jackson's Oxford Journal*, 19 Oct. 1867.

46 Max Beerbohm, *Zuleika Dobson*, 1911, ch. 1.

47 A portrait of the bearded Emperor Antoninus Pius (not one of the twelve) was, however, among several herms or terms representing Roman emperors which figured in a miscellaneous collection of historical and mythical herms/terms round the pool at Welschbillig, the Roman villa near Trier (for which see note 40 above).

48 John Harris, *William Talman*, 1982, p. 44.

49 British Library. Add. MS 9423, ff. 191–3, a description sent to Samuel Lysons in 1817 in connection with the Derbyshire volume of his *Magna Britannia*, published in that year. The owner of Bretby at the end of the seventeenth century was the 2nd Earl of Chesterfield, who would have seen Wren's screen when he received an honorary degree in the Sheldonian Theatre in July 1669.

50 Stephen Switzer, *Ichnographia Rustica*, iii, 1718, p. 120. I owe this reference to the late Gervase Jackson-Stops.

51 H.M. Colvin, *A Catalogue of Architectural Drawings . . . in the Library of Worcester College, Oxford*, 1964, pl. 105. Baily Park, Sussex, begun *c*.1705, but remodelled in 1898–1900, originally had a pair of facing caryatids on either side of the central window of the principal front: see the engraving of 1788 in Harrison's *Picturesque Views of Seats*.

52 *History of the King's Works*, ed. H.M. Colvin, v, 1976, p. 454.

53 Isaac Ware, *Compleat Body of Architecture*, 1756, pp. 250–1.

54 W. Chambers, *Treatise on the Decorative Part of Civil Architecture*, 1791, pp. 69–74. Chambers would doubtless have read the section on terms in the *Recueil d'Antiquités* of the French classical archaeologist the Comte de Caylus, published in 1750, in which (vol. i, p. 170), Caylus writes how, in Antiquity, terms, 'toujours placées dans les endroits le mieux cultivés . . . devoient produire des points de vue d'une charmante variété, et former les plus agréables spectacles pour le voyager'.

55 Alison Kelly, *Mrs Coade's Stone*, 1990, pp. 85–7.

56 Nicholas Penny, *Church Monuments in Romantic England*, Yale, 1977, pp. 154–5.

57 Le Queu's design is illustrated in *Visionary Architects* (exhibition catalogue, Houston, 1968), p. 201, Durand's temple in S. Villari, *J.N.L. Durand*, New York, 1990, figs. 51–2.

58 Homer Thompson, 'The Odeion in the Athenian Agora', *Hesperia*, xix, 1950, pp. 65–7.

59 E.B. Harrison, *The Athenian Agora*, xi, 1965, p. 140.

60 For Barry's interiors at Crewe Hall, Cheshire, as rebuilt after a fire in 1866, see *Country Life*, 29 March 1902. For Sir Ernest George and Harold Peto's design for a neo-Jacobean drawing room at Poles, Herts., *c*.1885, see John Harris, *The Design of the English Country House 1620–1920*, 1985, fig. 88. For atlantes flanking dormer windows on the Grand Hotel at Scarborough (*c*. 1865), see Derek Linstrum, *Towers and Colonnades. The Architecture of Cuthbert Brodrick*, Leeds 1999, fig. 135.

61 Loudon, *Encyclopaedia*, 1846, para. 1982; Mawson, *Art and Craft*, 1912, pp. 156–8.

62 *Country Life*, 21 Oct. 1916, 18 May 1940.

VII

THE SOUTH FRONT OF WILTON HOUSE

No english country house is more famous than Wilton, and none has been more frequently described. The grandeur of the state apartments and the serene beauty of the south front have always commanded unqualified admiration and proclaimed themselves to be the work of an outstanding architect. That that architect was Inigo Jones has often been taken for granted, and may indeed be substantially correct. But the precise extent of Jones's share in the design has never been clearly determined, and the chronology of the buildings themselves has been in some respects uncertain. In the absence of original accounts or correspondence dating from the time of the 4th Earl of Pembroke (1630–50) much in the architectural history of Wilton has had to be left to conjecture, which in the course of time has hardened into accepted fact. It is the purpose of this paper to review the crucial problem of the south front (figs. 115, 116) in the light of all the available evidence, including some which has not previously been known to architectural historians.

Inigo Jones's connection with Wilton was one of long standing, going back to the time of the third earl and to the reign of James I. In July 1615 his patron Lord Arundel was at Salisbury and wrote to his wife to say that the king would be dining at Wilton and that Lord Pembroke wished Jones to be there.[1] In what capacity his attendance was required is uncertain, but in a postscript Arundel goes on to refer to some portraits for which Jones had been negotiating in Rome, and there is no reason to suppose that Jones's visit had any architectural significance. In 1620 he was again summoned to Wilton at the king's command in order to carry out the first recorded investigation into the origin of 'the most notable Antiquity of Great Britain, vulgarly called Stone-Heng'.[2] But it was not until the reign of Charles I and the time of the 4th Earl of Pembroke that the Surveyor of the King's Works was invited to Wilton to consider the improvement of the house itself.

'King Charles the first,' says John Aubrey (himself a native of Wiltshire),

did love Wilton above all places, and came thither every summer. It was he that did put Philip . . . Earle of Pembroke upon making this magnificent garden and grotto, and to new build that side of the house that fronts the garden, with two stately pavilions at each end, all *al Italiano*. His Majesty intended to have it all designed by his own architect, Mr Inigo Jones, who being at that time, about 1633, engaged in his Majesties buildings at Greenwich, could not attend to it: but

115. The south front of Wilton House: measured drawing from H. Inigo Triggs and Henry Tanner, *Some Architectural Works of Inigo Jones*, 1901.

116. Wilton House: the south front as illustrated in Colen Campbell's *Vitruvius Britannicus*, ii, 1717, pls. 61–2. The central stairs never existed.

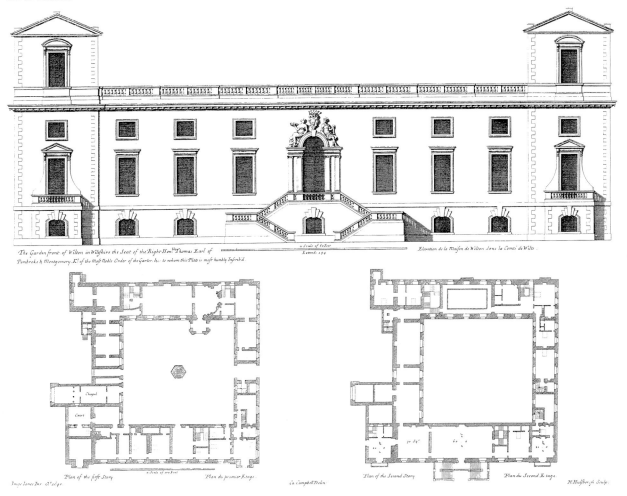

he recommended it to an ingeniouse architect Monsieur Solomon de Caus, a Gascoigne, who performed it very well; but not without the advice and approbation of Mr Jones: for which his Lordship settled a pension on him of, I think, a hundred pounds per annum for his life, and lodgings in the house. He died about 1656; his picture is at Mr Gauntlet's house at Netherhampton . . .

The south side of this stately house [he continues] that was built by Monsieur de Caus, was burnt ann. 1647 or 1648, by airing of the roomes. In anno 1648 Philip (the first) re-edifyed it, by the advice of Inigo Jones; but he, being then very old, could not be there in person, but left it to Mr. Webb, who married his niece.[3]

In another passage Aubrey gives a detailed description of the garden, 'a thousand foot long within the inclosure of the new wall, and about four hundred in breadth', with its parterres, green arbours, fountains and waterworks. Through the middle of it ran the river Nadder, whose irregular course was disguised by a 'grove' of trees or shrubs (see figs. 117, 118). Marble statues provided focal points and on two pillars there were metal crowns spinning with *jets d'eau*, evidently as a compliment to Charles I. Across the southern end there was a balustraded terrace, in the middle of which was the grotto, a classical building ornamented with frost-work, etc.[4]

Now Aubrey's statements were 'based upon his own knowledge of the mansion before the Civil Wars', upon information derived from Thomas, 8th Earl of Pembroke, the grandson of the 4th Earl, and from conversations with Dr Caldicot, who had been the family chaplain, and with Mr Uniades, 'who also held some appointment in the establishment'.[5] Their authority is therefore evident, and everything that Aubrey tells us deserves the closest attention. In one particular only does it seem that he was misinformed: Salomon de Caus was a Norman, not a Gascon, and as he left England in 1613 and died in France in the 1620s he cannot have been employed at Wilton in the 1630s. But Salomon de Caus had a younger relative, Isaac de Caus, who was certainly associated with Jones, both at the Banqueting House, where he constructed a grotto in the basement, and at Covent Garden, where he appears in the accounts as the 'executant architect' of some of the houses on the north side.[6] There is, in fact, documentary evidence, to be cited later, that it was Isaac de Caus who was employed at Wilton. Though primarily a contriver of gardens and grottos, he was certainly capable of architectural design and in 1638 it was in this capacity that the first Earl of Cork gave £5 to 'Mounsier decon [*sic*], the french architect who belongs to my L. Chamberleyn [i.e. Pembroke] . . . for drawing me a plott, for contriving my new intended bwylding over the great sellar at Stalbridge', that is, Stalbridge Park, Dorset.[7] Unfortunately nothing remains of the seventeenth-century house at Stalbridge, but the commission is important as evidence of de Caus' repute as an architect. Although he was naturalised in 1634,[8] he did not in fact remain in England for the rest of his life, dying in Paris early in 1648. In the register of the Huguenot cemetery there he is described as 'natif de Dieppe, agé de 58 ans, architeque.'[9]

With this correction, Aubrey's account may now be summarised as follows: there were two periods of building at Wilton, the first in the 1630s, under the direction of Isaac de Caus, 'but not without the advice and approbation of Mr Jones', the second after a fire in 1647 or 1648, under the direction of John Webb, again 'by the advice of' the now aged Jones.

So far as the first period of building is concerned, Aubrey's account is both confirmed and supplemented by three independent sources: the Receiver-General's accounts of Philip, Earl of Pembroke, for the years 1632/3 and 1634/5 (the only ones of this period that survive); a warrant of March 1635/6; and the account-book of the master mason and sculptor Nicholas Stone.

The accounts[10] contain only two relevant entries, but they show that extensive works on both house and garden were already in progress early in the 1630s:

1632/3 (f. 12ᵛ)   Et in denariis . . . solutis Johanni Bowles Ar.[11] (modo imprest) erga constructionem novi gardini apud Wilton per ordin[acionem] omnium officiorum . . . .   CCˡⁱ

1634/5 (f. 9ᵛ)   Et in denariis . . . solutis Antonio Hinton Ar.[11] erga constructionem novi gardini et domus domini Comitis apud Wilton per mandatum domini Comitis . . . MCCIIIIˣˣXIIˡⁱXVJˢ

[£1,292 16s. 0d.]

The record of expenditure in subsequent years is lost, but an entry in Lord Pembroke's official warrant-book as Lord Chamberlain shows that in March 1635/6 he gave orders to

Mr Isaak De Caux to take downe (wᵗʰ the advice of Mr Bowles) that side of Wilton house which is towards the Garden & such other parts as shall bee necessary & rebuild it anew wᵗʰ additions according to ye Plott which is agreed. And likewise to take downe ye Gardeners litle house & the Tennis Courte & sett up convenient houseing for ye Gardner in ye new kitchen garden which Garden Mr De Caux is to lay out in fitt proportions, walks & Quarters to bee planted wᵗʰ fruits, hearbes & rootes by Dominick Pile who is to have ye Custody thereof & to receave his direccions from Mr De Caux & the Officers for that which shall bee for his Loᵖˢ service. March 14 1635 [i.e. 1635/6].[12]

It was therefore in the spring of 1636 that work began on the south front under the direction of Isaac de Caus. According to George Vertue, who was well-informed about Wilton, it was completed in 1640.[13]

Meanwhile work had been proceeding on the garden, where the king's Master Mason, Nicholas Stone, was employed on the ornamental stonework. Stone's great-nephew Charles Stoakes says that Stone 'desined and built many curious workes for the Earle of Pembrock at his Honˢ. House att Wilton, near Salsbury and was well paide'.[14] George Vertue describes the 'Basso rilievo and water stone work' of the grotto as being the work of Stone's son Nicholas,[15] and in the elder Stone's account-book payments are recorded in 1637 for work done 'by Mr Decaus appointment', and again in 1639 for delivering a white marble cornice in six pieces 'by apoyntment of Mr de Caus', in both cases for Lord Pembroke.[16] From these references we may conclude with James Lees-Milne 'that Stone the elder probably

Le jardin de Vuilton scituant Sur l'tres noble et tres puissant Seigneur PHILIPPE COMTE DE PENBROOKE ET MONGOMERI Baron herbert de Cardif, Seigneur pare et Roisce de Cardell, Marmion, S.t quentin, et ... / Clanland, gardien de l'estanerie aux Contez, de Cornuall, et deson Chamberlain de la Maison du Roy, Chevalier du tres noble ordre de la Jartiere, Lieutenant general pour le Roy, aux provinces de Vuilts Summerset, et Irei: / Conceiller du Conceill Prive de sa Majeste'. / Isaac de caus Inuant

117. Wilton House: the formal gardens as seen from the house, an engraving from Isaac de Caus' *Wilton Garden*, published probably in the 1630s (the Provost and Fellows of Worcester College, Oxford).

built the grotto and other garden ornaments at Wilton, to the design and under the direction of Isaac de Caus'.[17]

So far as the gardens are concerned, De Caus' work is elaborately illustrated in the suite of engravings entitled *Wilton Gardens*, first published probably in the 1630s,[18] and the accuracy of the plates is vouched for by the contemporary descriptions left by Lieutenant Hammond in 1635,[19] by Lodewyk Huygens in 1652,[20] by Celia Fiennes in about 1685[21] and by that of John Aubrey quoted above. The Lieutenant's account is of especial interest, because he was shown round by the 'fat Dutch keeper thereof', evidently the Dominick Pile appointed as custodian of the kitchen garden by the earl's warrant of 14 March 1635/6, and as 'Dominick Pyle the old gardiner att Wilton' still in receipt of a 'pension' of £10 at the time of the earl's death in 1650.[22] The name Pyle occurs several times in contemporary records of foreigners resident in England, and the nationality is invariably registered as 'Dutch', that is (in contemporary usage) either a German or a native of modern

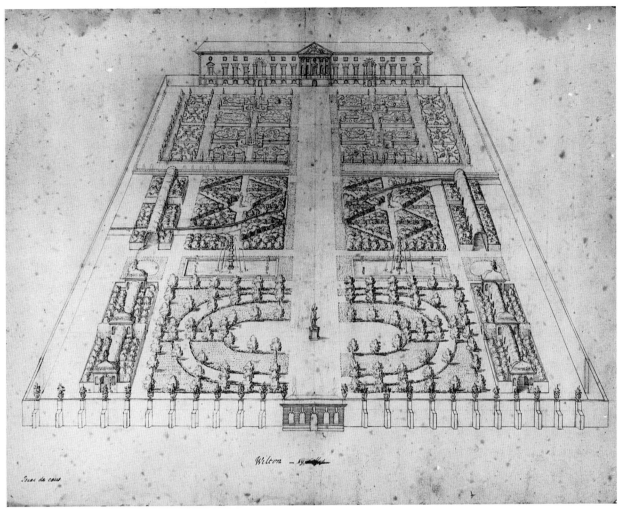

Wilton — by

Iean de caus

118. Wilton House: drawn design for the south front and garden corresponding to figure 117, but not engraved (the Provost and Fellows of Worcester College, Oxford).

Holland.[23] Pyle gave Hammond the impression that he, rather than de Caus, was the 'rare artist' responsible for designing the waterworks and there is perhaps a hint of friction between the two men in Aubrey's recollection that 'Monsieur de Caus had here a contrivance, by the turning of a cock, to shew three rainbowes, the secret whereof he did keep to himself', so that on his death this piece of hydraulic ingenuity was unfortunately lost.[24]

Although a view of the gardens from the house is the first of the set of engravings that comprise *Wilton Garden* (fig. 117), there is in that publication no corresponding view of the house from the garden. One was, however, prepared for engraving, for the original drawing is preserved in the library of Worcester College, Oxford (fig. 118). Loosely placed in Dr George Clarke's copy of *Vitruvius Britannicus*, it had escaped notice until discovered by the present writer and published to illustrate the original version of this essay in the *Archaeological Journal* for 1954. In the foreground is the grotto, then come the horticultural conceits already familiar from de Caus'

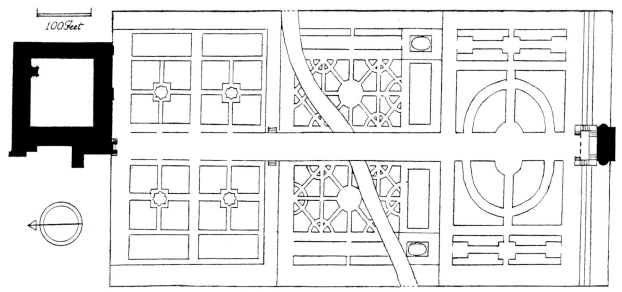

119. Wilton House: sketch-plan showing the relationship of house and garden in the seventeenth century.

published plates. The façade in the background is recognisable too, but at nearly twice its present length, and with a hexastyle portico of the Ionic order in the centre. Other divergencies from the existing front are the hipped roof, instead of one concealed behind a balustraded parapet, the absence of the pavilion towers and the substitution of circular for rectangular attic windows at either end. Otherwise the resemblance of the two flanking elevations to the one which exists at Wilton today is obvious. The miniature scale of the drawing makes it difficult to distinguish some architectural details, especially those of the portico, but the Ionic order with its pulvinated frieze is clear. The shadowing implies free-standing columns, but as there are no steps up to the portico, it is probably of slight projection. It should be added that the drawing, which is executed on paper with a watermark of an early seventeenth-century French type, bears the inscription 'Wilton – by Callot' in an eighteenth-century hand, but the name 'Callot' has been crossed out, and 'Isaac de Caus' written in the left-hand corner. Although the figures in the foreground of the corresponding view of the garden from the house are somewhat in the style of the celebrated French engraver, he died in 1635, and the attribution of either drawing to him is generally doubted.[25] Fortunately the identity of the draughtsman does not affect the value of the drawing as a unique representation of the south front as it was originally intended to be built.

That this great pedimented front, over 330 feet in length,[26] was seriously contemplated by the Earl of Pembroke and was not a mere paper scheme is indicated clearly enough by the way in which the garden was laid out in anticipation of its completion (fig. 119). House and garden were awkwardly related, the former occupying only half the width of the latter, in a manner that was commented on by Huygens in 1652,[27] but that today is disguised by the informal landscape garden that later replaced de Caus' elaborate walks. Such asymmetry in the relationship between the house and this otherwise most symmetrical garden is inexplicable unless it was intended to build the front to the full extent indicated by the drawing. Of the grand scheme we possess only the elevation; no plan remains. We do not know how much of the house would have been rebuilt behind the façade.[28] But we may guess that the intention was to have two matching apartments, as in the design for a great London house made for the earl by Jones's pupil John Webb in 1649.[29] This was the standard plan of a royal palace, here (as in other major country houses) introduced into the layout of a private house, no doubt in the expectation of such royal visits as we know from Aubrey that Charles I paid to Wilton. As in the proposed London house, the intention may have been to have a staircase or pair of staircases in the middle, depending on whether the earl contemplated rebuilding the west wing of the old house as well.

By 1636, when work began, this grand scheme had already been abandoned, the new south front reduced to approximately half the intended length, the portico omitted, and one of the two Venetian windows made into a substitute central feature. Why the change of plan? The explanation is probably financial. The death in January 1636 of the earl's newly-married son Charles resulted in the return of a colossal marriage portion of £25,000 that had been paid by his bride's father, the Duke of Buckingham. Faced with a choice between paying the eighteen-year-old widow a jointure of £4,000 per annum for life or repaying the £25,000, the earl chose the latter. His expenditure on his house in Whitehall was heavy, and he owed £64,000 when he died in 1650.[30] So the contraction of the garden front is hardly surprising.

It was evidently the contraction of the garden front that obliged Isaac de Caus to omit the intended view of the grand design from his set of engravings. *Wilton Garden* is a rare publication of which only nine copies have so far been traced,[31] and it has not hitherto been noticed that there are two (if not three) variant versions. The one best known to architectural historians, because a facsimile was published in 1982, has no list of contents.[32] But two copies exist which do have a list of contents, and the last item (No. XXIV) is a 'Dessein du front du batiment vers le jardin'. Now this 'dessein' is actually present in one copy (fig. 120) and an original drawing closely related to it is in the RIBA Drawings Collection (fig. 121). The drawing has long been attributed to Isaac de Caus, and the presence of an engraved version of it in his book obviously supports the attribution.

The engraving shows the grand design deprived of its porticoed centre, and reduced in effect to one wing. No scale or dimensions are provided, but assuming that the design corresponded in height to what was eventually built (cf. fig. 127), the front envisaged would have been some 20 feet shorter. Exactly how it was intended to relate either to the old house or to the garden is not clear. However, the fact that de Caus had this drawing engraved and included it in the list of contents suggests that at some stage – perhaps in 1635 or early in 1636, when the garden was nearing completion, but work had not yet started on the south front – this was the accepted design. Then the design in this form became obsolete in its turn, obliging de Caus to scrap both plate and list of contents at the last moment, and leaving *Wilton Garden* still without any view of the house or garden from the south to complement the one showing the garden from the north.

120. Wilton House: engraved design for the contracted south front forming plate XXIV of Isaac de Caus' *Wilton Garden*, according to the original list of contents (unique impression in a copy of *Wilton Garden* in a private library).

What made the plate obsolete was the addition of the two towers and of a balustraded parapet along the top of the wall between them. The balustraded parapet is one of several minor differences shown on the drawn version of the elevation already mentioned (fig. 121),[33] but the towers are absent. Aubrey states explicitly that they were part of the façade as built in the 1630s, and this has been borne out both by recent structural investigation in the course of repairs, and by the discovery of a topographical drawing in the library of the Society of Antiquaries, which shows the front as it existed in the 1640s (fig. 122).[34] The addition of the twin towers must have been suggested – perhaps even dictated – by those which already flanked the east front of the old house (fig. 123). A likely source for the

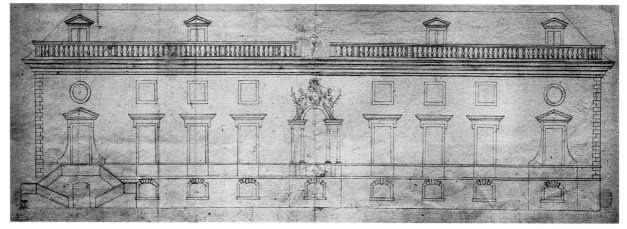

121. Wilton House: drawn design for the contracted south front in the Burlington–Devonshire collection of drawings by Inigo Jones and others (British Architectural Library).

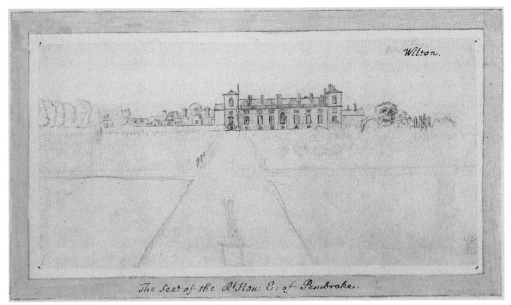

122. Wilton House: drawing of the south front as existing in the 1640s (Society of Antiquaries of London, Portfolio VII, 47).

123. Wilton House: the east front as shown in a survey of the lands of William, 1st Earl of Pembroke, made *circa* 1565 (the Earl of Pembroke and the Trustees of the Wilton House Trust, Wilton House, deposited in the Wiltshire Record Office).

form of the towers is a design in Scamozzi's well-known treatise on architecture published in 1615 (fig. 124). That they were an afterthought is suggested by an examination of the plan: there is no break in the wall, where the quoins are simply applied.[35] In the same way the cornice is unbroken from one end to the other. Had the towers been envisaged from the first, the wall would very likely have been brought forward a few inches to express them more clearly. Nevertheless, they effectively compensated for the absence of that vertical emphasis which would have been supplied by the missing portico. With their aid this fragment of a greater design was at once made self-sufficient: so self-sufficient, in fact, that it became one of the classics of English Palladian architecture, the archetype of Holkham, Hagley, Croome, Euston, Lydiard Tregose and other great country houses of the eighteenth century.

This, however, is to anticipate. For in 1647 or 1648, as Aubrey tells us, 'the south side of this stately house . . . was burnt . . . by airing of the roomes,' and in 1648 the Earl of Pembroke 're-edifyed it, by the advice of Inigo Jones,' who, 'being then very old, could not be there in person, but left it to Mr Webb'.[36] By now in his seventy-seventh year, Jones was no doubt relying more and more on the man he had 'brought up in the study of Architecture', and Webb, at thirty-seven, would have been perfectly competent to take charge of such an important commission. Certainly there is no reference to Jones in the accounts kept by the earl's executors, discovered among the Salisbury papers at Hatfield[37] by Professor Lawrence Stone, to whom I am indebted for the following extracts:

			£	s.	d.
1650	July	Paid to Mr Webb, Surveyor, for one quarters fee from Xmas to Lady day 1650	10	0	0
	Dec. 26	Paid to Mr Decritz upon a bill signed by Mr Webb for painting at the Cockpitt in 1642[38]	3	2	0
1650		To the London Workmasters in full of there bills for the building at Wilton	1,347	15	6
		To the Country workmen for worke and Materialls concerning the Buildings at Ramesbury & Wilton in part of 1,005. 12. 3½ in arrears due there	225	19	8
1651	March	Paid by Mr Mannings upon severall bills and debenters signed by Mr Webb the Surveyor due unto severall Country workmen imployed about the late buildings at Wilton, being in full of what is due to them upon the same	1,779	12	7½

But as the executors would be responsible only for the payment of debts due by the earl at his death in January 1650, their accounts do not necessarily record more than a part of the total expenditure. Nevertheless, they show that Webb was indeed the surveyor in charge at an annual fee of £40, and drawings by him for ceilings,

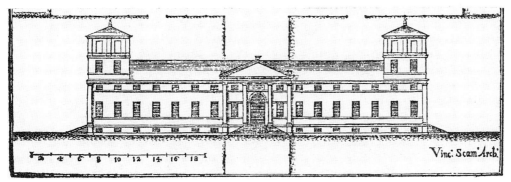

124. Elevation by Scamozzi for a villa farmstead designed according to Ancient precepts (from V. Scamozzi, *L'idea della architettura universale*, Venice, 1615, I (iii), p. 284).

a cartouche and several capitals, some of them dated 1649, show that he himself designed some important decorative features.[39] Other surviving drawings for doors in the state rooms were drawn by Webb but annotated by Jones (fig. 125).[40] In addition there are some much more accomplished designs for ceilings which are dimensioned in Webb's hand but similarly titled by Jones.[41] Formerly attributed to Jones, they are now believed to by Webb and to date from 1649.[42] Though presumably executed, the ceilings in question no longer exist.

Externally, the only significant alteration was the reinstatement of the towers with pedimented instead of pyramidal caps. But the interior had to be completely reconstructed. Repairs in 1988–9 revealed that the brick wall separating the Single and Double Cube Rooms was new,[43] and it seems likely that some of the original

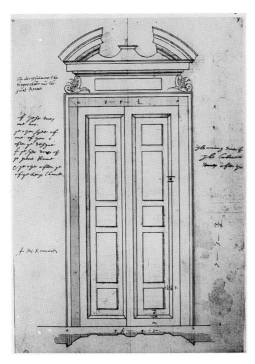

125. Wilton House: design for a doorway annotated in the hands of both Jones and Webb. The title at top left: 'The dores betwene the Kinges chamber and the Great Roome' is in Jones's hand, but the details on either side were written by Webb. The note 'for Mr Kennard' (lower left) evidently refers to the master joiner Thomas Kinward or Kenward, who was to execute the work (the Earl of Pembroke and the Trustees of the Wilton House Trust, Wilton House, deposited in the Wiltshire Record Office).

147

cross-walls had been timber-framed, thus allowing the fire to spread throughout the building. Their replacement in brick would therefore be a sensible precaution. Another important change was that the state rooms were given coved ceilings instead of flat ones, necessitating the blocking of the attic windows.[44] New chimney-pieces with elaborate overmantels were installed. Aubrey says that 'they were then [i.e. following the fire] built after the French fashion, with great figures of Playster above then, supporting scutchions of the Family, or the like.'[45] John Evelyn, too, remarks (1654) on the 'magnificent chimny-pieces after the French best manner.'[46] Elsewhere Jones made much use of Barbet's *Livre d'Architecture* (1633) as a source for chimney-pieces, so the French character of those at Wilton is not surprising. From George Vertue, who visited Wilton in 1731 and again in 1740,[47] and made sketches of the Double Cube Room,[48] we learn that some of the best London craftsmen were employed, including Edward Pierce, senior (painter), Matthew Gooderick (decorative painter) and Zachary Taylor (wood-carver).[49] To these may probably be added the names of the master carpenter, Richard Ryder[50] and of Thomas Kinward (Master Joiner of the King's Works from 1660 to 1682), who was to execute one of Webb's designs for doorways.[51]

Exactly how were the state rooms intended to function in the curtailed south range? As John Heward has pointed out, if circulation was from west to east, then the Single Cube would serve as ante-room to the Double Cube functioning as a Great Chamber, but if from east to west, then the single Cube would have been the withdrawing-room rather than the ante-room.[52] This is in fact the function assigned to it in Webb's designs for doors.[53] In either case the Double Cube Room, with its prominent window, externally 'Venetian' in form, but in fact of one light only (fig. 126), would have been the central feature both inside and out.

In 1704 there was another serious fire at Wilton,[54] but the south range appears to have escaped damage. Later in the eighteenth century there were some alterations to the state rooms in order to accommodate the Van Dyck portraits when they were moved to Wilton from the Pembrokes' London house, and again in 1824–5, when the present doors were made to the designs of Sir Richard Westmacott, but in other respects they remain much as they were in the late seventeenth century.[55]

Such is the story of the south front of Wilton House as far as it can be recovered from all the available evidence (fig. 127). It is the story of a minor architectural masterpiece produced, as architectural masterpieces sometimes are, by collaboration and improvisation rather than by a single creative inspiration. Externally, the awkwardly placed stairs down to the garden from the west pavilion were long a tell-tale relic of the grand scheme of the 1630s,[56] while inside, a lack of perfect symmetry in the fenestration and decoration of the state rooms is still an indication of some difficulties experienced both in stretching the reduced design as far as the central axis of the garden and in fitting a new wing onto an old house.[57]

Historically, there remains the problem of Inigo Jones's relations with the two men who supervised the work on the spot. Were they just the executants of a scheme closely controlled by Jones from London, or was Jones's role largely advisory, leaving de Caus and Webb to make designs that were submitted to him merely for criticism and approval? Any simplistic answer that sees the problem in

126. Wilton House: the central window in the south front (from H. Inigo
Triggs and Henry Tanner, *Some Architectural Works of Inigo Jones*, 1901).

1. The grand scheme of the early 1630s (cf. fig. 118)

2. The contracted scheme of *circa* 1635 (cf. fig. 120)

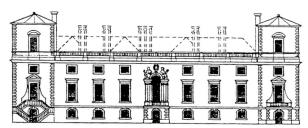

3. The south front as built in 1636–40 (cf. fig. 122)

4. The south front as rebuilt after the fire of 1648

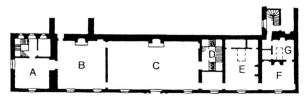

5. Plan of the south range after rebuilding in 1647/8 (key below)

METRES   FEET

127. Wilton House: the evolution of the south front, drawn by Daphne Hart (with acknowledgements to earlier versions by the Royal Commission on Historical Monuments for England and Mr John Heward).

Key to 5: A. Passage or Hunting Room; B. Single Cube (Withdrawing Room); C. Double Cube (Great Room); D. Staircase (later converted into Ante-Room); E. State Bedchamber (later Colonnade Room); F. Cabinet Room; G. Little Ante-Room.

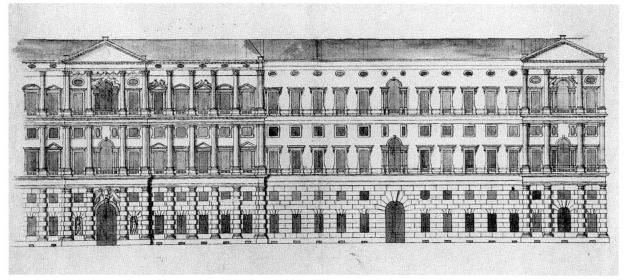

128. Design for Somerset House, London, made by John Webb in 1638 under Inigo Jones's direction (the Provost and Fellows of Worcester College, Oxford).

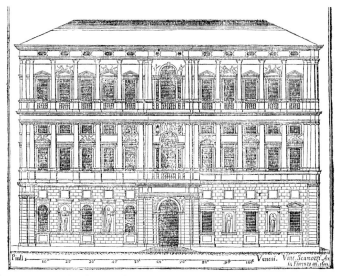

129. Design for a palace by Scamozzi, dated 1602 (from V. Scamozzi, *L'idea della architettura universale*, Venice, 1615, I (iii), cap. vii, p. 249).

terms of clear-cut alternatives, of either Jones or de Caus (or subsequently Webb) as the sole effective architect, must be ruled out. All three clearly had a hand in the evolution of the design: the problem is to define their respective contributions. Here an analysis of the grand design for the south front and of its reduced version may be helpful. An elevation of this kind (fig. 118), with central portico, astylar wings and plain ashlar wall surfaces, is more likely to have originated in the mind of Inigo Jones than in that of someone whose background was in French architecture, with its fondness for channelled and banded masonry. As Sir John Summerson pointed out, there is nothing here that is out of character with Jones's elevation for the Prince's Lodging at Newmarket of 1619;[58] or with the west front of the Queen's Chapel at St James's Palace (1632–5), with its round-headed window between two rectangular ones. A Venetian window as the central feature of an astylar wing flanking a pedimented centre block is a feature of a design for Somerset

130. Attic windows with swept architraves as a feature of the early seventeenth-century Hôtel Montescot at Chartres (C. Sauvageot, *Palais, châteaux, hôtels et maisons de France*, Paris, 1870, ii, pl. 44).

House made by Webb under Jones's direction in 1638 (fig. 128).[59] Moreover both this and many other designs by Jones and Webb were to have had pitched roofs, often with hipped ends as in the Wilton drawing, and so do certain published designs for *palazzi* by Scamozzi, which must have been a source for the Somerset House elevation (fig. 129). Some other features that at first sight seem more obviously related to de Caus' presumed French training than to Jones's Italian studies can also be found in the Somerset House design: one is the *oeil-de-boeuf* windows which, although undoubtedly popular in French architecture of the period, are also a prominent feature of the Somerset House elevation. Another is the swept architraves of the two end windows, a feature that cannot be found in Italian architecture, but is fairly common as a decoration of the prominent attic windows that are so prevalent in French domestic architecture of the sixteenth and early seventeenth centuries (fig. 130).[60] However, the appearance of swept architraves on two ranges of windows in Webb's Somerset House design (though admittedly in a much less pronounced form than those at Wilton), shows that by the late 1630s this feature had been assimilated into the Jones/Webb vocabulary. Whether at Wilton it was Jones or de Caus who so effectively exaggerated the sweep it is impossible to say, but in this form it recurs in the design that Webb made for rebuilding Belvoir Castle in the 1650s.[61] Thereafter it was to become a standard English 'Palladian' motif, to be found in many Georgian buildings by Kent, Keene, Paine and others.

So apart from the swept architrave, there is little that is specifically French about the grand design for the south front of Wilton House, and much that is paralleled in other products of Inigo Jones's office. Whoever drew the one surviving representation of the grand elevation for inclusion in de Caus' book, it shows a building that Jones could well have sketched out himself, leaving de Caus to work out the details. Certainly it is a design in which 'the advice and approbation of Mr Jones' may be supposed to have played an important part.

Turning to the reduced elevation as it was engraved, presumably in about 1635, for de Caus' publication (fig. 120), we find that one wing of the grand design has simply been cut off and set up on its own with no modification other than the addition of a small pedimented aedicule sitting on the cornice over the central window. Although Jones did include a similar feature in a design for a house, this was considerably larger in proportion to the length of the elevation and much more effective as a central accent.[62] Small features of this sort are, however, sometimes found in French architecture, notably at the Palais du Parlement at Rennes, built to the designs of Salomon de Brosse from 1624 onwards.[63] Evidently de Caus thought sufficiently well of the result to have the reduced design engraved for his book in this form, but was obliged to omit the plate when this design was superseded in its turn. In the form in which it was actually built between 1636 and 1640, the high pitched roof has gone,[64] the central aedicule has disappeared, and so have the *oeil-de-boeuf* windows and the aprons linking the first-floor windows with the top of the basement — the last a feature that (although used both by Palladio and by Jones himself, e.g. in the Banqueting House) would have detracted from the refined simplicity of the front as built. Above all, the façade has been given a new consequence by the twin towers, derived probably from the Italian Scamozzi, and, with their pyramidal caps, quite unlike the towers of any contemporary French châteaux. For these crucial improvements we may suppose that de Caus was once more indebted to the advice of Inigo Jones.

When, after the fire of 1647/8, the gutted south range was reconstructed by John Webb, again with Jones's advice, the outer walls were retained, but the twin towers (which had probably acted as funnels for the flames) were rebuilt with pedimented instead of pyramidal roofs. Unlike de Caus, Webb, as Jones's chosen pupil and assistant, would automatically have thought along similar lines to his master. It is therefore difficult to attribute any specific feature to the one rather than the other, and drawings for doorways and ceilings by Webb with inscriptions by Jones show the closeness of their collaboration (fig. 125).

If this analysis is accepted, it follows that the original design for the grand front may have owed quite as much to Jones as it did to de Caus; that it was Jones who probably transformed the latter's uninspired reduction of the grand design into a minor architectural masterpiece; and that after the fire of 1647/8 it was once more with Jones's advice that Webb gave the building its present form. The role of Jones as consultant architect was therefore important. Although none of the surviving drawings for Wilton can confidently be attributed to him, a number of them were titled by him, perhaps as an indication of his approval, and it is significant that (with the exception of Webb's designs for doorways, which remained at Wilton), all of them came from the collection of drawings passed on from Jones to Webb and sold by Webb's descendants to the predecessors of their present owners. Throughout the building history of Wilton in the first half of the seventeenth century Inigo Jones is the common factor. It is arguably to him more than anyone else that the south front owes its form. So those who, without full knowledge of its complicated history, have in the past attributed this icon of English Palladianism to Inigo Jones were perhaps not far wrong.

APPENDIX

A Note on Isaac De Caus' *Wilton Garden*

Nine copies of this set of engravings illustrating the seventeenth-century garden at Wilton have been located: in England at the British Library (1), the Bodleian Library (Gough Maps 33, ff. 16ᵛ–19ᵛ, incomplete (2), Worcester College Library, Oxford (3), Waddesdon Manor (the National Trust) (4) and a private library (5); and four in the USA, including one at Dumbarton Oaks (6). Of these I have personally examined only numbers 1–5.

The 'book' (described in the list of contents as 'ce livre') consists normally of a title (WILTON GARDEN) and an engraved description of the garden in either French (copies 3, 5, 6) or English (copies 1, 4), followed by 23 plates. In what was evidently its earliest form (before 1636) there was a list of contents in French (copies 2, 5), with roman numerals referring to engravings correspondingly numbered from I to XXIV. However, as subsequently published, presumably in the late 1630s (and certainly before 1641, when some of the offices attributed to Pembroke would no longer be appropriate), engraving XXIV ('Dessein du front du batiment vers le Jardin') is omitted, and the engravings (including the title and the description) are numbered in arabic figures from 1 to 26. The list of contents is absent. Engraving XXIV itself is present in only one copy (5) and is here reproduced as figure 120.

The English version was 'to bee sould by Thomas Rowlett att his shopp neare Temple Barre', perhaps in the 1640s. In 1664 the engraver and printseller Peter Stent, having acquired the plates, reissued numbers 1–25 as '*A Colecktione of Fountaines, Gardens and Statues*, P. Stentt Excudit 1654', this title being engraved on the plate showing the statue of the Borghese gladiator. A further edition of Stent's plates was advertised in 1662 as 'Twenty Plats of Wilton's Garden' (A. Globe, *Peter Stent, London Printseller*, Vancouver, 1985, pp. 159–60).

NOTES

1 Mary F.S. Hervey, *Life, Correspondence and Collections of Thomas Howard, Earl of Arundel*, Cambridge, 1921, p. 94.
2 J.A. Gotch, *Inigo Jones*, 1928, p. 16.
3 *The Natural History of Wiltshire*, ed. J. Britton, 1847, pp. 83–4.
4 Aubrey, *Natural History of Wiltshire*, pp. 86–7. The whole was clearly indebted to the Duke of Lorraine's garden at Nancy, as represented by Callot in an engraving of 1625 utilised by Jones in a design for a pastoral (S. Orgel and R. Strong, *Inigo Jones: The Theatre of the Stuart Court*, California, 1973, p. 519; T. Mowl and B. Earnshaw, *Architecture without Kings*, Manchester, 1995, p. 34).
5 Aubrey, *Natural History of Wiltshire*, p. 82. For Uniades see correspondence in *Times Literary Supplement*, 2–9 July and 31 Dec. 1954.

6 John Summerson, *Architecture in Britain 1530–1830*, 1953, p. 83; *Survey of London*, XXXVI, 1970, pp. 28, 71, 282.

7 *Lismore Papers*, ed. A.B. Grosart, 1st ser., v, 1886, p. 64. I owe this reference to Prof. Lawrence Stone.

8 W.A. Shaw, *Denization and Naturalisation* (Huguenot Soc., vol. xviii, 1911), p. 53.

9 *Bulletin de la Société de l'Histoire du Protestantisme en France*, 13, 1864, p. 227 (list of burials in the Huguenot Cemetery at Paris).

10 Now in the Wiltshire Record Office at Trowbridge (2057/A1/2).

11 John Bowles was Lord Pembroke's Steward and Auditor, Anthony Hinton a Receiver.

12 Published by A.A. Tait in *Burlington Mag.*, 106, 1964, p. 74, from PRO, LC5/133, f. 53. Two further warrants direct the housekeeper to remove 'all the stuffe in ye roomes & Lodgings of that side of the house which is to be pulled downe & rebuilt' and Mr Bowles 'to provide Timber . . . as shall be directed by Isaak de Caux'.

13 Walpole Society, *Vertue Notebooks*, ii, p. 32.

14 *The Note-Book and Account-Book of Nicholas Stone*, ed. W.L. Spiers (Walpole Soc., vii, 1918–19), p. 137.

15 *Vertue Notebooks* (Walpole Soc.), i, p. 91. The younger Nicholas Stone died in the same year (1647) as his father, aged only 29.

16 *The Note-Book*, etc., as above, pp. 115, 127. Examination of the MS shows that the editor's reading of 'Decans' on p. 115 can be corrected to 'Decaus'.

17 *The Age of Inigo Jones*, 1953, p. 100.

18 See Appendix on p. 154.

19 *A Relation of a Short Survey of the Western Counties*, ed. L.G. Wickham Legg (*Camden Miscellany*, xvi, 1936), pp. 66–7.

20 Lodewijck Huygens, *The English Journal 1651–2*, ed. Bachrach and Collmer, Leiden, 1982, pp. 132–3.

21 *The Journeys of Celia Fiennes*, ed. C. Morris, 1949, pp. 8–10, to which should be added William Schellinks in 1662 (*The Journal of William Schellinks' Travels in England 1661–1663*, ed. Exwood & Lehmann, Camden Fifth Series, I, Royal Historical Society, 1993, pp. 132–3).

22 Sheffield City Library, EM 1356 (accounts of Lord Pembroke's executors). He was, however, already on the earl's establishment in 1622/3 and 1634/5, receiving £10 a year (Receiver-General's accounts, as in note 10).

23 E.g., 'Returne of Aliens living in London', *Publications of the Huguenot Society of London,* X (ii), pp. 338, 410, 462, LVII, p. 329. The identity of the 'fat Dutch keeper' encountered by Hammond in 1635 has been more fully discussed by myself in a note in *Wiltshire Archaeological Magazine*, 85, 1995, p. 154.

24 Aubrey, *Natural History of Wiltshire*, pp. 86–7.

25 Mr John Peacock, the author of *The Stage Designs of Inigo Jones* (Cambridge, 1995) kindly informs me that in his opinion these two drawings are 'certainly not by Jones or Callot', and could well be by Isaac de Caus. He points out that by the time the Wilton drawings were made, Callot's style was widely diffused and imitated in France and England. As for Jones, his authorship is also ruled out on grounds of architectural draughsmanship, as convincingly argued by Dr Gordon Higgott in a letter published in *Country Life*, 26 March 1992, p. 74.

26 I am indebted to Mrs Daphne Ford for establishing the length of the proposed front as probably 334 feet, on the following basis. The height of the elevation to the underside of the cornice as existing is 37 feet. If this dimension is applied to the design engraved for de Caus' book, the distance between the centre of the Venetian window and the centre of the end window is 70 feet, and the overall length of the reduced front is 167 feet. Using these dimensions, the grand design works out at 334 feet overall, with a portico 45 feet wide. As drawn out in fig. 127 this agrees closely with the front represented in the Worcester College drawing, and avoids the awkward spacing of the windows in the Royal Commission volume (*Wilton House and English Palladianism*, 1988, fig. 32) and the excessive elongation of the portico in John Heward's drawing in *Architectural History*, 35, 1992, p. 96.

27 Huygens, *English Journal*, p. 132: 'the garden . . . was indeed very beautiful and symmetrical, except for the fact that it did not correspond well with the house.'

28 For the surviving remains of the Tudor house (and of the medieval nunnery from which it was adapted), see John Bold, *Wilton House and English Palladianism*, Royal Commission on Historical Monuments, 1988, and John Heward, 'The restoration of the south front of Wilton House: the development of the house reconsidered', *Architectural History*, 35, 1992.

29 John Harris and A.A. Tait, *Catalogue of Drawings by Inigo Jones, John Webb & Isaac de Caus at Worcester College, Oxford*, 1979, figs. 64–7.

30 Lawrence Stone, *The Crisis of the Aristocracy*, Oxford, 1965, pp. 618–19. The figure for the debt comes from the executors' accounts in Sheffield City Library. EM 1355.

31 See Appendix above.

32 Published together with de Caus' *New and Rare Inventions of Water-Works* by Garland Publishing, New York, 1982.

33 As Dr Bridget Cherry has pointed out, it cannot be taken for granted that the drawing is later than the engraving because it shows a balustrade, for the pedimented aedicule in the middle has been drawn in pencil over a section of erased balustrade. What it seems to represent is a period of indecision before the engraved version was decided on.

34 G. Popper and J. Reeves, 'The South Front of Wilton House', *Burlington Mag.*, 124, June 1982, pp. 358–61.

35 J. Heward, 'The restoration of the south front', p. 101.

36 Above, p. 138.

37 Private and Estate MSS, Accounts 168/2.

38 The earl's residence in Whitehall.

39 A cartouche and one capital are illustrated by John Bold, *Wilton House*, p. 50, figs. 56–7, from Webb's 'Book of Capitals'. One of the dated ceiling designs is at Worcester College, Oxford (Bold, fig. 48), the other in the Cotelle Album in the Ashmolean Museum, Oxford (Peter Thornton, *Seventeenth-Century Interior Decoration in England, France and Holland*, Yale, 1978, fig. 76).

40 Now in the Wiltshire Record Office (2057/H1/1a). Bold (*Wilton House*, pp. 46–7), argues that they were made by Webb under Jones's direction in the 1630s and reused for the reconstruction after the fire. If so, the inscription 'For Mr Kennard' on one of them would have been added after the fire, as it presumably refers to Thomas Kinward, who was Master Joiner of the King's Works from 1660 onwards.

41 John Harris and A.A. Tait, *Catalogue of Drawings*, figs. 40–7.

42 John Bold, *Wilton House*, p. 47. Although formerly attributed to Jones by Harris and Tait in 1979, they are now generally accepted as the work of John Webb and do not figure in John Harris and Gordon Higgott, *Inigo Jones, Complete Architectural Drawings*, 1989. In addition to the principal dimensions, in Webb's hand, which are written in the margins and could have been added by him to drawings made by someone else, there are within several of the drawings themselves minute annotations of dimensions in Webb's hand.

43 Observations made in 1988–9 by Mr David Sumpster and Mr John Harris show that, unlike the east wall of the Double Cube Room, the west wall, separating it from the Single Cube, was a new brick wall inserted after the fire. I am grateful to Mr Harris for showing me photographs which substantiate his observations. If Heward ('The restoration of the south front', p. 99) is correct in stating that the positions of the present cross-walls were all determined by 1636, any previous timber partition would no doubt have been in the same place as its brick replacement.

44 Heward, 'The restoration of the south front', p. 104; photographs of blocked windows taken by Mr Harris.

45 Bodleian Library, Aubrey MS 2, f. 30^v.

46 *The Diary of John Evelyn*, ed. E.S. de Beer (Oxford Standard Authors 1959), p. 343.

47 Walpole Society, *Vertue Notebooks: Index*, p. 289.

48 Reproduced by John Harris in *Country Life*, 15 Sept. 1988, pp. 238, 241, from the originals in the Lewis Walpole Library at Yale. There are similar sketches by Vertue in Bodleian, MS Gough Drawings a.1, ff. 13–14.

49 Walpole Society, *Vertue Notebooks* ii, p. 59.

50 Ryder charged Lord Salisbury, for whom he designed an addition to Cranborne Lodge, Dorset, for coming over from Wilton on two occasions during the years 1647–50 (Hatfield Muniments, Bills 239).

51 See note 40 above.

52 Heward, 'The restoration of the south front', pp. 106–9.

53 The positions of the doors are specified in such a way as to make it quite clear that the withdrawing room was the room immediately to the west of the 'great room' (i.e. the 'Double' Cube) and that in its north wall there was a door opening into the west range of the old house.

54 Narcissus Luttrell, *A Brief Historical Relation of State Affairs*, iv, 1847, p. 503; *The Diary of John Evelyn*, p. 1114.

55 For these alterations, see John Harris in *Country Life*, 15 Sept. 1988, pp. 238–41.

56 In his plate of Wilton, published in *Vitruvius Britannicus* in 1717 (fig. 116), Colen Campbell shows a staircase beneath the central window, but it is quite clear that no such staircase has ever existed. All the early views show the staircase attached to the western pavilion (and therefore on the central axis of the garden). By 1747, however, Rocque's engraved view shows that it had been removed to a less

conspicuous position on the west side of the same pavilion. In 1757 the 10th Earl took up Campbell's hint and actually obtained an estimate from a local mason (William Privett) 'to set up a Flight of stairs (according to a Sketch given in with this Estimate) leading to the center Window of the Salloon Room . . . at Wilton', but nothing was done, and the stairs remained round the corner at the west end until they were removed by Wyatt in the course of his alterations early in the nineteenth century. The absence of any direct communication between the upper floor and the garden was, however, found to be inconvenient, and round about 1900 a flight of steps, this time of wood, was once more placed beneath the western window of the south front. There they remained until just before the Second World War, when they were removed by the 15th Earl.

57 Heward, 'The restoration of the south front', pp. 99–100. Among other discrepancies in the Double Cube Room, neither chimney-piece nor principal window is quite central, and as the former is 4 feet too far east and the latter only 2 feet, they are not exactly opposite one another.

58 *Architecture in Britain 1530–1830*, 1991, p. 130: 'we have only to compare the fenestration [of the south block of Wilton] with that of the second design for the Prince's Lodging at Newmarket to see how much of Jones it contains.' It is difficult to accept John Harris's verdict that 'de Caus' front speaks a quite different language to that of Jones' (*Inigo Jones, Complete Architectural Drawings*, 1989, p. 301).

59 Harris and Tait, *Catalogue of Drawings*, pls. 16–17. The garlanded Ionic capitals of the Wilton window (fig. 126) were a feature not apparently used by Jones elsewhere, but they recur as an interior feature in one of Webb's designs for the Double Cube Room (see his 'Book of Capitals', no. 14) and in his designs for Belvoir Castle (*RIBA Drawings Catalogue: Jones and Webb*, fig. 108).

60 E.g. at Villers-Cotterets, a royal château in the Loire valley, built in the mid-sixteenth century (F. Gebelin, *Les Châteaux de la Renaissance*, Paris, 1927, pl. lxxvii), at the Parisian Hôtels Zamet (1580–1) (Rosalys Coope, 'John Thorpe and the Hôtel Zamet in Paris', *Burlington Mag.*, 124, 1982, fig. 25) and Savourny (1586), at the Hôtel de Montescot at Chartres (c.1610, cf. fig. 130), and at the Château of Wideville, Seine-et-Oise (c.1630).

61 *RIBA Drawings Catalogue: Jones and Webb*, fig. 109; W. Kent, *Designs of Inigo Jones*, ii, 1727, p. 24.

62 Harris and Higgott, *Inigo Jones, Complete Architectural Drawings*, 1989, p. 261.

63 Rosalys Coope, *Salomon de Brosse*, 1972, pls. 199–201.

64 I follow John Heward ('The restoration of the south front', p. 102) in interpreting the drawing in fig. 122 as showing the roof of the N range on the other side of the courtyard and the chimney-stacks rising from the courtyard side of the south range (though it might be difficult to distinguish these from chimney-stacks rising from the south side of the N range).

VIII

THORPE HALL AND ITS ARCHITECT

THE ARCHITECTURAL HISTORY of England in the seventeenth century is dominated by two figures – Inigo Jones and Sir Christopher Wren: Jones, who introduced an Italianate classicism based on the precepts of Serlio, Palladio and Scamozzi; Wren, whose long life saw the development of a mature baroque style out of the academic essays of his scientific youth. It is one of the surprises of English architectural history that, in a century which saw the building of so many country houses, neither of these two great architects should have been directly involved in the designing of more than two or three of these symbols of wealth and territorial power. Both of them were essentially Court architects, too busy working for State and Church to be able to accept many commissions from private clients. Even when, at Charles I's behest, Inigo Jones was asked to design a new south front for the Earl of Pembroke's house at Wilton, he was too deeply committed to the works then in progress at Greenwich Palace to do more than recommend a tried subordinate, and offer to provide him with help and advice.[1] As for Wren, with fifty churches and a cathedral to rebuild after the Great Fire of London, plus his official responsibility, as Surveyor of the King's Works, for half a dozen royal palaces, he could not possibly undertake the long journeys that were the inevitable accompaniment of country-house commissions.[2] Between them, in any case, there was the hiatus of the Commonwealth and Protectorate, during which Jones, already in failing health (in 1646 he explained to a parliamentary commission that 'his age and weakness of body [had] not permitted him to goe much abroad in this tyme')[3], died (June 1652). A decade was to elapse before Wren began to show a serious interest in architecture. During the years of Jones's decline, and after his death, the leading English architect was his pupil John Webb (1611–72), and it is to Webb that virtually every classical building erected between the death of his master in 1652 and the Restoration of Charles II in 1660 has at one time or another been attributed. There is, indeed, abundant evidence that Webb continued to practise freely throughout the Interregnum, in the course of which he designed premises in London for the College of Physicians, and built or altered several country houses, including Wilton (1648–50),[4] The Vyne (1654–6), Lamport (1655–7), Belvoir (1655 onwards), Syon (1656–60), Gunnersbury (c.1658–63) and Amesbury (c.1659–61).[5] But as long ago as 1933 Geoffrey Webb pointed out that there was a group of houses built mostly in the 1650s which deviate more or less from the classical

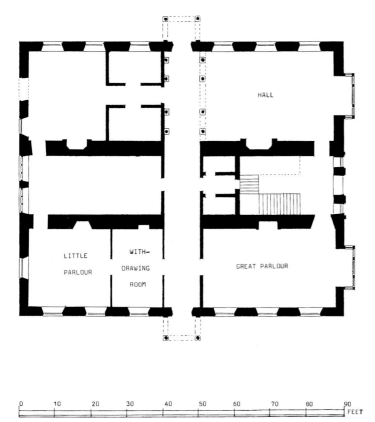

131. Plan of Thorpe Hall, showing the ground floor before the alterations of 1850–2: based on the plan published by A.W. Hakewill in 1852 and the modern survey by F.R. Roberts published in the *Georgian Group Journal* for 1993. North is at the top. The names of the rooms on the south side are derived from drawings of the interior dated 1710 in the Victoria and Albert Museum.

discipline that is so evident in Webb's documented works.[6] The earliest is the so-called Cromwell House, Highgate, built in 1637–8 by Richard Sprignell, a wealthy Londoner who was later to be an active supporter of the Parliamentary cause.[7] Three of the remaining five were built by eminent Parliamentary politicians, namely Wimborne House, Wimborne St Giles, Dorset, by Anthony Ashley Cooper, a member of the Protectorate Council of State, begun in 1651;[8] Thorpe Hall, near Peterborough, built by Oliver St John, Chief Justice of Common Pleas, 1654–6; and Wisbech Castle, Cambridgeshire, built by John Thurloe, Secretary of State, *circa* 1655–7.[9] The others are Tyttenhanger, Hertfordshire (Sir Henry Blount), *circa* 1655[10], and Thorney Abbey House, Cambridgeshire (William Russell, Earl of Bedford), 1660–2.[11]

Of these 'six houses in search of an architect' (as Geoffrey Webb called them), Thorpe Hall has generally been regarded as the outstanding example. Despite its relatively modest dimensions (90 by 75 feet), it struck John Evelyn as a 'stately palace' when he passed it (still under construction) in 1654,[12] and soon after the Restoration its repute as a model country house led the Earl of Clarendon to covet it, though he lost interest when informed that it contained only 'five or six rooms on a floor'.[13] Built of the finest ashlar masonry on a neatly rectangular plan (fig. 131), it stands 'foursquare and solid', with walled gardens to north, south and east and offices to the west.[14] Both the garden gateways (figs. 132 and 134) and the office range exhibit mannerist features of considerable sophistication, but the two identical north and south elevations of the house itself achieve a classical poise with the minimum of architectural effort (fig. 133). But for one detail they might have come

132. Thorpe Hall: one of the principal gateways.

133. Thorpe Hall: the south front.

134. Thorpe Hall: another gateway.

Scale 1 0 1 2 3 4 5 of Feet.

135. Thorpe Hall: the east front.

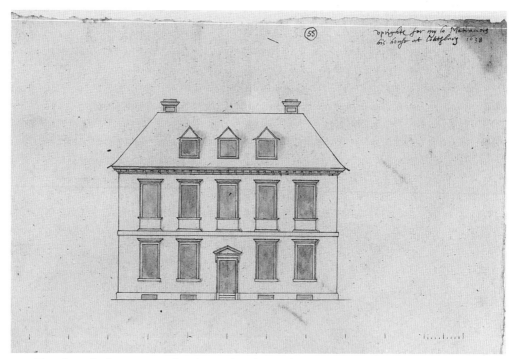

136. Elevation of a house in London for Lord Maltravers by Inigo Jones, dated 1638 (the Provost and Fellows of Worcester College, Oxford).

straight from Webb's office. Indeed, as Dr Giles Worsley has pointed out, they have much in common with a design by Inigo Jones for a house in Lothbury, London, made for the Earl of Arundel's son, Lord Maltravers, in 1638, and intended for business purposes (fig. 136), and this in turn may well derive from a published design for a small house (fig. 137) by Sebastiano Serlio.[15] But the architrave of the central window (fig. 138) on both fronts is broken out with a lug supported by half pilasters rising from scrolls in a manner that neither Jones nor Webb would have

137. Sebastiano Serlio: design for a house published in *l'Opere d'Architettura*, Venice, 1619.

138. (*facing page*) Thorpe Hall: detail of the window over the south doorway.

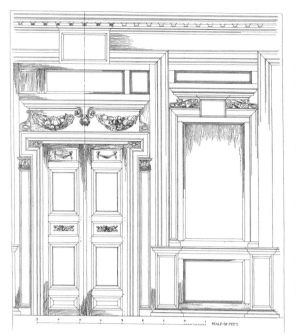

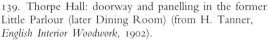

139. Thorpe Hall: doorway and panelling in the former Little Parlour (later Dining Room) (from H. Tanner, *English Interior Woodwork*, 1902).

140. Thorpe Hall: chimney-piece in the former Withdrawing Room.

sanctioned.[16] This tell-tale detail, elegant variations of which are to be found inside the house both in the joinery and in two of the chimney-pieces (figs. 139–40), is one which Thorpe shares with four of the five other houses in Geoffrey Webb's list.[17] At Thorpe it is one expression of the mannerist taste that has already been noted in the gateways and outbuildings, and that manifests itself again if one examines the east front (fig. 135). With its elaborately varied fenestration of two-storeyed pedimented bay windows on either side of a central tripartite one, topped by an attic containing one circular, two square and two rectangular windows, this east front is very different in character from the two principal ones. The bay windows look like Jacobean oriels classicised, and are examples of that cross between a mullioned and transomed window and a Venetian one (already used as early as early as 1636 in the library of St John's College, Oxford) that became so popular in urban vernacular architecture a little later in the century (fig. 141).[18] Simpler groups of pedimented bay windows were once not uncommon in London streets (figs. 142–3) and suggest possible links between the architecture of Thorpe Hall and that of the City. So do the mullioned and transomed windows paired beneath a single cornice that are a feature of the west front, overlooking the service courtyard (fig. 144).

So stylistically Thorpe Hall is something of a hybrid: either a mannerist house subjected to a measure of classical discipline or an orthodox design of the Jones/Webb school carried out with mannerist deviations. The mannerist features are so pervasive and so sophisticated of their kind as to make the first alternative much the more likely, and there is documentary evidence, to be cited later, to show that this was in fact the case. In his 1933 paper, Geoffrey Webb mentioned as possible

141. Mullioned and transomed window incorporating a 'Venetian' tripartite window at St John's College, Oxford, 1636.

142. (*top right*) London: seventeenth-century houses, formerly numbers 413–414 Strand (Rowland Paul, *Vanishing London*, 1894).

143. (*right*) London: a house formerly in Bishopsgate Street Without, with a pedimented version of the mullioned and transomed 'Venetian' window. Inside there was an 'artisan mannerist' chimney-piece (*Transactions of the London and Middlesex Archaeological Society*, i, 1880, p. 161).

144. Thorpe Hall: the west front.

architects of the group of houses he had identified, Edward Carter (d. 1663), Edward Marshall (*c.*1598–1675), and 'those obscure figures, the city surveyors, Mills, Oliver and Jarman'. Carter, now recognised as the likely architect of the remodelling of Forde Abbey in Dorset for the Parliamentary Attorney-General, Edmund Prideaux, was a good suggestion, for not only is a variant form of the lugged architrave motif to be seen at Forde, but there are chimney-pieces in the principal rooms that might well be at Thorpe.[19] In fact, however, it was Peter Mills who was the architect of Thorpe Hall. A contemporary copy of one of the contracts for building the house happens to be preserved in the British Library (and was published in 1952 in the original version of this essay). It is dated 8 February 1653/4, and by it two Ketton freemasons contract with Oliver St John to make thirty-eight windows for the north and south fronts, 'of such order mouldings and size and bignesse respectively as is expressed and sett forth in a Draught or map of the said intended House made by Peter Mills of London Surveyor'.[20] Each window in the first and second storeys was priced at 40s., those in the 'uppermost story' at 35s.

Comparison of the fenestration described in the contract with that of the house as it was built reveals two discrepancies. The first concerns the number of windows. There are twenty windows in each front as against nineteen in the contract. This is easily explained if we assume that the enriched central window was made the subject of a separate contract, together perhaps with the doorcase which it sur-mounts. The second discrepancy concerns the form of the first-floor windows. There is no mention in the agreement of the cornices and pediments with which

166

they are alternately decorated. Moreover, it is apparent both from the prices stated and from the specification of the 'perpoint stones' – that is, jamb stones bonded into the walls, which were to be the same in number (six) for the windows 'in the two nethermost storyes', but only four for those in the 'uppermost story' – that the ground- and first-floor windows were to be of the same height, whereas in fact the first-floor windows are considerably taller. Evidently the design was altered after the contract was drawn up, the middle row of windows being enlarged and given greater prominence by the addition of cornices and pediments in the Palladian manner. But for this alteration the fenestration would have been similar to that of Wisbech Castle, as represented in a seventeenth-century painting (fig. 145). The only other architectural detail specifically mentioned in the contract is an architrave

145. Wisbech Castle, Cambridgeshire: a painting of the demolished house in the Wisbech Museum (*Country Life*).

146. Thorpe Hall, a drawing by Peter Tillemans dated 1721 (British Library, Add. MS 32467, f. 154).

moulding over the 'peers' (i.e. the sections of wall) between the upper windows. This is a feature of the design both of Thorpe Hall and of Wisbech Castle, though much more prominent, if the painting is to be trusted, at Wisbech than at Thorpe, where its attenuation might have resulted from the pushing up of the attic windows to allow for the heightening of those below.

A glance at figures 135 and 145 will show several other resemblances between Thorpe Hall and Wisbech Castle, and the similarity would be still more striking if Thorpe had not lost the cupola which once surmounted the flat platform on top of the roof, together with the balustrade noted by a visitor in 1676, though apparently missing by the time Tillemans drew his view (fig. 146).[21] Both houses were built within a few years of one another by prominent members of the Protectorate government who were close friends of long standing, and there can be little doubt that they were both designed by the same architect, and that architect was, in the words of the contract, 'Peter Mills of London Surveyor'. Indeed, 'Mr Mills' is mentioned in a letter from St John to Thurloe dated 24 September 1657 in a way which makes it clear that there was 'business at Wisbech', presumably of an architectural kind, in which he was concerned.[22] By this time Thurloe's house must have been almost finished, for in January 1655/6 his steward had written to report that the roof was covered with lead and that the carpenters were at work on the staircase and the balustrade round the 'plattforme' on which the 'turret' stood.[23]

The name of Peter Mills, associated in 1952 almost exclusively with the survey

168

of London streets which he carried out after the Great Fire, is now well known as that of a leading London architect of the mid-seventeenth century and as the builder of houses which formed part of what in the eighteenth century was recognised as 'the first regular street in London'.

Mills was a bricklayer by trade, and the records of the Tylers' and Bricklayers' Company show that as 'Peter Mills, son of John Mills of Eastdean, Sussex, Taylor', he was apprenticed on 30 November 1613 to John Williams, tyler and bricklayer of London.[24] He had been baptised at East Dean on 12 February 1597/8. His apprenticeship was due to terminate in 1621, but owing to a gap in the records of the Company the date when he took up his freedom is not recorded. We know, however, that in 1629 he took his first apprentice, and that in October 1643 he was appointed Bricklayer to the City of London. He was Master of his Company in 1648–9 and again in 1659–60. In 1648 he was appointed a member of the Committee for the City of London Militia – presumably an indication that his political sympathies were on the Parliamentary side.[25] In 1654 a new office of City Surveyor was created for him and his colleague Edward Jerman, the City Carpenter. After the Great Fire Mills was one of the four surveyors appointed by the City authorities to supervise the rebuilding of London in conjunction with Wren, May and Pratt, and it was in this capacity that he made the survey of the devastated area already mentioned. He was the author of a plan for rebuilding the City, of which nothing is known except that it was considered inferior to that submitted by Robert Hooke.

In the summer of 1667 Mills became seriously ill, but he continued to receive his salary as one of the City Surveyors until his death in 1670. In his will, dated 20 July 1670, he mentions his own 'great losses by the dreadfull fire'. These included the destruction of some property at Garlick Hythe, part of whose site he was afterwards obliged to surrender for street widening, and three tenements in Budge Row which he held under Pembroke College, Cambridge, by a lease dated 10 April 1662. This was to have expired in 1702, but in July 1668, the college, 'in consideration of his great losse susteyned by the Fire', agreed to extend it on condition that the houses were rebuilt 'with all convenient speed' and in accordance with the 'Act of Parliament lately made for the Rebuilding of the Citty of London'. Mills also played an active part in the rebuilding of the property of St Bartholomew's Hospital, Smithfield, of which he had become a Governor in December 1644. He lived in a house in Bartholomew Close which he rented from the Hospital, and his will provides for a legacy of ten shillings each to the twenty Governors 'that most frequently meet at the Compting House about the affairs of the Hospital whom I desire may be at my Funerall . . . to buy each of them a Ring'. He died in August 1670, and was buried in the church of St Bartholomew the Less.

Mills's reputation as an architect is shown by a resolution of the Gresham Trustees appointing Edward Jerman as surveyor of the Royal Exchange on 25 April 1667, the committee 'being very sensible of the greate burthen of businesse lying upon him [Mills] for the City att this time; and considering that Mr Jerman is the most able knowne artist (besides him) that the City now hath'. One of the chief proofs of Mills's abilities as an 'artist' must have been the houses which he built

147. London: houses in Great Queen Street built by Peter Mills *circa* 1640 (from H. Inigo Triggs and Henry Tanner, *Some Architectural Works of Inigo Jones*, 1901).

nearly thirty years before in Great Queen Street, Lincoln's Inn Fields (fig. 147). For it was these houses, built of fine red brick, with uniformly pilastered fronts, which (in Summerson's words) 'laid down the canon of street design which put an end to gabled individualism, and provided a discipline for London's streets which was accepted for more than two hundred years'[26]; and, according to that assiduous student of seventeenth-century art and architecture, George Vertue (1684–1756), they were 'designed and built' by Mills.[27] The latter part of his statement is confirmed by documentary evidence that the site of numbers 66–68 Great Queen Street was leased to Mills on 15 September 1639,[28] and as all the houses on the south side of the street were built at approximately the same time according to a uniform pattern, very likely insisted on by the commissioners on building (the London planning quango set up by royal authority), there seems no reason to doubt that Vertue was correct in attributing their design to Mills. Indeed, the moulded labels set over the windows are a mannerist touch that shows that the elevations were the work of a City artisan rather than of a Court architect. In considering Mills's work as an urban developer in London it is unfortunate that no visual record seems to survive of the houses he built in Castle (now Furnival) Street, Holborn,

148. Pembroke College, Cambridge: part of the Hitcham Building, probably designed by Peter Mills in 1659 (Michael Clifford).

on land leased to him in 1642 by Oliver St John himself. They were to be of brick, three storeys high, and 'in the same uniformitie and beauty' as some adjoining houses to be built in accordance with a royal licence dated August 1641.[29] The world of the city artisan is also apparent in the block called Sir Robert Hitcham's Building at Pembroke College, Cambridge (1659–61), which was almost certainly designed by Mills (fig. 148). For, as Dr Timothy Mowl has pointed out, we find here the same windows paired beneath a pediment and set one above another that were to be seen in London streets and that probably influenced Mills's design for the east front of Thorpe Hall.[30]

Whatever leanings Mills may have had towards the Parliamentary side in the 1640s, they did not prevent his employment at the Restoration both to construct the triumphal arches set up in the City to celebrate Charles II's coronation (covertly designed by the disgraced Sir Balthazar Gerbier with Mills's assistance) and to organise the 'shews and pageants' on the Thames with which the City welcomed Charles and his queen to Whitehall on 27 August 1662.[31] Nor did the royalist Duke of Lennox scruple to employ Mills to rebuild the centre of his mansion at Cobham in Kent in 1661–3.[32] At Cobham, moreover, Mills showed that by then he had learned to conform closely to the conventions of English domestic architecture as practised by contemporaries such as Hooke, May and Pratt, only the principal doorcase still betraying a trace of mannerist taste.

In 1665 Mills received £5 10s. for drawing 'several platformes' for Colfe's Almshouses at Lewisham, which were built to his designs in 1664–5. These almshouses, demolished after bomb-damage in the last war, consisted of a simple brick range with a raised centre to accommodate an unpretentious chapel.[33] In 1667–8 he prepared plans for a 'Compting House, Court Roome and School' for Christ's Hospital, which seem to have been built, at least in part, before his death in 1670.[34]

So the architect of Thorpe Hall was a leading London artificer and architect who probably shared the political convictions of his patron, and had previously been employed by him in the City in the 1640s. When St John acquired property near Peterborough on which he decided to build a country seat befitting his status as a Lord Chief Justice, it was therefore entirely natural that he should decide to employ Mills as his architect.

Two questions remain. Does Mills's responsibility for the design of Thorpe Hall and Wisbech Castle mean that any of the other 'six houses in search of an architect' should be attributed to him? And what are the implications of the change in the fenestration of the north and south fronts? Does the classical restraint of these two façades as built imply any knowledge by Mills of such studiedly simple designs by Inigo Jones as that for Lord Maltravers' house?.

Mills certainly had no monopoly of what has been called the 'artisan mannerist' style, and it would be unwise to assume without further evidence that he was the architect of any of the other houses in question. As a brick house within twenty miles of London, Tyttenhanger (fig. 149) is an obvious candidate for attribution to him, but there are differences in both plan and architectural detail that counsel caution. As for Mills's relations with Inigo Jones, on the only occasion (in 1637) when we know that they were both professionally involved in the same building, it was as representatives of clients (the Privy Council on the one hand and the churchwardens of a City parish on the other) whose architectural ideas did not coincide: in fact, it was an architectural confrontation which was typical of the bad relations that existed between Court and City in the 1630s.[35] But because on this occasion Mills was probably defending a semi-Gothic or mannerist classical design against something more in the style of St Paul's, Covent Garden, that does not mean that he was incapable of learning from Jones's example. Although he is unlikely to have seen the design for the Maltravers house (which appears not to have been carried out), other houses with astylar fronts of this sort were built in London and the south of England in the 1630s and 1640s.[36] The man who in the 1660s could so far conform to contemporary architectural fashion as to design the new front of Cobham Hall must be credited with the ability to absorb something of the Jones/Webb manner in the 1640s and 1650s. It is, of course, possible that the alteration was prescribed by the client, Oliver St John, even perhaps that he had consulted some other architect about the design of his house. The fact that there are ceilings at Thorpe that are similar to contemporary ceilings in houses designed by

149. Tyttenhanger, Hertfordshire, *circa* 1655.

John Webb (one, indeed, is a variant of a design for a ceiling at Wilton made by Webb himself in 1648 or 1649)[37] might even point to the direct intervention of that architect at St John's behest. But no other features of the interior reflect Webb's style, and, at a time when master workmen (especially plasterers) habitually made their own designs, it is much more likely that the form of the ceilings was due to the employment of a master plasterer who had previously worked at Wilton, or elsewhere under Webb. As for the exterior, the stylistic trademark of the lugged architrave over the two principal entrances suggests that Mills was still in control. Whatever lay behind the decision to modify the elevations in 1654, the enhancement of the first-floor windows gave Thorpe Hall a degree of authority that was lacking in its twin at Wisbech and that has always marked it out as one of the most notable architectural works of the mid-seventeenth century in England.

APPENDIX I

A Note on the Lugged Architrave with Half Pilasters

In English architecture the first dated example of this motif appears to be the the south doorway of St Helen's Church, Bishopsgate, London, dated 1633 (fig. 150), but a version of it (with putti instead of pilasters) had already appeared in sculpture on the monument in Westminster Abbey to Elizabeth Fane, who died in 1618. Thereafter it is found in two important houses in the neighbourhood of London: at Cromwell House, Highgate, 1637–8 (fig. 151), and in joinery in the north drawing-room at Ham House, Surrey, 1637. Then it occurs in the woodwork of the Selden End of the Bodleian Library at Oxford (1638–40), at Forde Abbey, Dorset (c.1650), Thorpe Hall (1654–6), Wisbech Castle (c.1655–7), Tyttenhanger (c.1655) and Thorney Abbey House (1660–1), and on many funerary monuments of the mid and later seventeenth century.

The lugged architrave was an Italian mannerist invention of the sixteenth century, and is, for instance, a prominent feature of a design for a frame by Pirro Ligorio (c.1515–1583) in the Ashmolean Museum at Oxford. Who first added the half-pilaster remains to be determined, but in this form it probably reached England from northern France or the Low Countries, where it is particularly associated with the influence of Wendel Dietterlein's *Architectura*, first published at Nuremberg in 1593–4, of which there was a second edition in 1598. Dietterlein himself was not an architect but a painter, and some of his more fantastic compositions were scarcely capable of realisation in stone. However, architectural features derived from 'Ditterling' (as he was generally called) were to be seen here and there in England, e.g. at Charlton House in Kent and at Bolsover Castle in Derbyshire, and one of his designs for gateways was actually built at Wentworth Woodhouse in Yorkshire (figs. 152–3). The lugged architrave and the half pilaster figure in some of his plates (fig. 154), and it was probably from this source and others of it kind (e.g. Bernardino Radi's *Varii Inventioni per Depositi*, Rome, 1618 and 1625) that this mannerist feature found its way into the repertoire of the London architects of the mid-seventeenth century.

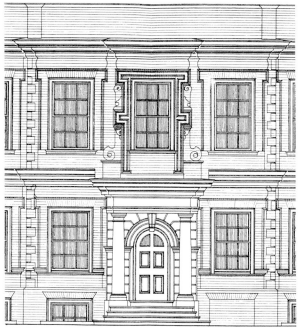

150. St Helen's Church, Bishopsgate, London: south doorway dated 1633.

151. Cromwell House, Highgate, North London: the centre of the principal front (from Philip Norman, *Cromwell House, Highgate*, Survey of London, 1926).

152. (*above left*) Wendel Dietterlein, design for a gateway (from his *Architectura*, Nuremberg, 1598).

153. (*above right*) Wentworth Woodhouse, Yorkshire: an early seventeenth-century gateway copied from Dietterlein's engraving.

154. Wendel Dietterlein, design for a gateway with a lugged architrave and scrolled half-pilaster (from his *Architectura*, Nuremberg, 1598).

APPENDIX II

The Thorpe Hall Building Contract (British Library, Additional MS 25,302, f. 153)

Articles of agreement Indented and made agreed and concluded upon this 8th day of February 1653 between John Ashley [*sic*] and Sampson Frisbey of Ketton in the County of Rutland Freemasons on the one part and the Right Honorable Oliver St John Lord Chief Justice of the Court of Common Pleas at Westminster of the other part. Witnesseth as followeth, That is to say.

First. The said John Ashbey [*sic*] and Sampson Frisbey for themselves their Heires Executors and Administrators do hereby Covenant and grant to and with the said Oliver St John his Heirs Executors and Administrators That they the said John Ashbey [*sic*] and Sampson Frisbey their Heirs Executors or Administrators or some of them shall and will att their proper costs and charges provide make and finish for him the said Oliver St John his Heyres etc. 38 windows of Freestone raised at Ketton pitts in the County of Rutland to be placed in a mansion House intended to be built by him the said Oliver St John at a place called Hill Close in Longthorpe in Com. Northampton, the one half of the said windowes to be placed in the north front and the other half in the south front of the said intended House, and to be of such order mouldings and size and bignesse respectively as is expressed and sett forth in a Draught or map of the said intended House made by Peter Mills of London Surveyor. And further that the stone of the said windows shall be so wrought as to conteyne part of the Ashler and Splays of the said House and that in every window in the two nethermost storyes of the said intended House there shall be six perpoint stones viz.[t] 3 on each side and in every of the said windowes in the uppermost story of the said intended House 4 perpoint stones vix.[t] 2 on each side, every of the said perpoint stones to be a foot square at the least. And shall likewise make and finish of Ketton stone aforesaid the Architrave Moulding as well over the said uppermost windowes as over the Peers between the same windowes, and shall joynt and return the same according to the order expressed in the Draught or mapp aforesaid and shall from time to time deliver the said windowes faire and workmanly wrought and noways defaced at the Place in Hill Close aforesaid where the said House is to be built in such manner and proportion as the proceeding of the Building of the said House shall require so as the same shall not at any time be hindred for want of the said windowes or any of them or any part of them, in Consideration whereof The said Oliver St John for himself his heires Executors etc. doth covenant and grant to and with them the said John Ashley [*sic*] and Sampson Frisbey their Executors administrators etc. to pay the several summs of mony hereinafter expressed over and above 5.[l] already paid. That is to say, for every window to be placed in the first and 2.[d] story of the said intended house made and finished as aforesaid forty shillings. For every of the said windows to be placed in the uppermost story of the said House thirty five shillings, and for every foot of the said Architrave moulding over the Peers between the windows in the said uppermost story proportionally according to the rate and quantity of the same windowes. The said severall summs of money to be paid from Time to Time according to the proceeding of the said intended House and delivery of the said windowes and premises at the place aforesaid.

In witnesse etc.

A Bond of 60.[li] to performe Covenants

They are to have 30.[li] advanced

Coppy

1 Above, pp. 136–8.

2 Below, p. 193.

3 *History of the King's Works*, ed. Colvin, iii, 1975, p. 157.

4 Above, pp. 146–7.

5 H. Colvin, *A Biographical Dictionary of British Architects 1600–1840*, 3rd ed., 1995, pp. 1030–1.

6 Geoffrey Webb, 'The Architectural Antecedents of Sir Christopher Wren', *RIBA Journal*, 3rd ser., 14, 27 May 1933, pp. 573–83.

7 Philip Norman, *Cromwell House, Highgate* (Survey of London Monograph 12, 1926), and Arthur Oswald in *Country Life*, 26 May 1966. For Sprignell's membership of numerous Parliamentary committees in the 1640s see the index to *Acts and Ordinances of the Interregnum*, ed. Firth and Rait, 1911.

8 *Country Life*, 10, 17, 24 Sept. 1943; Royal Commission on Historical Monuments, *Dorset*, v, 1975, pp. 94–7.

9 Demolished in 1815, but recorded in a 17th-century painting (see fig. 145).

10 *Country Life*, 4, 11 Oct. 1919; H.A. Tipping, *English Homes*, Period IV, vol. i, 1929, pp. 63–84; J.T. Smith, *English Houses 1200–1800* (Royal Commission on Historical Monuments, 1992), pp. 67–70. Sir Henry Blount was a Royalist during the Civil War, but by the 1650s had accepted the Parliamentary regime (Clutterbuck, *History of Hertfordshire*, i, 1810, p. 210).

11 *Country Life*, 27 Sept. 1919: H.A. Tipping, *English Homes*, pp. 53–62. The building contract with John Loven of Peterborough, mason, was published by Gladys Scott-Thompson in *Family Background*, 1949, pp. 180–4. The structure was to be built 'according to the draught and order of works designed for the same and now delivered in . . . under the hand of the said John Loven', but it did not cover the joinery, in which the mannerist features associated with this group of houses are chiefly in evidence.

12 *The Diary of John Evelyn*, ed. E.S. de Beer (Oxford Standard Authors, 1959), p. 351.

13 Mark Noble, *Memoirs of the Protectoral House of Cromwell*, 1787, ii, p. 21.

14 As described by Nikolaus Pevsner in *Bedfordshire and the County of Huntingdon and Peterborough* (Buildings of England, 1968), p. 353. According to the present county boundaries, Thorpe is in Cambridgeshire.

15 Giles Worsley, *Classical Architecture in Britain*, Yale 1995, p. 10. See also Worsley's previous article on the house in the *Georgian Group Journal*, 1993.

16 For this motif see Appendix I.

17 At Wimborne House the window in the middle of the N front which led Webb to include it in his list appears in fact to date from 1740 (RCHM, *Dorset*, v, 1975, p. 95).

18 A well-known example is at Sparrowe's House, Ipswich, of *c*.1670. Such windows are rare in country houses, but appear to be indicated in Kip and Knyff's engraving of the E front (date uncertain) of Hampstead Marshall, Berkshire (*Britannia Illustrata*, i, 1714, pl. 45). At Thorpe structural evidence shows that the bay windows, though slightly altered in the nineteenth century, are an original feature of the house, and their presence is indicated, albeit sketchily, in Tillemans' view of 1721 (fig. 146). They are also shown, almost exactly as at present, in an early nineteenth-century drawing by Edward Blore (1787–1879) in the British Library, Add. MS 42020, f. 100.

19 For the attribution of Forde Abbey to Carter see J.J. West in *Archaeological Journal*, 140, 1983, pp. 27–8. The house is described in *Country Life*, 14 March–4 April 1963, and in RCHM, *Dorset*, i, 1952, pp. 240–6.

20 Printed in full (Appendix II) from Add. MS 25302, f. 153. The document had in fact been published fifty years earlier by one L. Gaches, but in so obscure a periodical (*Fenland Notes & Queries*, iv, 1898–1900, pp. 272–3) that no one, including the writer, had noticed it.

21 Quoted by Arthur Oswald from the travel diary of John Conyers of Walthamstow (*Country Life*, 19 August 1949, p. 529).

22 Thurloe Papers: British Library, Add. MS 4158, f. 33. St John writes that he has 'not adventured from hence and therfore can give you noe information of your busines att Wisbich which will be better done by Mr Mills'. See also Add. MS 4157, f. 86 for another letter from St John dated 26 August 1656 in which he tells Thurloe that he has visited 'your house att Wisbich and with the enlargements it will be a very fine seate'.

23 Thurloe Papers: Bodleian Library, MS Rawlinson A 22, f. 369.

24 For the documentation of Mills's career see my *Biographical Dictionary of British Architects 1600–1840* (3rd ed., 1995), pp. 655–8, and the introduction to *The Survey of Building Sites in the City of London after the Great Fire of 1666*, ed. Jones and Reddaway, London Topographical Society, 1967.

25 *Acts and Ordinances of the Interregnum*, ed. Firth and Rait, i, 1911, p. 1138. See also p. 1131.

26 John Summerson, *Georgian London*, rev. ed., 1969, p. 34.

27 *Vertue Notebooks* (Walpole Society), i, p. 130.

28 *Survey of London*, v (St Giles in the Fields), pp. 44, 86.

29 Huntingdonshire Record Office, dd M 69/4/1. John Thurloe was a witness.

30 T. Mowl and B. Earnshaw, *Architecture without Kings*, Manchester, 1995, p. 143.

31 J. Ogilby, *Relation of His Majestie's Entertainment passing through the City of London to his Coronation with a Description of the Triumphal Arches*, 2nd ed., 1662; John Tatham, *Aqua Triumphans; being a true Relation of the Honourable the City of London's Entertaining their Sacred Majesties upon the River Thames*, etc., 1662. The original drawings for these arches, which survive in the British Architectural Library's Drawings Collection, were presumably drawn by Gerbier, though they are certainly not by the same hand as the design for gate piers at Hampstead Marshall, Berkshire (Bodleian Library, MS Gough Drawings a.2, ff. 24–5), which is inscribed 'Sr Balthazar Gerbier Baron Douly Fecit'.

32 H. Colvin, 'Peter Mills and Cobham Hall', in *The Country Seat*, ed. Colvin and Harris, 1970. Three of the craftsmen employed here had also been employed on the triumphal arches, i.e. Thomas Wratten, carpenter, Thomas Whiting, joiner, and Richard Cleer, joiner, and it is not unlikely that Cleer, at least, had also been employed at Thorpe Hall, as suggested by Geoffrey Beard, *Craftsmen and Interior Decoration in England 1660–1820*, Edinburgh, 1981, fig. 45, although the drawing there reproduced is not a contemporary design but an early 18th-century drawing of an existing doorway at Thorpe Hall.

33 See the illustration of it in W.H. Godfrey, *The English Almshouse*, 1955, fig. 39b.

34 For these and other commissions mentioned above, see references in my *Biographical Dictionary*, s.v. 'Mills'.

35 H. Colvin, 'Inigo Jones and the Church of St. Michael le Querne', *The London Journal*, 12 (1), 1986.

36 See Giles Worsley, *Classical Architecture in Britain*, Yale, 1995, ch. 1.

37 As first pointed out by Tipping in *English Homes*, Period IV (i), 1929, p. 41. The drawing is at Worcester College, Oxford. For further discussion of the interior decoration see John Cornforth's article on the house in *Country Life*, 31 October 1991. The panelling formerly in the Great Parlour is now at Leeds Castle, Kent.

IX

CHESTERTON, WARWICKSHIRE

THERE IS SCARCELY an English county in which (as James Lees-Milne once observed), 'some Jacobean house with, say, a window, gable or porch displaying a more or less regular use of the classical orders, has not been classified by over-zealous topographers as an Inigo Jones building'.[1] Though in most cases such ill-informed attributions can be dismissed out of hand, they are sometimes worth investigation, for the influence of Inigo Jones spread far beyond the narrow Court circle to which his own architectural activities were confined, and for many years after his death his buildings were studied and admired by many architects and builders for whom (as a German traveller noted in 1740)[2] Jones was 'the Palladio of England'. What we find is unlikely to be an authentic work of the master (or even of his pupil John Webb), but may well prove to be an imitative work by one of those master builders who were the backbone of English architectural practice in the seventeenth and eighteenth centuries.

Chesterton in Warwickshire is a case in point. Every guidebook to the county contains a reference to the vanished seventeenth-century mansion of the Peytos, 'designed by Inigo Jones and demolished in 1802 by Lord Willoughby de Broke', and draws the visitor's attention to the still surviving windmill, likewise said to have been 'erected from designs by Inigo Jones'.

For further information we turn to Dugdale's *Warwickshire*, and to the manuscript collections of the Revd Thomas Ward, now in the British Library.[3] From these two authorities we learn the essential facts in the history of the Peyto family: how they claimed descent from a Poitevin ancestor reputed to have come to England in the reign of Henry II, how in the fourteenth century John de Peto acquired the manor by marriage, how in the fifteenth Sir John de Peto rebuilt the manor-house and filled the windows with heraldic glass, how in the sixteenth the family produced its most famous son, that William Peto who was made a cardinal under Queen Mary, and how in the seventeenth Sir Edward Peyto was 'a strenuous asserter of the Parliament against King Charles I' and held Warwick Castle in the face of the royal army.

Sir Edward Peyto died in 1643, and it was his son, another Edward, who in about 1655 began to pull down the old manor-house and 'to build a Mansion House and other buildings necessary for his habitation' on the hill overlooking the church. But in 1658 he died at the early age of thirty-two, leaving a widow to bring up his heir and five other children. During his last illness he had told his servant Robert Smoak that 'if he should dye before the said buildings was finished his desires were that the same should be compleated', and in his will he accordingly directed that 'the building I have begun at Chesterton may be finish'd out of the rents of the lands in Chesterton which belong after my decease to my son Edward Peyto . . . towards which I do give and appoint that all the Bricks, Stones, Timber and other materialls provided for that building shalbe therein imployed.'[4] True to her trust, Elizabeth Peyto carried on the work with the aid of the faithful Smoak, and it is their accounts (now divided between the Willoughby de Broke archives at Stratford-on-Avon and those in the British Library)[5] which enable the progress of the work to be followed to its completion in about 1662. The masons chiefly employed were Thomas Bonde, father and son, but they were both paid by the day, and were evidently local men with little capital who were not prepared to take a contract for the masonry as a whole; or, if they were, Elizabeth Peyto was too prudent a manager of her son's heritage to put out the mason's work 'by the great', a manner of proceeding which was regarded as risky by most seventeenth-century writers on building. As for the plan and elevation, they had of course been settled by Edward Peyto in his lifetime, and are consequently not mentioned in his widow's accounts. But there were certain details for which drawings had still to be obtained, and so in October 1659, she gave £1 to 'Mr Stone for Drawing the Draught of the head of the Pillars for Chesterton'. In the following year she paid John Stone £2 'for the 2 capitalls of the arch at the Staires', and a further £6 as part 'of the Bargaine he made for the 10 Capitalls of the lower Row of pillars, and to Caius Gabril Cibbers for the same work £4'. Further entries show that in 1660–1 Cibber carved the ten capitals of the upper order and the staircase doorway, for which he received in all £24.

John Stone (1620–67) was a member of a family of London master masons, and Cibber, afterwards a well-known sculptor, and father of Colley Cibber the actor and playwright, was at this time acting as his foreman. John's father, the famous Nicholas Stone (1587–1647), had served as master mason under Inigo Jones at the building of the Banqueting House in Whitehall in the reign of James I, and had been one of the most distinguished monumental sculptors of his day, designing and erecting many splendid tombs in churches all over the country. Among them, as we know from his notebook,[6] was the one in Chesterton Church to the memory of William Peyto (d. 1609) and his wife Eleanor (d. 1635), which he made in 1639, and 'for the which I had well payed unto me 150£' (fig. 155). Now in 1639 Nicholas Stone also made a monument in St Mary's, Warwick, to Sir Thomas Puckering, the owner of Warwick Priory, 'for the which Ser Daved Cyninghem my Nobell frend payed 200£', and a few years before he had been paid £180 by Sir David for erecting a very similar monument at Charlton in Kent to Sir Adam Newton, Puckering's brother-in-law, and father of Sir Edward Peyto's wife Elizabeth.[7] The similarity between the two monuments was not accidental, for in his will Sir Thomas Puckering had directed that the 'materialls, forme and proporcion' of his tomb were to be 'sutable to that erected in Charlton Church for my brother Newton'.[8] As for Sir David Cunningham, he had been one of Sir Adam

155. Chesterton Church, Warwickshire: monument to William Peyto (d. 1609) and his wife Eleanor, made by Nicholas Stone in 1639.

156. Chesterton Church, Warwickshire: monument to Sir Edward Peyto (d. 1643), made in Nicholas Stone's workshop.

Newton's executors, and when Sir Thomas Puckering's executors required a duplicate of Newton's monument in 1639 it was natural that he should be consulted. He was evidently interested in architectural matters, for he was the builder of the house in Lincoln's Inn Fields, now known as Lindsey House, which is one of the earliest examples of what Sir John Summerson has called 'the purer type of Artisan classicism', and which he suggests may have been designed by Stone himself.[9] Whether or not the Peytos were personally acquainted with Stone's 'noble friend', they would certainly have known the monument to Lady Peyto's father which he had commissioned, and it may well have been this family connection which led to the sculptor's employment at Chesterton. When Sir Edward Peyto the Parliamentarian died in his turn in 1643, and was buried in Chesterton Church, his monument too (fig. 156) was evidently made in Stone's yard, for not only does it closely resemble the two monuments ordered by Sir David Cunningham, but

Dugdale procured an engraving of it for his *Warwickshire* which bears the signature 'Ioh. Stone delin. et fecit'. It was John Stone who in 1660 supplied the black marble ledger-stone which covers the remains of the second Edward Peyto, for among the family papers at Stratford-on-Avon is his receipt for £5 from Mrs Elizabeth Peyto 'in full payment as well for all works done for her as for particularly a gravestone sent down for her husband deceased'. John Stone, like his father, was a mason as well as a sculptor, and we have it on the authority of his brother-in-law, Charles Stoakes, that he was also 'an excellent architect'.[10] Hitherto nothing has been known of his architectural activities, but in view of the continuous patronage of his firm by the Peyto family over a period of some twenty years, and the fact that he was employed by Elizabeth Peyto in 1659 to make the 'draughts' for the capitals of the superimposed orders which were the principal feature of Chesterton House, it is reasonable to conclude that it was he to whom Edward Peyto had gone for a design when three or four years previously he had 'resolved to build a Mansion House and other buildings necessary for a habitation'.

Had the house which he designed survived to the present day, there can be no doubt that it would have been regarded as one of the most interesting examples of the architecture of its time (fig. 157). Its dependence on the Banqueting House (fig. 158) is obvious, and shows how faithfully John Stone followed the Palladian formulas which his father had learned from Inigo Jones. Had Jones himself been its author, the relation of the ends to the centre would no doubt have been managed

157. Chesterton House, Warwickshire, demolished in 1802: a drawing by the Revd Thomas Ward (1770–1850) (British Library, Add. MS 29264, f. 190).

158. The Banqueting House, Whitehall, built by Nicholas Stone in 1619–22 to the designs of Inigo Jones.

more adroitly, while the centre itself would certainly have been emphasised by something more effective than the row of niches whose swan-necked canopies nod to one another between the urns. Nevertheless, the elevation of Chesterton avoids the *gaucheries* of the seventeenth-century wing at Brympton D'Evercy in Somerset, another building whose designer borrowed features from the Banqueting House, and managed them so badly that the terminal pediment at one end is segmental in form while that at the other is triangular (fig. 159). Here, as at Hinton St George in the same county, the controlling discipline of the orders is omitted, leaving

159. Brympton d'Evercy, Somerset: the south front built *circa* 1670–80.

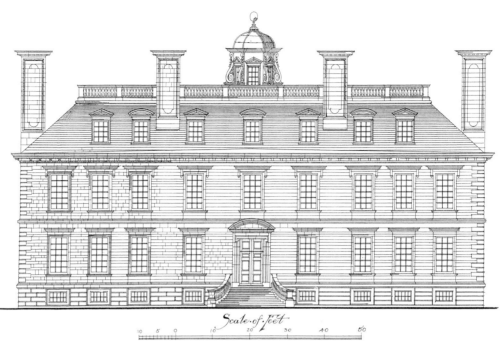

160. Coleshill House, Berkshire, completed in 1662 to the designs of Sir Roger Pratt (from H. Inigo Triggs and Henry Tanner, *Some Architectural Works of Inigo Jones*, 1901).

only the two rows of pedimented windows to recall the source. A more profitable comparison may be made with Coleshill in Berkshire (fig. 160). Designed by Sir Roger Pratt for his cousin Sir George Pratt, Coleshill was completed in the same year as Chesterton, and likewise owed a good deal to Inigo Jones. Both represented the new type of compact, rectangular house introduced by Jones and his pupil Webb, and Chesterton, like Coleshill, was probably what Pratt called a 'double pile', that is, a house two rooms deep divided along its length by a corridor. How the stairs were arranged is not recorded, but payments for the making and carving of what were apparently stone capitals 'for the arch at the Staires' and for 'the Stare Case Dore' suggest a formal architectural treatment. So far as the exterior was concerned, the problem was to give interest to what might easily become a somewhat monotonous succession of identical windows. In both houses this was achieved by a skilful variation in the spacing of the windows, and, in the case of Chesterton, by the additional embellishment of superimposed orders and pedimented architraves. There can be no doubt that in the refined simplicity of Coleshill Pratt achieved a better composition than Stone did with his architectural parade at Chesterton. But it would be unfair to judge Chesterton solely by the surviving representations of the principal front (fig. 157),[11] for Cibber's carving was no doubt much more competent than Thomas Ward's rather coarse drawing would suggest, and on a fine day the parade of half-columns and pilasters must have been extremely handsome.

The young Edward Peyto did not long survive his father, and Chesterton passed to his brother William, who died in 1699. The last male member of the family was

161. Chesterton, Warwickshire: the surviving brick gateway between the church and the grounds of the house.

William, son of William, and nephew of Edward Peyto, who, in the words of Thomas Ward, 'lived here at Chesterton in no little honor, being one of the first rank in this County, and representing it in several Parliaments as one of the Knights of the Shire . . . and being fond of the sports of the field, for he kept a Pack of Fox Hounds'. Unfortunately he was also too fond of the bottle, and died at Warwick in 1734, while overcome with liquor after a dinner at the Castle. Ward says that he was 'unfortunately strangled' as he lay helpless in his bed, 'his servant having neglected loosing his Neckcloath'. He died unmarried and intestate, having destroyed a will made made not long before on discovering that the lawyer – one 'Will' Wright of Warwick (so called 'on the account of his making wills') – had surreptitiously inserted a clause leaving a handsome legacy to himself. His heir at law was his aunt Margaret Peyto, who died in 1746 at the age of eighty-eight, leaving the Chesterton estate to her cousin Lord Willoughby de Broke. But her 'kind bequest' was disputed by collateral branches of the family, and when the 6th Lord Willoughby had the house pulled down in 1802 it was reported that he did so 'to prevent possession being taken' by any rival claimant. The materials were taken to Birmingham and sold, and today nothing remains of the Peyto mansion except a walled garden and a brick gateway (fig. 161) leading from the churchyard to the site of the house.

Half a mile to the north-west, on the highest point in the parish, stands the windmill (fig. 162), and not far away, at the end of a small lake, is the charming building illustrated in figure 163. Long adapted for use as a watermill, it was presumably designed as a dwelling. The windmill is dated 1632, and must therefore

185

162. Chesterton, Warwickshire: the windmill dated 1632.

have been built by Sir Edward Peyto (d. 1643). The façade of the watermill is evidently of the same period, and the two buildings may therefore be considered together. Both are beautiful examples of seventeenth-century mason's work whose classical formality can hardly, at this early date, have been due merely to a local master builder. But despite the persistent attribution of the windmill to Inigo Jones, it is very unlikely that he designed either building, and, in the absence of any documentary evidence,[12] it is tempting to suggest that their real designer was

186

163. Chesterton, Warwickshire: the watermill.

Nicholas Stone. However, it is equally possible that Sir Edward was his own architect, for he had a number of architectual textbooks in his library,[13] from which he could have derived the classical detailing, and the mathematical skill with which he is credited on his monument, where he is described as *vir bonarum literarum maxime mathematicarum peritissimus*, would no doubt have enabled him to help a competent master mason to work out the stereotomy of the circular windmill.

In addition there is in Thomas Ward's manuscript a sketch (fig. 164) of a curious building known as the Lodge, which once stood near a clump of trees (now felled)

164. Chesterton, Warwickshire: the demolished lodge, sketched by Thomas Ward (d. 1850) (British Library, Add. MS 29264).

The Lodge at Chesterton on a high Hill a Wood behind

called Lodge Wood. It was, Ward says, 'a kind of Summer House, having two Rooms one over the other, and both wainscotted. In the lower Room was a cupboard in which was painted very masterly a large loaf of bread and a cheese half of which was cut, a cucumber and onion, plate, knife, etc., which being seen at a small distance gave every appearance of things in reality: and the edifice becoming out of repair, through chinks and fissures in the door and windows, many looking through have been much deceived.' This whimsical conceit has long disappeared, but Ward's sketch shows that it was square in plan, with windows corbelled out over the angles like the bartizans of a Scottish castle. Whether it had any practical function, such as a hunting-stand or a keeper's lodge, or was merely an early example of a folly, it is difficult to say. Its foundations were said still to be visible in the 1950s.

NOTES

1 *The Age of Inigo Jones*, 1953, p. 105.
2 *The Letters of Baron Bielfeld*, trans. Hooper, 1770, iv, p. 99.
3 Add. MS 29264, ff. 189–90. For Ward see Geoffrey Tyack in *Architectural History*, 27, 1984, pp. 534–51.
4 P.C.C. 62 NABBS.
5 Shakespeare Birthplace Trust Record Office, DR 98/1540; BL, Egerton MS 2983, ff. 126–33.
6 *The Note-Book and Account Book of Nicholas Stone*, ed. W.L. Spiers (Walpole Soc., 1919), p. 76.
7 Ibid., pp. 65, 76.
8 P.C.C. 157 GOARE.

9   *Architecture in Britain 1530–1830*, 1991, p. 151.

10   *The Note-Book of Nicholas Stone*, p. 26.

11   A simplified view of the house reproduced by Geoffrey Tyack (*Warwickshire Country Houses*, 1994, p. 49) from a mid-eighteenth-century estate plan, agrees in general with the drawing reproduced here, but abbreviates the front by two bays.

12   Some payments for the completion of the windmill in 1633 have been discovered among the Willoughby de Broke papers by Mr Philip J. Wise and published in *Warwickshire History*, ix, no. 4, 1994/5, but they do not throw any fresh light on the responsibility for the design of the building.

13   The late Philip Styles kindly drew my attention to the catalogue of the library at Chesterton, drawn up in 1733 and now among the Willoughby de Broke papers at Stratford (DR 98/1741). The architectural works included three editions of Vitruvius, a Palladio (1601), Scamozzi (1615), Alberti (1553 and 1565), Philibert de l'Orme (1626), Vredeman de Vries (1619) and Rubens's *Palazzi di Genova* (1622).

165. Ramsbury Manor, Wiltshire, from the north-east (B.T. Batsford Ltd).

X

ROBERT HOOKE AND RAMSBURY MANOR

RAMSBURY MANOR IN Wiltshire is a much-admired example of an English country house of the late seventeenth century. Dignified without ostentation, it has an air of comfortable domesticity that to many is more sympathetic than the grandeur of a Chatsworth or the sophisticated elegance of a Harewood or a Kedleston. Historically it is precious because it has survived to the present day with no significant alterations to its exterior and only minor ones to its interior. Architecturally, it is notable as an excellent example of the 'double pile' plan that was so frequently adopted by English architects of the period when designing houses for the gentry (figs. 165–6).

Ramsbury Manor was built by Sir William Jones, a successful lawyer who, after acquiring a 'capital practice' in the Court of King's Bench, had successively held the offices of Solicitor-General and Attorney-General. Resigning in 1679, he entered Parliament as an opponent of the Court and was a prominent supporter of the Bill to exclude James, Duke of York, from the succession to the throne. For such a man it was a natural ambition to establish himself as a country landowner, and in 1676 he purchased the Ramsbury estate from the Earl of Pembroke and set about building a new house there.

He was not, however, to enjoy it for long, for in May 1682 he died at the age of fifty-one. As the rainwater heads on the house are dated 1683 we may conclude that it was probably begun in about 1680 and completed shortly after Jones's death. This is confirmed by his will, which contains a codicil dated 30 April 1682, in which he directs that 'the building of my house at Ramsbury . . . shall proceed and the workmen thereof shall be paid out of my personall estate according to the agreement I have made with them.'[1] Unfortunately neither the workmen in question nor any surveyor are named in the will.

Who Jones's architect may have been is a question that has exercised the minds of more than one generation of architectural historians. To Avray Tipping, writing in 1920, there was about Ramsbury 'so perfect a sense of proportion, and also so free and personal a touch within the limits of the prevailing style, that failure to identify its designer is a matter of regret'.[2] Christopher Hussey, writing in 1961 of this 'exceptionally interesting and satisfying building', reviewed the stylistic evidence, but was equally unable to suggest the name of its designer.[3] Sir John Summerson points out that the house 'is very close to Hugh May's work' (for

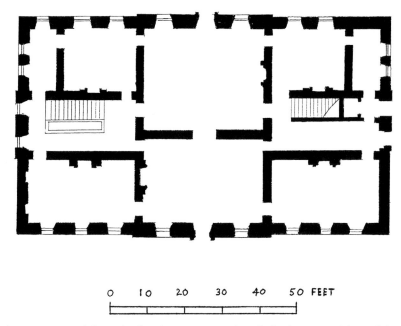

166. Ramsbury Manor, Wiltshire: plan based on one in Nathaniel Lloyd, *History of the English House*, 1931. North is to the right.

example, at Cornbury), Mr John Cornforth observes judiciously that the architect 'was probably a London man in the Wren atelier, well versed in the ideas of Pratt and May'.[4]

Despite the 'personal touch' noticed by Tipping, there is in fact nothing so distinctive about the architecture of Ramsbury as to point compellingly to any one of the leading architects of the period in which it was built. Hooke, May, Pratt and Winde all designed houses of the type to which Ramsbury belongs, but none of their surviving works has any characteristic that immediately claims Ramsbury for the same drawing-board.

To anyone who has read his diary attentively, Robert Hooke must be the favourite candidate for the honour of being Ramsbury's architect. For Sir William Jones was one of his regular acquaintances. From the date the diary commences in August 1672, to the end some ten years later, there are numerous references to Jones.[5] The exact nature of the relationship between the two men does not emerge clearly from the telegraphic entries in Hooke's journal, but they were evidently on friendly terms. What is more, Hooke more than once acted as Jones's architectural adviser. In 1673, for instance, he 'drew designs' for Sir William Jones, and 'saw his survey of Country house' – perhaps in connection with a proposed purchase that proved abortive, for nothing more is heard of it. Then in 1680 Hooke paid several visits to Jones's house in Bloomsbury, apparently to supervise the installation of sash windows.

The termination of the printed text of the diary in December 1680 might seem to preclude any hope of proving that Hooke was Jones's architect at Ramsbury as

192

well as in Bloomsbury. But the diary does not in fact end in December 1680. A disarming editorial note warns the reader that there are further entries up to May 1683 which the editors did not consider 'of sufficient importance to publish'. The original manuscript is in the Guildhall Library and easily accessible. On examination it soon becomes apparent that, although the entries do become somewhat irregular after 1680, there is still much of interest to the student both of architecture and of science, and that the omission of these final two and a half years must be condemned as editorially indefensible.

But what of Ramsbury? Five meetings with Sir William Jones in the course of 1681 leave us tantalisingly ignorant of their purpose, and it is not until after Jones's death in May 1682 that at last we find conclusive evidence that Robert Hooke was concerned in the building of his country house. On 7 August he set out from London in a coach in company with one Heblethwait. This Heblethwait was Jones's trusted servant, who had witnessed his will and received a legacy of £50. They dined at Maidenhead and spent the night at Reading, where they 'saw monastery and Drunken Justices'. On the following day they continued their journey westwards, dining at Speenhamland near Newbury, inspecting Donnington Castle, and supping (probably at Hungerford) with 'Mr. Pelham, Lem, Avis, Davis'. On the 9th the whole party 'viewed Ramsbery & D[ined] at Swan' before returning to London via Speenhamland, Reading and Maidenhead. A drink of cider and a 'Deo Gratias' conclude Hooke's account of what must have been a tiring expedition that had taken up the best part of a week.

The object of the journey was presumably to take stock of the state of the half-finished house following its owner's death. 'Mr. Pelham' was Thomas Pelham, Jones's son-in-law and principal executor. Joseph Lem, Joseph Avis and Roger Davies were three prominent figures in the London building world. What is more, they were all men whom Hooke had regularly employed for some years past. At the College of Physicians (1672–8), for instance, Lem had been one of the master bricklayers, Avis one of the carpenters and Davies the joiner. In 1674 it was 'with Lem' that Hooke had 'contrived Design of Merchant Taylors' School', while Davies, a first-class joiner, had been employed under Hooke at the Bethlehem Hospital and at Montagu House as well as at several of the City churches. So it was a well-tried architectural team that met Hooke in Berkshire on 8 August 1682, and it can hardly be doubted that if the building accounts of Ramsbury Manor should ever be found, they would reveal that the house was built to Hooke's designs by Lem, Avis and Davies.[6]

Now that the case for identifying Robert Hooke as the architect of Ramsbury Manor has been made, it is worth while to look again at his other documented works to see if any instructive resemblances can be observed. Here the Bethlehem Hospital of 1675–6 is the most rewarding building to consider, for in the two long pedimented blocks on either side of the central pavilion we see something like an elongated version of the east and west fronts of Ramsbury (fig. 167). Subtract four bays at either end and insert a central doorway and it is apparent that something very close to Ramsbury emerges.

There can therefore be no difficulty in accepting Ramsbury as an addition to the

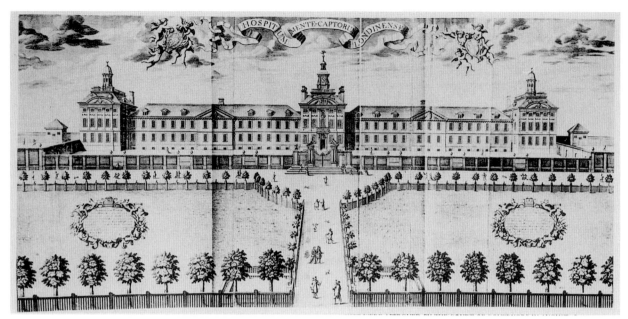

167. The Bethlehem Hospital, Moorfields, London, built to Robert Hooke's design in 1675–6 (engraving by Robert White, published in 1677).

list of Hooke's authenticated works. It is a building well within the capacity of an architect who, although not perhaps of outstanding ability, was a close colleague of Wren and an able designer in that agreeable domestic style of which Ramsbury Manor is such an attractive example.

NOTES

1   P.C.C. 58 COTTLE.
2   *Country Life*, 2 Oct. 1920, p. 439.
3   *Country Life*, 7–14 Dec. 1961.
4   *Architecture in Britain 1530–1830*, 4th. ed., 1963, p. 150; Oliver Hill and John Cornforth, *English Country Houses: Caroline*, 1966, p. 178.
5   *The Diary of Robert Hooke*, ed. H.W. Robinson and W. Adams, 1935.
6   Some of the building accounts have in fact been found by Dr Hentie Louw among the papers of Thomas Pelham as executor of Sir William Jones, which form part of the Townshend archives at Raynham Hall, Norfolk. The names of Lem, Avis and Davies duly appear, and in addition those of Thomas Davis, probably the London mason and sculptor of that name, Thomas Burton, plasterer, and Daniel Houghton, 'plaisterer', who supplied the copper globe and vane in 1686. Hooke is mentioned only as a mourner at Jones's funeral, but there is a 'Valluation of the Designe for the new house at Ramsbury' totalling £2,171 13s. 8d. The payments indicate that the interior was not finished until 1686, and in view of the fact that Sir William did not obtain full legal title to the manor until 1681, it is likely that building started in that year rather than in 1680. Dr Louw suggests that in addition to providing the window-dressings and door-surrounds, Thomas Davis may have been employed to make Jones's monument in Ramsbury Church (H.J. Louw, 'New Light on Ramsbury Manor', *Architectural History*, 30, 1987).

XI

THE REBUILDING OF
THE CHURCH OF ST MARY ALDERMARY
AFTER THE GREAT FIRE OF LONDON

EVER SINCE THE publication of *Parentalia* in 1750 it has been taken for granted
that all the 'fifty-one parochial churches of the City of London' listed there by
Christopher Wren, junior, were indeed 'erected according to the Designs, and
under the Care and Conduct, of Sir Christopher Wren'.[1] That Wren could not
personally have designed every detail of so many churches has long been recognised, and it is well known that in most cases the fittings, and in some even the
architectural details, were designed by the craftsmen employed. Even if Wren
'originated the design of every church', 'in many cases the working out and
supervision was done by somebody else' – generally by Robert Hooke or Edward
Woodroffe, or after Woodroffe's death in 1675, by John Oliver, Wren's deputy as
Surveyor of St Paul's Cathedral.[2] Of the many surviving drawings, relatively few are
in Wren's own hand. Some are clearly by Hooke, whose characteristic draughtsmanship is fairly easy to recognise, some no doubt are by Woodroffe, and some
must be by the draughtsmen named in Wren's accounts for rebuilding the churches:
first William Walgrave, who in or about 1673 was paid £2 10s. 'for taking the
ground platts of 12 churches yet unbuilt', then Henry Hunt, who received £6 10s.
for thirteen similar plans in 1676/7, and finally Thomas Lane, who between
1676/7 and 1682 was regularly paid 'for coppying the Designes of severall
Churches', then 'for drawing the designes for severall Churches', and finally for
'drawing and making designes for severall Churches'.[3]

Even if the share of these intriguing but shadowy figures in the designing of the
City churches remains ill-defined, there can be no doubt that it was Wren's
architectural intentions that they were interpreting. Many of what must be their
drawings remain in Wren's personal collection at All Souls College, and all the
payments for workmanship and materials were made by his authority and are duly
registered in the original accounts now in the Guildhall Library and in the two great
volumes of abstracts among the Rawlinson manuscripts in the Bodleian Library.
There is, however, a small group of churches for which Wren's responsibility is by
no means clearly established: churches that were badly damaged but not wholly
destroyed in the Great Fire and were reconstructed by their parishioners without

any direct supervision by Wren and his staff. The churches in question are St Dunstan-in-the-East, St Mary Aldermary and St Sepulchre, Holborn. In the case of St Dunstan-in-the-East and St Sepulchre, Holborn, what appears to have happened was that the parishioners were allowed to go ahead and engage workmen on their own initiative on the understanding that they would be reimbursed by the trustees of the Coal Dues. In this way St Sepulchre's got £4,993 4s. od. in instalments between 1670 and 1677, St Dunstan's £1,075 18s. 2d. in 1671–2, but in neither case was any direct payment made to the workmen by Wren's office.[4] In both cases the result was a building that incorporated the patched-up shell of the medieval fabric, so that externally it retained much of its medieval character, although internally the Gothic arcades were replaced by Tuscan ones. Relatively little would have been needed in the way of architectural designs, and the City craftsmen would have had no difficulty in performing their tasks without the supervision of an architect. Over twenty years later Wren was to add a celebrated Gothic steeple to the body of St Dunstan-in-the-East, but that was a quite separate operation, carried out under his direction from start to finish.

St Mary Aldermary differs in two respects from the two churches already mentioned. It is wholly Gothic in style, both inside and out, and was entirely financed by a private benefaction, without any help from the Coal Money. So consistent an example of Gothic architecture amid the many classical churches designed by Wren has naturally attracted attention and demanded explanation. The explanation that has long been current is that here the use of the Gothic style was prescribed by the benefactor who paid for the rebuilding. Over thirty years later Wren was to remind Dean Atterbury that in some of the City churches he had been 'oblig'd to deviate from a better Style',[5] and St Mary Aldermary seemed to be a case in point. Thus John Whichcord, in an article written in 1859, conjectured that Wren was bound by 'instructions to restore the Church . . . in its Gothic type'.[6] Wheatley and Cunningham averred in 1891 that 'the present church was intended by Wren to be a copy of [its predecessor,] a sum of £5,000 having been left . . . with the express proviso that the new church should be a copy of the old one',[7] while in 1929 the Royal Commission on Historical Monuments, in describing the church as 'the finest example of Wren's Gothic', stated it as a fact that 'the bequest of Henry Rogers' (the benefactor in question) was 'conditional to its being a copy of the old building'.[8] All of them were wrong, for not only is there no stipulation as to style in Henry Rogers's will, but there is in that document no mention whatever of St Mary Aldermary, and (whatever instructions may have been given by those responsible) it is by no means certain that the architect who received them was Sir Christopher Wren.

With the medieval origins of St Mary Aldermary we are not here concerned: 'Aldermarie church' was already known as such in the eleventh century,[9] and according to Stow it owed its name to the fact that it was reputed to be 'elder than any church of St Marie in the Citie'.[10] Early in the sixteenth century it was entirely rebuilt, largely at the expense of Sir Henry Keeble, Lord Mayor of London in 1511. A set of verses, formerly hanging over his tomb, commemorated him as 'a famous worthy wight, Which did this Aldermary church erect and set upright'. When he died in 1518 the tower at least was not yet finished, and it remained a mere stump until 1626, when two legacies enabled it to be completed. One of these stipulated that it should 'follow its ancient pattern and go forward and be finished, according to the foundation of it laid one hundred and twenty years since by . . . Sir Henry Kibbel'.[11] The churchwardens' accounts show that the work was carried out in 1627–8 at a cost (in masonry alone) of £534 8s. 7d.[12]

How much of the Tudor church survived the Great Fire of 1666? In 1917 Philip Norman wrote that

> of the body of the church before the Great Fire much still exists, portions of the walls being incorporated in the present fabric, which is thought to stand entirely on the old foundations, and as far as the ground plan is concerned appears to be a good example of a late mediaeval City church . . . It was discovered many years ago that the traceried heads of the windows in the south aisle were of Caen stone, dating from before the Fire.[13]

Philip Norman's belief that much of the fabric of the old church survived the Fire is borne out by the churchwardens' expenditure during the next ten years. For although the parishioners were obliged to attend services held in a 'tabernacle' or temporary wooden church set up on the site of the neighbouring church of St Thomas the Apostle (one of those that were not to be rebuilt, its parish being amalgamated with St Mary's), they continued from time to time to spend a certain amount of money on the fabric of their church, which we should probably envisage as a burnt-out shell rather than as a total ruin. Thus in 1669/70 one labourer was paid 'for carrying the stones which fell from the battlements', and in 1674 another for 'clearing the stones in the church'. In 1674–5 the tower was taken in hand with the approval of the commissioners administering the Coal Dues. Their minutes record that, as it was 'well built' and 'reparable if preserved in time', 'encouragement was given by our Officers to the Churchwardens to cover the same with a new roofe leaded.' It was accordingly floored, roofed and provided with a clock and bell. The structural work, amounting to £74 9s. 6d., was paid for out of the Coal Dues, but the cost of the clock and bell was found by the parishioners.[14] The tower would obviously not have been repaired in this way had a completely new church been in contemplation, but made good sense if in due course it was hoped to restore the body of the existing church. A payment of 2s. 6d. to a glazier 'for mending the church windows' in 1674/5 is further evidence that some part at least of the church remained intact at that date, while in January 1676 Robert Hooke noted in his diary that he had found a workman taking down 'the greatest part of the parapet 17 bricks high' at 'Aldermary church' and 'Forbid him taking down any more'.[15]

So far there had been no indication of any attempt to get the church itself rebuilt out of the Coal Dues, three-quarters of whose yield was from 1670 onwards allocated to the rebuilding of the City churches. Although this enabled the rebuilding of eighteen churches to get under way in 1670 or 1671, the limited amount of money and materials available, and the numerous calls on the time and attention of Sir Christopher Wren and his two assistant surveyors (Hooke and

Woodroffe), necessarily delayed the starting of others. Indeed, in 1671 the Lord Mayor formally directed that no more churches were to be begun for the time being, 'in so much that the number of Churches in hand are as many as are suitable, to the Time, mony, Workemen, and Materialls, requisite to the Orderly finishing of them', and it was not until 1686 that work began on the last of the forty-nine churches wholly or partially paid for out of the Coal Money.[16]

The first move to get St Mary Aldermary into the queue of waiting churches appears to have been made on 10 July 1676, when the churchwardens spent 6s. 'in goeing to Sir Christopher Wren'. However the outcome was a payment to them of only £30, from which £3 was deducted for some further repairs to the steeple. Precisely how the remaining £27 was spent is not apparent, but in 1677/8 the church was surveyed by 'Mr Wyse the Mason', that is Thomas Wise, who became Master Mason to the Crown in June 1678.[17] But no further progress appears to have been made until 1678/9, when help was offered from an unexpected source. A lady bountiful appeared on the scene, with £5,000 to spend on rebuilding a church in the City. Her name was Anne Rogers.

Anne Rogers was the niece and one of the executors of Henry Rogers, a wealthy Somerset squire whose family had acquired extensive monastic lands at Cannington in that county in the reign of Henry VIII. When he died without issue in September 1672 his landed estate (being held in tail male) reverted to the Crown,[18] but his will made provision out of his personal estate for some considerable charitable benefactions to the poor of Cannington, Porlock and Thrupton. He also left £1,000 apiece to his nephews Warwick Bampfield and John Winter, and £500 to his niece Anne Rogers. Together with Thomas Warre of Shepton Beauchamp, these three were named as Rogers's executors.[19]

Henry Rogers's will was made in May 1672, but on 1 September 1672, only ten hours before his death, he added a codicil declaring that such sums of money as were left in his closet at Cannington were to be disposed of by Anne Rogers in such a manner as he had privately directed her. Rogers died at his house in Westminster, but he was buried at Cannington and after the funeral the closet was opened and the money therein was found to amount to no less than £7,500. Anne Rogers then disclosed that her uncle's wish was that the money 'should be layd out in the building of a church in London where was most need and that the residue should be disposed to other charitable uses'. Her fellow executors, however, refused to acknowledge the validity of the codicil, made (so they said) at a time when Rogers was no longer *compos mentis,* and proceeded to divide the money amongst themselves, Bampfield and Winter taking £1,800 apiece, Warre (who unlike the other executors, received no benefit under the will) £2,500. Anne Rogers was offered £1,250 as her share of the spoil.[20]

But Anne Rogers refused to be bought. True to her trust, she instituted suits both in the Prerogative Court of Canterbury and in the Court of Chancery. On 6 November 1677 she emerged triumphant from the latter court with an Order directing the £7,500 to be brought into the Court, and as a result the greater part of the misappropriated money was recovered – £2,500 from Warre and £1,250 from Bampfield and Winter. Together with the £1,250 left in Anne's own hands this added up to £5,000 – enough to rebuild a City church. By 1679 she had fixed on St Mary Aldermary as the object of her uncle's posthumous benefaction. Like him, she lived in Westminster, and there appears to be no evidence that she or any members of her family had any special connexion with St Mary Aldermary. What inquiries she made and whose advice she took in the matter we do not know. But, as she informed the Lord Chancellor in November 1679, 'the provision [made] by the late Act of Parliament for rebuilding churches falling short & the parishoners not being able to rebuild the same', she

> did propose to the Archbishop of Canterbury and to the Lord Mayor of London and Court of Aldermen that the said £5,000 might be applyed for building the said Church and the same being approved of by them, Mr Oliver one of the City Surveyors hath surveyed the ground & computed the charge and workmen have undertaken to build the same and have already soe farr proceeded in the building and buying materialls as that there was neere £500 expended.

The capital, however, was still lying 'dead' in the Court, and on 20 November 1679 the Lord Chancellor agreed that it should be paid into the Chamber of London, where it would earn interest at the rate of three per cent until it was needed. The Chamberlain would pay it out as Anne Rogers 'should from time to time direct'.[21] Neither his accounts nor hers have been preserved, but among the City records there still survive many of the individual orders signed by Anne Rogers authorizing payments to the workmen in accordance with the Order in Chancery of 20 Novemember 1679.[22] The last of them are dated 16 June 1681, and an inscription in the church records that it was opened in 1682.

The process of rebuilding is also reflected in the records of the two parishes of St Mary Aldermary and St Thomas the Apostle which under the Act of 1670 were henceforth to share the church. In 1678/9 (the precise date is not given) the churchwardens of the former parish spent 6s. 'to treat Mr Oliver', while in the following year their colleagues of St Thomas's parish paid 10s. to 'Mr Oliver for looking after the Church ground' (that is, presumably, the site of their demolished church). Then from 1680 onwards the St Mary's accounts contain the record of periodical gratifications to the 'workmen in the church' and, more specifically, to the masons, carpenters and joiners. On 23 February 1680/1, for instance, they 'spent with Mr Spinage, Mr Oliver and the master workemen of the Church 8s. 6d'. Again, on 4 April 1681 3s. 3d. was laid out 'to treat Mr Oliver and the Master Workmen'. The master craftsmen employed were all well known in their respective trades: Samuel Fulkes, the mason, was employed at several of the other City churches, as were John Longland, the carpenter, Stephen Leaver the smith, Mathew Roberts the plumber, Henry Doogood the plasterer and Jonathan Maine the carver. The last-named received £50 out of Henry Rogers's money in December 1680 and another £50 in May 1681, probably for the pulpit and reading-desk, for the altarpiece was the gift of Dame Jane Smith, widow of Sir John Smith, who died in 1673 and was buried in the church, and the pewing was separately paid for by the two parishes, St Mary's employing a joiner of their parish called Thomas Bayley, St Thomas's one from theirs named Thomas Powell. Although the distinct identities of the two congregations were thus expressed in two distinct sets of pews, uniformity of design was assured by the employment of Thomas Creecher, an eminent master joiner, to make 'draughts' for both sets. The terms of the agreement with Thomas Bayley have not survived, but Thomas Powell undertook 'that his stuffe and workmanship shall in every respect equall that in the Parish Church of St Lawrence Jury, London'. These agreements were made in February 1681/2, and an inscription put up by the churchwardens records that 'This church was pewd and wainscoted at the charge of both parishes . . . and also opened in the year of our Lord God, 1682.' There appears to have been no formal ceremony of reconsecration, but the approximate date of the reopening may be indicated by an entry in the churchwardens' accounts showing that in June 1682 the grateful parishioners spent £3 3s. od. on 'a haunch of venison and twenty bottles of Rhenish wine to present Madame Rogers', and gave her maid the handsome tip of a guinea.[23] As the parish was a peculiar of the Archbishopric of Canterbury, the diocesan was William Sancroft, and it was he who composed the elegant Latin inscription (formerly over the west door, now at the west end of the south aisle) which acknowledges the 'pious benevolence' of Henry Rogers and draws attention to his relationship to Sir Edward Rogers of Cannington (d. c.1567), a stalwart Protestant in the time of the Marian persecution.[24]

On one important matter the surviving records of the rebuilding of St Mary Aldermary are not explicit: there is no payment which clearly establishes the identity of the architect. After 1676 there are no more of those payments for gratuities to Sir Christopher Wren that abound in the accounts of the churches for whose rebuilding he was financially and architecturally responsible. For St Mary Aldermary Wren had, as we have seen, no financial responsibility. Thanks to Anne Rogers, the rebuilding of the church was accomplished without any call on the Coal Money. Did Wren nevertheless have any architectural responsibility for the church? For this there is absolutely no evidence. Not a single plan or elevation connected with St Mary's survives among Wren's drawings at All Souls College, nor among the drawings from the Bute Collection sold in 1951. Nor does Wren's name occur in any of Anne Rogers's orders to the Chamberlain of the City. The name that does occur is that of John Oliver. It was 'Mr Oliver, one of the City Surveyors', not Wren, to whose preliminary survey and computation of cost Anne Rogers referred in her suit before the Lord Chancellor, and it was Mr John Oliver to whom she directed the Chamberlain to pay £100 'to defray incident charges in the rebuilding' of the church on 16 June 1681. It was Oliver, too, with whom we have seen churchwardens and master workmen in conference during the rebuilding of the church. Clearly the work was carried out under his immediate direction. This does not prove that Oliver was the designer of St Mary Aldermary, for his name occurs often enough in the churchwardens' accounts of other churches for whose design Wren was unquestionably responsible. As one of the City Surveyors (the others were Hooke and Mills), and as Wren's deputy at St Paul's Cathedral, Oliver was intimately involved with Wren's architectural activities in the City. At St Mary Aldermary he could therefore have been executing a design made by Wren. Or he could equally well have been executing a design made by himself,

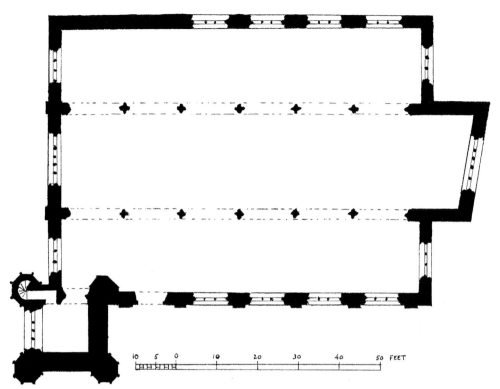

168. St Mary Aldermary Church, London: plan showing the church before the addition of buttresses and other alterations in 1876.

perhaps with some help from Wren. Although he was an architect in his own right, with the halls of two City Companies to his credit,[25] it is perhaps unlikely that he would have designed a City church without some friendly consultation with his superior at St Paul's. Architecturally St Mary Aldermary is too idiosyncratic to permit significant stylistic comparisons. The piers and the windows follow well-established Tudor Gothic forms and probably conform closely to the work of 1511. That would have followed from the retention (noted by Philip Norman) of much of the outer walls and the reuse of the existing foundations (fig. 168). Only the decoration of the spandrels of the arcades and of the plaster ceilings of the nave and aisles clearly proclaims the church's seventeenth-century date. The use of small fan-shaped conoids in conjunction with other forms of real or simulated vaulting does of course have Tudor prototypes (notably at Hampton Court), but the great dish-shaped traceried panels which dominate the St Mary Aldermary ceilings are a fancy that is obviously Carolean rather than Tudor (fig. 169). There is nothing quite like it in any other of Wren's Gothic work, which tends to be sturdier and less 'busy', but where so little was built, such negative comparisons are of little value. What, then, can be said about the responsibility for the design of St Mary Aldermary? First, that the customary inclusion of the church in the list of Wren's authenticated works is scarcely justified by the available evidence. Second, that John Oliver had, at the very least, much to do with it.

Although St Mary Aldermary was once more in use from 1682 onwards, the

170. St Mary Aldermary Church, London: view of the west end of the nave and of the tower as completed in 1701–3 (T.H. Shepherd, *London in the Nineteenth Century*, 1830).

tower remained in a patched-up condition, bereft (we may suppose) of parapets or pinnacles. These were at last supplied in 1701–3 and paid for out of the Coal Money. This time the parish records leave us in no doubt about Wren's responsibility. Not only did the churchwardens wait on him in person in 1700/1 and again in 1703/4, they attended 'My Lord Mayor about Sir Christopher Wren's workmen at Guildhall' in 1701/2, and spent £3 17s. od. 'on workmen and on Sir Christopher Wren's Account about the Steeple' in the same year. More than once they sought to expedite their business by timely gifts to 'Sir Christopher Wren's Clerke', and on two occasions they entertained 'Mr Dickinson'. These references to William Dickinson are important because in his capacity as Deputy Surveyor of Westminster Abbey he was later to make designs for a central tower for the abbey church which have the same elongated bottle-shaped pinnacles as the tower of St Mary Aldermary.[26] It seems very likely that it was Dickinson who designed the new upper stage of the tower (fig. 170) under Wren's direction. Its general form was prescribed by the octagonal panelled buttresses of 1511 and 1627–8, but the tall pinnacles, the belfry windows and the pierced parapets have a distinctive character that clearly marks them out as a product of Wren's office.

169. (*facing page*) St Mary Aldermary Church, London: the plaster ceiling of the nave.

Although St Mary Aldermary escaped serious damage in the Second World War, the interior unfortunately lost most of its original furniture in 1876 at the hands of Messrs Tress and Innes, and the almost total refacing of the exterior in Portland stone early in the present century has removed not only those interesting traces of fire-damaged Caen stone which were once visible in the windows of the south aisle, but also those variations in the external masonry of the tower which formerly distinguished the three successive periods at which it was built. According to Birch, the mouldings of the 'parapets, strings, buttresses, plinths, and window-heads' of the church have also been altered in the course of successive restorations, 'more in conformity with the style of the fifteenth century than with that of the closing years of the seventeenth'.[27] Nevertheless, St Mary Aldermary remains as a precious if in some respects enigmatic example of seventeenth-century architectural taste and as a monument not only to the well-advertised benevolence of Henry Rogers, but also to the less publicized integrity of his niece, Anne Rogers.

NOTES

1 *Parentalia, or Memoirs of the Family of the Wrens*, compiled by Christopher Wren, Jr, but published by Stephen Wren, 1750, p. 309.

2 John Summerson, *Sir Christopher Wren*, 1953, pp. 82–3.

3 Bodleian Library, MS Rawlinson B. 389, ff. 115–23[v]. Henry Hunt is mentioned more than once in Hooke's diary. On 12 April 1675 Hooke 'left at Sir Ch. Wren's the 14 Ground plats of churches Harry [Hunt] had drawn' (*Diary of Robert Hooke*, ed. Robinson and Adams, 1935, p. 158). Thomas Lane may have been a joiner of that name employed by Wren at St Paul's Cathedral.

4 Bodleian Library, MS Rawlinson B. 388, ff. 11–12, 103–4.

5 In his report on Westminster Abbey, made in 1713 (*Wren Society*, xi, p. 20). In the context of Wren's report, which was largely concerned with his proposals for a central tower and spire, the examples of Gothic design that he had chiefly in mind could well have been the steeples of St Alban, Wood Street (1682–5), St Dunstan-in-the-East (1697–9) and St Mary Aldermary (1701–4, see below) rather than the bodies of any of these churches.

6 John Whichcord, 'Church of St Mary Aldermary, Bow Lane', *Trans. London & Middlesex Archaeological Soc.*, 1, 1860, p. 264.

7 *London Past and Present*, 11, 1891, p. 491.

8 RCHM, *London*, vol. 4 (*The City*), p. 81.

9 H.A. Harben, *A Dictionary of London*, 1918, p. 389.

10 John Stow, *Survey of London*, ed. Kingsford, 1908, i, pp. 252–3.

11 John Stow, *Survey of London*, ed. Strype, 1720, Book III, p. 18.

12 Guildhall Library, MS 6574. The contracting masons were Henry Walton and Thomas Leech.

13 P. Norman, 'St Mary Aldermary', *Trans. St Paul's Ecclesiological Soc.*, viii, 1917.

14 Guildhall Library MS 25,540/1 (minutes of the commissioners for rebuilding the parish churches), 29 April 1675; MS 4863/1 (churchwardens' accounts of St Mary's Aldermary); Bodleian Library, MS Rawlinson B. 389, f. 115.

15 *Diary of Robert Hooke*, ed. Robinson and Adams, 1935, p. 209.

16 Guildhall Record Office, ex-Guildhall Library MS 307 and Misc. MS 157.14; *Wren Society*, x, pp. 12–13.

17 Guildhall Library, MS 4863/1, under years cited.

18 *Cal. State Papers Domestic 1672*, p. 263.

19 PRO, PROB 11/340, f. 391 (PCC 157 EURE).

20 PRO Chancery Decrees and Orders, 1679, B., f. 46ᵛ (C33/254).

21 Ibid.

22 Guildhall Record Office, ex-Guildhall Library MS 320 and Misc. MS 157.6. The 18 surviving orders together account for an expenditure of some £3,852.

23 Guildhall Library, MS 4863/1 (churchwardens' accounts of St Mary Aldermary), MSS 662/1 and 663/1 (churchwardens' accounts and vestry minutes of St Thomas the Apostle).

24 Drafts of the inscription by Sancroft are in Bodleian, Tanner MS 89, f. 240. It may be regretted that in the end Sancroft rejected an alternative wording which acknowledged Anne Rogers's faithful discharge of her duties as her uncle's executrix.

25 For Oliver's architectural career see H. Colvin, *A Biographical Dictionary of British Architects 1600–1840*, 3rd ed 1995, pp. 714–15.

26 Illustrated in *Wren Society*, xi, pl. v (initialled 'W.D.' and dated 1722).

27 G.H. Birch, *London Churches of the XVIIth and XVIIIth Centuries*, 1896, p. 147. Profiles of some of the original mouldings will be found in Whichord's article cited in note 6 above.

XII

AUBREY'S
CHRONOLOGIA ARCHITECTONICA

WHEN EASTLAKE SET out to write the history of the Gothic Revival, he began, quite rightly, by devoting a good deal of space to the historians and antiquaries of the seventeenth and eighteenth centuries. For it was they who created that awareness of the medieval past without which no revival of its architecture would have been possible, and it was they too who provided illustrations of abbeys, castles, and funerary monuments for Georgian architects to translate into churches, villas and chimney-pieces. But, as Eastlake noted, 'an interval occurred between the works of Dugdale and Dodsworth, of Herbert and Wood, on the one side, and those of Grose, Bentham, Hearne, and Gough, on the other – between the men who recorded the history of Mediaeval buildings in England, and the men who attempted to illustrate them.'[1] Dugdale's works were, of course, embellished by Hollar's engravings, but these were for the most part views of a general kind, often unreliable in matters of detail, and well over a century elapsed before men like Carter, Capon, Pugin and Blore began making measured drawings of specific architectural features which could serve as exemplars for the Gothic Revivalists. The gap was filled, after a fashion, by the views of the brothers Buck, whose amateurish engravings constituted – then as now – the only record of many a ruined castle or mouldering abbey. But neither Buck's views, nor those of other Georgian topographers such as Stukeley, provided an adequate basis for the serious study of Gothic architecture, nor was there, as yet, much interest in Gothic as a style of architecture with its own historical evolution. For most educated men it was, in the words of Roger North, 'a mode introduc't by a barbarous sort of people, that first distres't then dissolved the Roman Empire'.[2] 'The Goths', wrote Sir John Clerk of Penicuik,

> were those barbarous nations from the north of Europe, who overspread Italy and ruin'd the Roman Empire. They likewise broke and destroyd all monuments of antiquity, statues & ornaments of all kinds which fell in their way. They introduced a bad manner not only in Architectory but in all other arts & sciences. We have been for upwards of 200 years endeavouring to recover ourselves from this Gothicism. Yet there still are too many amongst us whose bad taste neither example nor precept will ever rectify & therefore are to be left to themselves. For Goths will always have a Gothic taste.[3]

206

There could be no point in studying the architecture of such barbarians. Clerk, like Horace Walpole, had 'no curiosity to know how awkward and clumsy men have been in the dawn of arts, or in their decay'.[4] For him the only past that was worth investigating was that of the ancient world, and he was (in the words of his friend Sandy Gordon) all out for the 'Extirpation of *Gothicism*, Ignorance and a bad Taste'.[5]

Despite the stigma of barbarism which thus attached to it, Gothic architecture drew reluctant admiration from those who could appreciate its technical daring. 'To doe those good men that built our churches right,' says Roger North,

> I must . . . profess that in the ordinance of walls and abbutment they have done as much as is possible, to make the stone and lime work its utmost, and that now wee have not any that will venture to set such weight upon so small support, and I question whether they are able, or have the skill they had, to calculate those propositions. To give one instance, there is the cathedrall of Salisbury . . . There is nothing in appearance to support the tower but 4 uprights, and the weight is prodigious. But observing it with some curiosity, I found abbutments wrought very cuningly in the walls 8 severall ways by 2 half arches, the uppermost resting upon the 2^d pillar from the tower, and the undermost upon the next to it. These two arching abuttments appear in crossing the windoes next to the tower, so that at seting on, the tower hath a very broad support, otherwise it were impossible it should stand.

He also found much to admire in King's College Chapel, a building 'wonderfully thought & executed, the abuttment being small, & the roof broad & massy', while at Gloucester he 'never saw anything neater then some of their monachal cloysters'. What attracted him particularly at Gloucester was the fan-vaulting, which he thought 'admirably pretty' and even superior, for its purpose, to 'regular' (i.e. classical) vaulting.

Having got so far, North found it 'no unpleasant thing to observe the course of proceeding in that sort of building, which prevailed in our nation, till almost King James the first' – in other words, to trace the history of English Gothic. 'Now [he continues] I give three periods, exemplified in the building of the respective times.' The first, 'seen in the church of Durham', he attributed to the period before the Danish invasions.

> The order is round upright lumps for columnes, with perfect semi-circular arches . . . derived from the Greek & Roman Regular columnes, but for want of art, and learning . . . so rudely executd as wee see. But devious from the right as it is, none can deny but, it bears not onely an air of grandure, but hath a strength and reasonableness . . . such as an extraordinary high spirited judicious barbarian might be supposed originally to invent . . . This round work lastd to the inroads of the Danes, the next order was the birdsey arch & diagonall collumne[6] which I propose lasted to the Edwards' time, and then a still finer sort of building came in, which is exemplified in the Cathedrall of New Sarum, which church, for the area of it, I beleeve stands upon the least support of any in the world. It is all of one order, and instead of the diagonall thredded columne it is composed of

rounds, whereof one is the middle, and four about it much smaller, upon which the thredds of the arches fall, & are therefore diagonall to the range. This conceipt is taken from the Temple Church in London, which is more ancient, but its columnes are four rounds consolidated . . . These are the 3 periods of the Gothick building, which is now expired in the world, and the Regular taken from old ruins and books succeeds it.[7]

Despite the acuteness of some of his observations, Roger North was, of course, as wrong in his dating as he was confused in his attempt at stylistic analysis. In a letter to the Dean of Westminster his contemporary, Nicholas Hawksmoor, came somewhat nearer the mark in distinguishing between the round-arched Romanesque, which he recognized as 'the most Antient style in the Gothick or Monastick manner', the pointed Gothic of Henry III's time (exemplified in the Abbey) and the later manner which 'is what the ingenious Masons call Tracery'.[8] But his chronology was vague (he thought St Albans Abbey Church was the work of King Offa), and it was not until 1763 that anything like a correct historical analysis of English Gothic appeared in print as part of Thomas Warton's *Observations on Spenser's Faerie Queene*. Fifty years of antiquarian investigation followed before in 1817 Rickman produced the definitive classification of styles which remained in use throughout the nineteenth century. The importance of Rickman's work was to propound an evolutionary sequence of forms whose logic was so compelling that there could be no doubt as to its essential correctness. Much remained to be done before the history of medieval English architecture was fully understood (especially in its relationship to French prototypes), but Rickman's *Attempt* provided the basic stylistic chronology without which no medieval church could make historical sense.

A century and a half before Rickman, a hundred years before Warton, another treatise on English Gothic had been written by a man whose contribution to the subject has never been generally recognized.[9] The name of John Aubrey (d. 1697) is well known to prehistorians for his *Natural History of Wiltshire* and for his *Monumenta Britannica*, works in which he laid the foundations of British field archaeology. Less well known is the original manuscript of the *Monumenta*, now in the Bodleian Library.[10] It is divided into four parts, the first (*Templa Druidum*) dealing with prehistoric monuments, especially Avebury and Stonehenge, the second with Roman remains, the third with barrows, pottery, earthworks and burials, and the fourth with a variety of antiquarian topics including heraldry, palaeography, the history of prices and the history of dress. It is in this fourth section that we find the *Chronologia Architectonica*, a treatise of some fifty pages written, it appears, chiefly in the 1670s.[11] Like all Aubrey's works, it is half a collection of notes, half a connected essay. On the title-page there is a direction to the printer to 'begin to print this Treatise at page 31', and here we find some cursory remarks about Roman architecture in Britain, followed by an account of its degeneration 'into what we call Gothick, by the inundation of the Goths'. This 'barbarous fashion [he goes on] continued till Henry 7th of England about which time the old Roman Architecture began to be revived in Italie, by Palladio'.

'Twas first revived in England, in the time of King Edward the sixth. Seymour Duke of Somerset Ld Protector of England, sent for Architects & workmen out of Italie, who built Somerset-house in the Strand, and that august House of Longleate in Wiltshire, which is great enough to receive the King's Court: it is 3 stories high (above the stately vaults under ground) adorned with Doriq, Ioniq and Corinthian pillars, leaded on the top. The first Tombe that I have seen of Roman Architecture is Bishop Gardiner's in the Cathedral Church at Winchester: and at this time the Clavies, or mantle-pieces of Chimneys were Ioniq, or Corinthian Cornices, which about that time generally came in vouge. In Queen Elizabeth's time Architecture made no growth: but rather went backwards: great wide windowes, which were not only cold, but weakned the Fabriq. Burleigh-House and Audeley-end were the two best piles of her raigne. Earl of Salisbury's [at] Hatfield was built *tempore* Jac. I.

The next step of Roman Architecture was the New Exchange in the Strand, which was surveyed by Mr Inigo Jones, and after that, A° Dni 16 [12]was that magnificent building of the Banquetting-house at White-hall, built by King James I with the £10,000 which the City of London was fined, for the Prentices killing Dr Lamb in the streetes for a conjurer, which was donne by Mr Inigo Jones his Majestie's Surveyor and is so exquisite a piece, that if all the Books of Architecture were lost, the true art of Building might be retrived thence. The Hall and staire-cases of Greenwich &c. there, were also of Mr Inigo Jones surveying. But the stately new Building by the Thames side there, was donne by Mr Webb Surveyor to King Charles II, A° Dni 166_ and since that, the old Roman fashion is become the common Mode.

As a brief history of the progress of English classical architecture during the previous century this is by no means bad. Almost every significant building is mentioned and the perspicacity of the remark about Elizabethan architecture going backwards will not be lost on those who have read Dr Mark Girouard's paper on 'Elizabethan Architecture and the Gothic Tradition'.[13] Elsewhere we find further scattered notes about Elizabethan and Jacobean architecture, including a sketch of two sorts of sixteenth-century window-mouldings, an anecdote about Queen Elizabeth at Burghley ('Will,' she said to Lord Treasurer Burghley, 'thy witt and my money have made a stately House'), and an interesting characterization of the architecture of Northumberland House as 'Ditterling (as they call it)'.[14] John Evelyn (to whom the manuscript was evidently lent) initials various additional observations of his own, including an aside about the Queen's House at Greenwich being built 'like a pair of panniers for the sake of the high way very foolishly'. None of this — least of all the conventional remarks about the Goths — prepares us for the main body of the treatise, which is nothing less than an attempt to establish the chronology of English medieval architecture. The enterprise was one in which (remembering that Aubrey was a Fellow of the Royal Society) we can recognize the influence of contemporary scientific thought. For its purpose was to classify and to compare, and classification and comparison were both features of the new 'experimental philosophy' to which the Royal Society was dedicated. The method was to find examples of window-tracery and other characteristic details to which a date could be attached, if possible by documentary evidence, to sketch them in diagrammatic fashion, and then to arrange the sketches in chronological order so as to establish a continuous sequence. For information about buildings and documents Aubrey was able to turn to his many learned and antiquarian friends. On the very first page we find a memorandum of a conversation about freemasons which Aubrey had had with Wren and Dugdale and a note that Bishop Seth Ward had told him that 'the Bull for the building our Ladies church at Salisbury is (or was) in the Archives of that church'. Elsewhere Dr Plot informs him that at Dover there is 'a good deale of Roman building', while Sir Thomas Browne 'affirmes to me, that the Cathedrall Church at Norwich, was built tempore Willelmi Rufi; the arches there are semi-circular, and so at the Castle'. Sir Thomas Browne is also the source of information about tombs of Saxon kings supposed to be at Blythburgh in Suffolk. 'I wish,' Aubrey writes, 'I could have had the leisure to have gone thither, quaere somebody, what kind of architecture there.'

Luckily one rich source of information was easily available in Wood's recently published *Antiquities of Oxford*. Here Aubrey 'found in what King's reigne & yeare of the Lord such or such part of a College was built'. It was at Oxford that the main body of the manuscript was written,[15] and Oxford buildings figure prominently among the drawings. First we have a two-light Romanesque window 'at the Checquer-Inne in Oxford, heretofore Kempe-hall', and an early Gothic one in the tower of St Giles's church, supposed by Aubrey to have been built *tempore regis Stephani*[16] (fig. 171). Then there is a fully developed Gothic window in the chapel at Woodstock Manor, rightly compared with Henry III's work at Westminster Abbey, another with intersecting tracery from St Mary's tower, and a third, with reticulated tracery, from St Aldate's church (fig. 172). The second is wrongly ascribed to the late fifteenth century (the date, as Aubrey knew, when the body of the church was rebuilt), the last correctly to the year 1335, when it was commissioned by Sir John of Ducklington.[17] Merton, Magdalen, All Souls, Corpus and Christ Church all contribute dated examples to Aubrey's corpus, and there is a valuable sketch of the moulded plinth of 'the magnificent chapelle or cathedral intended by Cardinal Wolsey, which did runne from the College to the Blew-bore-Inne; and was pulled downe by Bishop Fell, about 1671' (fig. 173). Other examples were derived from London (Westminster Abbey, Westminster Hall, Old St Paul's, St Bartholomew Smithfield, Clifford's Inn), from his native Wiltshire (Kington St Michael, Bishop's Lavington, Devizes), from Herefordshire, the county from which the Aubreys sprang (Abbey Dore, Wigmore, Goodrich and Penyard Castles, Hereford Cathedral), from Somerset (Wells), Sussex (Battle Abbey), Winchester and Norwich. But in almost every case he went on to note the existence of similar windows elsewhere. 'The arches of this church of St Marie's [at Devizes] are of the fashion in the margent: and likewise some of the windowes of the Tower' we read on folio 154. A memorandum then draws our attention to the east window of Wimborne Minster, which is 'like those of Sarum Castle, but ha[s] a great deal of moulding. The west end of Hereford Minster is just such work as at Winburne ... The other windowes of that church are of later structure, as will hereafter appear.' Altogether there are over fifty drawings, and at least eighty buildings are either illustrated or mentioned.

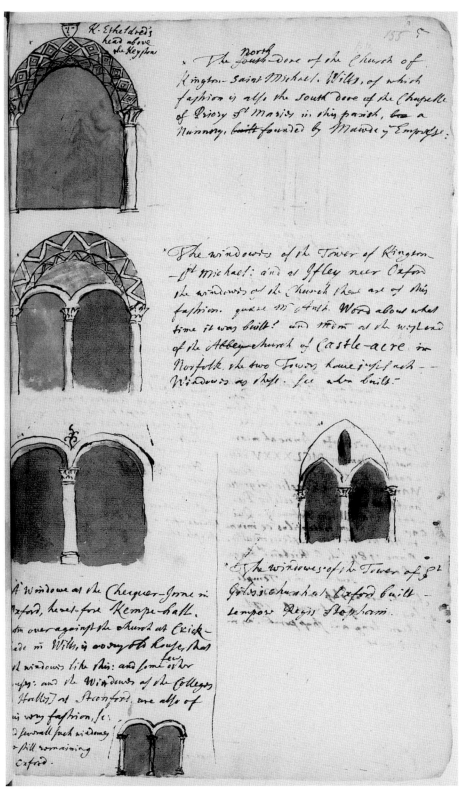

171. Sketches by John Aubrey of Romanesque and early Gothic windows from Kington St Michael Church, Wiltshire, Kemp Hall, Oxford, and St Giles' Church, Oxford (Bodleian Library, MS Top. Gen. c. 25, f. 155).

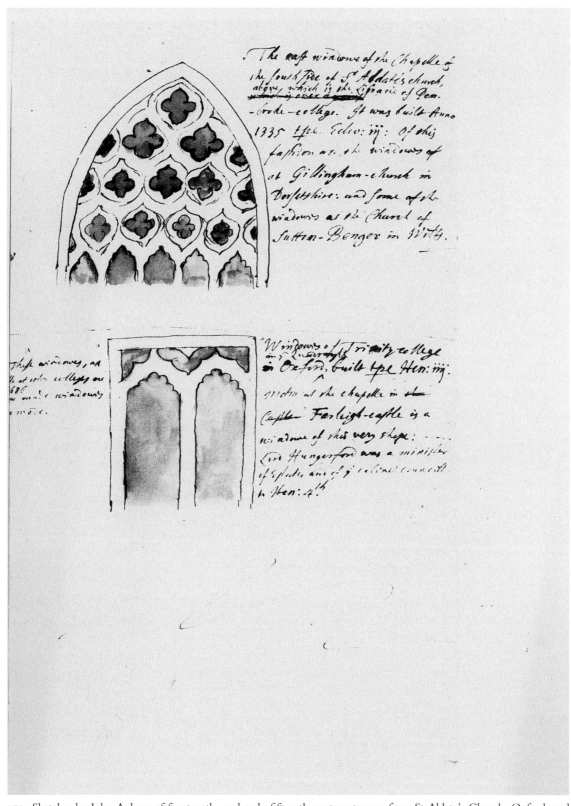

172. Sketches by John Aubrey of fourteenth- and early fifteenth-century tracery from St Aldate's Church, Oxford, and Trinity College, Oxford (Bodleian Library, MS Top. Gen. c. 25, f. 159).

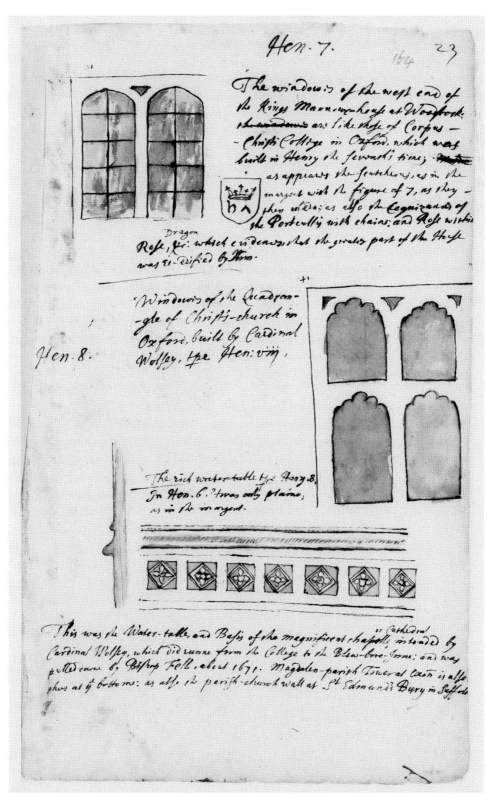

173. Sketches by John Aubrey of Tudor windows from Woodstock Manor and Christ Church, Oxford, and of the plinth of Cardinal Wolsey's unfinished chapel at Christ Church (Bodleian Library, MS Top. Gen. c. 25, f. 164).

Though the facts were not invariably correct, the method was sound, and the arrangement of the drawings shows that Aubrey was feeling towards a typological sequence which would serve to date other buildings for which no documentary evidence was available. 'The fashions of building,' he noted, 'do last about 100 years, or less; the windows the most remarqueable, hence one may give a guess about what Time the Building was.' He made no attempt to give his examples stylistic labels, but anyone who turns over the pages of the manuscript can see at a glance the development of Romanesque into what Rickman was to call 'Early English', of 'Early English' into 'Decorated', and of 'Decorated' into 'Perpendicular'. Thanks to Aubrey's careful delineation of the Oxford examples, one can even trace some of the changes in 'Perpendicular' window-tracery analysed by R.H.C. Davis[18] (fig. 174).

To John Aubrey, therefore, must go the credit for being the first to think historically about medieval English architecture. As a child, Aubrey's 'greatest delight' had been 'to be continually with the artificers (e.g. Joyners, carpenters, coupers, masons)' who came to his father's house at Easton Piers, and thus to 'understand their trades'. 'At 8,' he tells us, 'I was a kind of Engineer; and I fell then to drawing, beginning first with plaine outlines, e.g. in draughts of curtaines.'[19] He was, therefore, predisposed to look at buildings with an eye for significant details such as mouldings, and he had the skill to sketch what he saw in a manner that, if not very elegant, was adequate to his purpose. What he lacked, unfortunately, was the ability to get his work into print. The archaeological part of the *Monumenta Britannica* had had its origin in a command given by Charles II to publish an account of Avebury, which Aubrey assured the King 'did as much excell of Stoneheng as a Cathedral does a Parish Church'. But, as Oliver Lawson Dick tells us, 'Aubrey had proceeded so slowly with the work and had added so many facts about other antiquities that five separate dedications of the book were made, as death took away one hoped-for patron after another, before it even got near the press.'[20] The direction to the printer on the first page of the *Chronologia Architectonica* seems to imply that its author regarded the manuscript as ready for publication, but no compositor would have been able to make sense of it as it stood. And so, like the rest of his written work, it remained unpublished and unknown except to the small circle of learned friends with whom Aubrey discoursed of antiquities. At the time of his death in 1697 all four parts of the *Monumenta* were in the hands of a bookseller named Awnsham Churchill, who had borrowed the manuscript to help in the preparation of a new edition of Camden's *Britannia*, and it was not until 1836 that they joined the rest of Aubrey's collections in the Bodleian.[21] While it was in private hands, Hutchins, the historian of Dorset, made a copy of the manuscript from which some 'rude etchings' illustrating the 'Fashion of Windows in Civil and Ecclesiastical Buildings' were made by Francis Perry as a supplement to his *Series of English Medals*, published in 1762.[22] Perry's book did not, however, have a very wide circulation, and the supplementary plates seem to have attracted little notice in the antiquarian world. By the time Britton drew attention to them in the preface to his *Architectural Antiquities of Great Britain* (1826) Rickman's book had reached its third edition, and Aubrey's work had been superseded. Now its only value is as a

The Tower of Merton-college was built ~~ye Hen 6~~, Anô 1421. 4imo Henrici 5ti

The windowe of the Chapelle of Priory St Maries juxta Kington - S michael.

Part of the windowe of the northcrose aisle of Merton-college: which is a very statly one. this part hath resemblance with that of Priory St Mary windowe & I guesse them to have been built about Hen 6

The Windowe of Magdalen College Tower built about 149?, ~~ye~~ Hen. 7. built by Cardinel Wolsey.

174. Sketches by John Aubrey of Perpendicular tracery from Merton and Magdalen Colleges, Oxford, and Kington Priory, Wiltshire (Bodleian Library, MS Top. Gen. c. 25, f. 162).

partial record of some buildings, such as Woodstock Manor, that have long since disappeared. But in an essay written to honour the author of *The Buildings of England* it may not be inappropriate to pay a belated tribute to one who deserves recognition, not only as our first archaeologist, but also as our earliest architectural historian.

NOTES

1 C.L. Eastlake, *A History of the Gothic Revival*, 1872, p. 42.

2 Roger North, *Of Building*, ed. Colvin and Newman, Oxford, 1981, p. 110.

3 This passage forms one of the notes to Clerk's poem, 'The Country Seat', the MS of which is among the Clerk of Penicuik papers deposited in the Register House, Edinburgh.

4 *Letters of Horace Walpole*, ed. Toynbee, x, 1904, p. 313 (to William Cole, 1 Sept. 1778).

5 Quoted by Stuart Piggott, 'The Ancestors of Jonathan Oldbuck', *Antiquity*, xxix, 1955, p. 152. Cf. the well-known remarks of John Evelyn in his *Account of Architects and Architecture*, 1706, p. 9.

6 In another passage North indicates that this was the style in which Westminster Abbey was built.

7 Roger North, *Of Building*, pp. 110–12.

8 K. Downes, *Hawksmoor*, 1959, Appendix A, no. 147. Compare Wren's observations on the same subject in *Parentalia*, ed. S. Wren, 1750, pp. 297, 306–7.

9 It was, however, appreciated by John Britton (see his *Memoir of John Aubrey*, 1845, p. 3), and Stuart Piggott briefly indicated the significance of Aubrey's work on Gothic architecture in his essay on 'Antiquarian Thought' in *English Historical Scholarship in the Sixteenth and Seventeenth Centuries*, ed. L. Fox, 1956, p. 109.

10 MS Top. Gen. c. 25, ff. 152–79. A facsimile of the archaeological part of the manuscript was published in a limited edition by the Dorset Publishing Company in 1980–2, under the title *John Aubrey's Monumenta Britannica*, ed. John Fowles and Rodney Legg.

11 The date 1671 appears on the intended title-page, but passages in the text bear various dates from 1656 (f. 153ᵛ) to 1672 (f. 156), and on the first page there is a reference to Wood's *Antiquities of Oxford*, which was not published until 1674. On f. 166 there are notes, obviously added later, about architectural changes under James II and William III. It is clear, therefore, that the MS is a composite work of various dates.

12 This and the next date are left incomplete in the MS.

13 *Architectural History*, vi, 1963.

14 In his *Natural History of Surrey* Aubrey mentions 'a handsome Ditterling gate' at Byfleet (*Surrey Archaeological Collections*, 50, 1946–7, p. 102). For the German Wendel Dietterlin see above , p. 174.

15 'I writ this at Oxford & left it with Mr Anth. Wood.' The introductory essay was written 'at London, not having the other part by me'.

16 This was the date, recorded by Dugdale, when the church was given to the nuns of Godstow.

17 Cf. J. Peshall, *City of Oxford*, 1773, p. 146 (based on Wood's Collections).

18 R.H.C. Davis, 'The Chronology of Perpendicular Architecture in Oxford', *Oxoniensia*, xi–xii, 1946–7.

19 *Aubrey's Brief Lives*, ed. O. Lawson Dick, 1962, pp. 11, 13.

20 Ibid., pp. 94–5.

21 R. Gough, *British Topography*, ii, 1780, p. 369, n. g.

22 In *English Romanesque Art* (Arts Council 1984), p. 362, Dr Thomas Cocke points out that Aubrey's manuscript was also used by the antiquary Charles Lyttelton (1714–68), who stated in 1757 that it was to a 'loose sheet of Mr Aubrey's manuscripts in the Ashmolean' that he 'took the first hint' of 'Saxon' (i.e. Romanesque) architecture.

XIII

GOTHIC SURVIVAL AND GOTHICK REVIVAL

IT USED TO be customary, when discussing the origins of the Gothic Revival, to begin by paying a brief tribute to 'the rivulet of Gothic construction, which flowed on in a sluggish, bucolic, but not a contemptible stream'[1], far into the eighteenth century, before turning to consider the influences, literary and historical, which produced the Revival itself. The reader was left with the impression that 'in rural England from Tudor days on . . . the essentials of Gothic craftsmanship never actually died out but remained *sub rosa* or *sotto voce*, so to speak, ready to appear again with the Revival'[2] – that Gothic survival merged imperceptibly into Gothic revival, and that the continuity of Gothic architecture in this country was in fact never broken. Eighteenth-century classicism, according to this view, was a parasitic growth imposed on English architecture by aristocratic pressure – an exotic product of the Grand Tour rather than a natural expression of English taste. Once the pedantry of Palladianism was broken (so the argument went), the native style burst forth once more 'like the fresh green sprouts which owe their existence to the life still lingering in some venerable forest oak',[3] only perverted at first by the dilettante enthusiasm of amateurs like Horace Walpole, or by the ignorance of architects like James Wyatt.

The unfavourable attitude towards English classical architecture implied by this argument is now [1948] in full retreat, but so far no serious attempt has been made to discover whether there is any truth in this legend of the continuity of Gothic. Was there really a subterranean current of Gothic craftsmanship waiting to be tapped as soon as the rules of taste were relaxed in favour of medieval forms? To answer this question it is not enough merely to demonstrate chronologically that Gothic churches were still being built up to the very date when Walpole and Bentley were busy planning Strawberry Hill. It is necessary either to show that the revivalists employed country masons who still practised Gothic building, or to prove that the local masons who were still at home with buttress and pinnacle themselves built Gothick villas or churches which might have passed the Strawberry Hill Committee.

As for the first possibility, there is, as Sir Kenneth Clark has rightly said, nothing to show that Walpole or his kind sought for such men.[4] Their craftsmen, like their architects, were more accustomed to classical than to Gothic work, but when their patrons demanded Gothic, they executed it – in brick and plaster. Walpole himself admited that 'neither Mr Bentley nor my workmen had *studied* the science [of Gothic]',[5] and at Strawberry Hill and elsewhere it was employed, not as an unaccustomed method of construction, but as a style of decoration of much the same character as 'Chinese' (with which indeed it was sometimes confounded). At Strawberry Hill there was singularly little mason's work, the only important exception being the miniature Chapel-in-the-Woods, which had a Portland stone front copied from Bishop Audley's tomb in Salisbury Cathedral.[6] This was executed by Thomas Gayfere the elder (*c.*1721–1812) who, as master mason to Westminster Abbey, may be supposed to have possessed more than a superficial familiarity with Gothic architecture. But there is little to support this supposition. Gayfere was the son of a mason of Wapping, and almost certainly served his apprenticeship under Andrews Jelfe, one of the mason contractors for Westminster Bridge, before becoming the Abbey mason.[7] Jelfe, who designed the classical town hall at Rye in Sussex, was not the man to train his apprentices in Gothic traditions, and when the Jerusalem Chamber in the Deanery was remodelled in 1769 to the designs of Henry Keene, the Abbey surveyor, with Gayfere as mason, the elaborate Gothic detail was all carried out in woodwork and plaster.[8] If Gayfere is 'the only definite link between survival and revival', he is not a very strong one.

There were, however, parts of the country where the tradition of Gothic masoncraft had survived both Reformation and Civil War and was still alive in the early eighteenth century. One of these was Oxford. Here, as elsewhere, the monasteries had disappeared as corporate patrons of architecture, but the colleges survived, and much building had taken place during the early seventeenth century. Most of it was conditioned by a 'deep sense of tradition',[9] and even in the early eighteenth century a whole quadrangle at University College could be built in a sub-Gothic style scarcely distinguishable from that of the previous century. By then the university was notoriously Tory in its politics, and in the past there has been a temptation to see a connection between the political conservatism of Oxford and the 'late, or debased, Gothic buildings' so carefully described in Parker's *ABC of Gothic Architecture* (1881). No one would dispute that Oxford is the *locus classicus* for seventeenth-century Gothic. But Sir Kenneth Clark has questioned the view that this was due to mere conservatism. Gothic, as he points out, was still the normal way of building churches, chapels and colleges in the seventeenth century, and the late Gothic of Oxford owes its prominence simply to the accident that comparatively few other ecclesiastical or collegiate buildings were erected at the time.[10] But such as there were − Fulmer Church, Buckinghamshire (1610), Lincoln's Inn Chapel (1620–3), the steeple of Godmanchester Church, Huntingdonshire (1623), Charles Church, Plymouth (begun in the 1640s, but not consecrated until 1665), the remarkable church at Staunton Harold in Leicestershire, built between 1653 and 1665 (figs. 175–6),[11] or those at Foremark in Derbyshire (fig. 177) and Low Ham in Somerset (fig. 178), consecrated in 1662 and 1669 respectively − are at least as Gothic as the more familiar Oxford examples. Indeed, apart from St Paul's, Covent Garden, what is now Marlborough House Chapel, and a small church at Hale in Hampshire, rebuilt in 1631–2, no completely classical church was built in England until after the Great Fire of London.[12] It was

175. Staunton Harold Church, Leicestershire, built by Sir Robert Shirley, 1653–5.

176. Plan of Staunton Harold Church, Leicestershire.

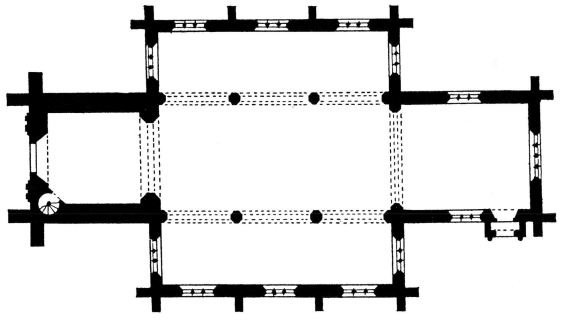

177. Foremark Church, Derbyshire, consecrated 1662.

178. Low Ham Church, Somerset, consecrated 1669.

not until Wren rebuilt the City churches that the architecture of English Protestantism emerged in the form of which St James's, Piccadilly, is the prototype.[13] Until 1666 Gothic was still normal for ecclesiastical architecture, and there was nothing singular in its employment by the clerical dons of Oxford.

Nor did Oxford by any means enjoy a monopoly of masons who worked in Gothic. Merton Great Quadrangle (1608), the Arts End of Duke Humphrey's Library (1610–12), and the Schools Quadrangle (begun 1613) were designed and built by Yorkshire masons,[14] and when Dean Fell commissioned the hall staircase at Christ Church, with its fan-vaulted roof, he got one Smith, 'an artificer from London', to build it.[15] In 1638–40 the tower of Goudhurst Church in Kent (fig. 179) was rebuilt in the traditional style by three London masons – one of them a past, another a future Master of the Masons' Company.[16] Here, as at Steane Chapel, Northamptonshire (1620) (fig. 180), and at Staunton Harold, it is only a classical doorway that betrays the true date of the building. At St John's, Leeds (1631–4), it is the characteristic Jacobean furniture (fig. 181), but 'from the outside it could be mistaken for a church of the late 15th century'.[17] Gothic in the seventeenth century was still a living style, one which was practised in the towns as well as in the country.

But in London the masons' trade was transformed by the Great Fire. The ancient

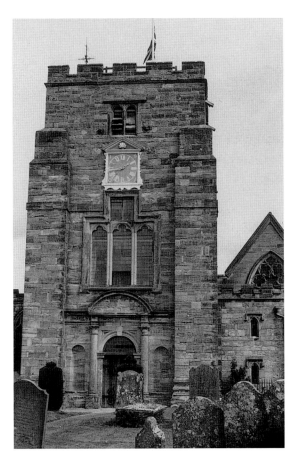

179. Goudhurst Church, Kent: the west tower built by London masons in 1638–40. Pinnacles 20 feet high were provided for in the contract but were either not built or have since been removed (the late Jill Allibone).

180. Steane Chapel, Northamptonshire, built by Sir Thomas Crewe, 1620.

181. St John's Church, Leeds, built 1631–4: part of the interior, drawn by R. Norman Shaw, 1881.

monopoly of the Masons' Company was broken down by the necessity of admitting 'foreigners' to assist in the rebuilding, and what the masons working under Wren on St Paul's Cathedral and the City churches learned from him was the architecture of post-Renaissance Europe, not the principles of Gothic. If here and there the retention of a patched-up pre-Fire church made it appropriate to rebuild the tower in Gothic form, it was architect's rather than mason's Gothic. After 1666 no one would have thought of sending to London for a mason to build a Gothic church. He would have had no difficulty, however, in any part of the country where the mason, rather than the carpenter or the bricklayer, still dominated the building

222

trade. For Gothic is essentially a mason's architecture (what carpenter's Gothic could be like Batty Langley was soon to demonstrate), and its survival was bound up with the survival of the mason as an independent craftsman. In eighteenth-century London the mason was losing ground as a designer to the new profession of architect, and as a builder to the expanding trade of bricklayers, neither of which understood Gothic traditions.

And so Gothic retreated with the mason to the stone districts of the Midlands, the West and the North. Here it was kept alive almost exclusively by church-building and repairs. But of this there was far more than is generally realised (thanks largely to the thoroughness of Victorian 'restoration'), and much of it was carried out in by no means contemptible Gothic. It was the work of masons who were architects in the sense in which *The City and Countrey Purchaser and Builder's Dictionary* (1703) defines the term: 'A master-workman . . . who will contrive a Building, and draw a Draught, or Design thereof, as well as most (and better than some) Surveyors'. The Smiths of Warwick, the Grumbolds of Cambridge, the Townesends of Oxford are familiar examples of men of this kind, 'who dominated a locality, and yet were not confined to it',[18] and there are many more who await identification by the architectural historian. It is the purpose of this article to introduce the reader to Thomas Sumsion of Colerne and the Woodwards of Chipping Campden, because their careers throw some light on the problem of the continuity of Gothic which has been discussed above.

Colerne is a Wiltshire village lying at the south-east extremity of the Cotswolds, between Bath and Chippenham. It is built wholly of the local stone, and in the churchyard the diligent searcher will find a table-tomb with inscriptions to a family of masons surnamed Sumsion or Sumption. Those on the south and west sides of the monument are quite illegible, and those on the east and north sides almost so. One of the legible inscriptions, however, commemorates 'Thomas Sumsion of this parish Freemason who died October the 21, 17[44][19] aged 72 years'. No doubt there are cottages in Colerne built by Sumsion and his family (a mason of his name still [1948] lives in the village), but it is twenty miles away to the north, at Dursley in Gloucestershire, that we first find any record of Sumsion as more than a village mason. Dursley steeple fell down on 7 January 1698/9, and was rebuilt in 1708–9 with the aid of a Brief. The churchwardens' accounts for 1708 record the spending of 5s. 3d. 'Att ye Bell wn ye tower builders came first', and an account of the expenditure of the money raised by the Brief contains the entry 'paid Barker and Samsion for building the Tower £500 0s. 0d.' Who Barker was I do not know, but a comparison between the towers of Dursley and Colerne churches will leave no doubt that 'Samsion' was Thomas Sumsion. For Dursley tower (fig. 182) is essentially a copy of the still existing fifteenth-century tower at Colerne (fig. 183). The north, south and west faces of both towers are almost identical: first a large four-light Perpendicular window (a common feature of church towers in this area), then a rectangular traceried panel occupying almost the whole of the second stage, with a central niche flanked by narrow, single-light windows, and finally paired belfry windows with pierced stone panels almost filling the upper lights above the transom. Even the offsets and string-courses occur at identical intervals, though at

182. Dursley Church, Gloucestershire: the west tower built in 1708–9 by Thomas Sumsion of Colerne.

183. Colerne Church, Wiltshire: the fifteenth-century west tower.

Dursley the buttresses are diagonally placed, whereas those at Colerne are set at right-angles to the walls. The only other conspicuous difference appears in the parapet, which at Colerne is formed of a series of trefoils, while Dursley boasts the pierced battlements and openwork pinnacles of the 'Gloucester coronet'.[20]

The tower at Dursley is one of the most impressive examples of Gothic survival in the country. Completed the year before the Act for Building Fifty New Churches which gave London St Mary-le-Strand and St George's, Bloomsbury, only the detail of the niches and the shallow reveal of the windows and panels betray its true date, and if it be objected that this is a mere copy of another and an earlier tower, then in this the methods of its builders were fully in accordance with medieval precedent. For John Harvey assures us that in the fifteenth century the conscious imitation of existing buildings was already a common feature of building contracts.[21] Unfortunately the contract for Dursley tower does not survive, so it is impossible to say whether Colerne was deliberately chosen as the exemplar with the approval of the churchwardens, or whether they left the masons to determine the design themselves. It may, however, be suspected that the latter was the case, for at Sherston, near Malmesbury, there is another late Gothic tower reminiscent of that at Colerne, and here the churchwardens' accounts leave no doubt that Sumsion was the architect. It was found necessary to take down the old central tower in the spring of 1730, and on 23 March one Moses Rice received a shilling 'for his sones goeing to Collourn to give notice to Thoms. Sumption to come the second time'. The tower was demolished in April, and on 9 May, £1 15s. 0d. was paid to 'Thomas Sumshon for the draught of ye Tower & Journeys'. For this modest sum Sumsion provided the churchwardens with another version of the tower of his native village, repeating the elaborate pierced parapet and pinnacles which he had built at Dursley. But the buttresses had to be left out in a central tower, and the mouldings are noticeably inferior to those at Dursley (fig. 184). The whole tower is, in fact, much less convincingly medieval than its twin at Dursley, and this may be due to the fact that the mason employed was not Sumsion, but one Thomas West, who came from Corsham. He completed his work in 1733, and on Guy Fawkes Day that year the churchwardens were once more able to spend their customary five shillings 'for ringing ye 5th of Novem.'

Sumsion died in 1744, but he was not the last of his kind, for when the detached bell-tower of Berkeley Church became so unsafe in 1748 that it had to be taken down, its successor was built in the same conservative tradition as those of Dursley and Sherston (fig. 185). Unfortunately the parish records are not explicit as to the designer: in 1747, when the state of the tower first gave cause for alarm, £1 7s. 6d. was paid 'to the Masons for giving in a plan for the Tower and Expens. at meeting ye same time'. These masons are not named, but the contractor, who received £740 for his work in 1753, was a certain 'Mr Clark'. Neither his trade nor his place of origin is mentioned in the accounts, but it is tempting to identify him with William Clark, of Leonard Stanley, Glos., carpenter, who in 1750 contracted, together with John Bryan of Painswick and Joseph Bryan of Gloucester, masons, to take down and rebuild the tower of Great Witcombe Church.[22] For this little tower, which cost only £80, and was completed within a few months of the

184. Sherston Church, Wiltshire: the central tower built in 1730–3 to the designs of Thomas Sumsion of Colerne.

signing of the contract in July 1750,[23] is yet another example of the survival of Gothic in the Cotswolds and its belfry windows are similar in form to those of the Berkeley bell-tower (fig. 186). The same William Clark is doubtless to be identified with a master carpenter of that name who was one of the innumerable witnesses in a forgotten *cause célèbre* of eighteenth-century architectural history, the repair of Tetbury Church in 1740–1,[24] but this does not help us to decide whether he designed the towers at Berkeley and Witcombe, and it may be that, as a carpenter and not a mason, he is a doubtful candidate.

185. Berkeley Church, Gloucestershire: the detached bell-tower, built in 1750–3.

186. Great Witcombe Church, Gloucestershire: the west tower built in 1750. The lower west window is a nineteenth-century insertion. The porch is eighteenth-century.

Whoever designed them, the record of these Gloucestershire steeples proves that in the first half of the eighteenth century Gothic was still the accepted style for church towers in the Cotswolds, and that, as late as 1750, there were still men who were capable of building something which, superficially at least, is scarcely to be distinguished from the work of 300 years before.[25] It illustrates the tenacity of Gothic in a district where stone was still the only regular building material, but it does not prove that there was any continuity between the Gothic of Berkeley tower and that of Sanderson Miller's Edgehill eye-catcher (fig. 187), between the Gothic of a Sumsion and that of a Palmer of Bath.[26] Yet there are monuments at Colerne to men who made their fortunes as builders in Bath a generation after Sumsion,[27] and Thomas was by no means the last of his family to follow the mason's trade. But architecturally as well as socially Bath followed the standards and conventions of London, and its Gothick chapels have no connection with the rural Gothic of the Cotswolds. When Horace Walpole visited Berkeley in 1774 he merely noted that the 'steeple' had been 'rebuilt, but at a distance from the body'.[28] Its builders were not in search of 'the true rust of the barons' wars' and the creator of Strawberry Hill displayed no more interest in their work than if it had been put up by a London

187. Edgehill, Warwickshire: the Gothic tower built by Sanderson Miller in 1745–7.

bricklayer. Their Gothic was wholly local in inspiration, and owed nothing to the antiquarianism of a Walpole or a Miller. For them it was the natural way of designing church towers, and fundamentally the only way in which their work differs from that of their medieval predecessors is the lack of that experimentalism which was so rarely absent from medieval work. Gothic for them was a traditional way of building, not a continuously evolving technique of planning, arching and vaulting. The Berkeley bell-tower, it is true, presents all the essential features of a great Gothic steeple, except a spire, but it is almost devoid of mouldings, and quite without any of those enrichments which a medieval mason would have wanted to introduce – and which architects of the Strawberry Hill school were apt to mistake for the spirit of Gothic itself. Even the openwork battlements are reduced to a series of simple uprights and cross-bars, and the pierced 'sound-holes' of the belfry windows fulfil a strictly utilitarian function. In spite of these shortcomings Berkeley tower is an impressive thing – perhaps the last considerable monument of native Gothic. But its qualities are entirely inherited, and it is difficult to see in it any encouragement for those who believe that Gothic had further fields to explore had it not been killed by the great frost of classicism. The Sumsions and their kind were

229

living on the architectural capital of the Middle Ages, and Berkeley tower shows that by 1750 that capital was very nearly exhausted.

But further north there was another family of Cotswold masons whose work deserves investigation before we conclude that Gothic survival and Gothic Revival had nothing in common. The Woodwards of Chipping Campden are [1948] unknown to architectural scholarship, but their work is to be found in three counties, and their name deserves to be recorded as that of a leading family of West Midland masons in the first half of the eighteenth century. A tomb in Chipping Campden churchyard, supplemented by the wills of several members of the family, provides the essential genealogical facts.[29] Thomas Woodward (*c*.1672–1748) was the father of Edward, Robert and Thomas Woodward. It was Edward, who died in 1766 at the age of sixty-nine, by whom 'this Tomb was built'.[30] He also 'made and

188. Chipping Campden, Gloucestershire: the fifteenth-century west tower of the parish church, features of which were copied by the Woodwards at Blockley and Worcester.

erected' a tablet in the neighbouring church of Mickleton to his grandfather Thomas of Aston Subedge (who died in 1716, aged seventy-one), which is surmounted by the masons' arms, and so proves that at least three generations of the family were in the building trade. In 1719 Thomas (d. 1748) took a lease of the local Westington quarries which he bequeathed to his youngest son Thomas.[31]

The first work of any consequence that can be connected with a Woodward is the rebuilding of the tower of Blockley Church in 1726–7. Blockley lies in a detached portion of Worcestershire not far from Campden, and the original contract, with plans and elevation attached, is among the documents from Northwick Park now in the County Record Office at Worcester.[32] It places on record that for £500 Thomas Woodward the elder of Chipping Campden, mason, will, before 24 June 1727, 'in the best and most complete workmanlike manner, well and substantially erect, build, sett up and finish a new Tower at and to the parish church of Blockley. . . . according to the Modell, several platforms, Draughts, or Schemes thereof hereto annexed'. He was also to provide floors and bell-frames, to cover the tower with lead and to glaze the windows at his own charge, and bound himself in £1,000 for the performance of his contract. Payment was to be in seven instalments, carefully related to the progress of the work. The drawing is unsigned, and may have been made by another master mason,[33] but in his *History of Gloucestershire*, published in 1791, Bigland stated that the tower was 'desiged and conducted by Thomas Woodward',[34] and the fact that the belfry windows are copied from those at the latter's native Campden (fig. 188) tends to confirm his statement. The tower Woodward built is medieval in outline, with offset buttresses, Gothic belfry

189. Blockley Church, Worcestershire: the west tower built by Thomas Woodward the elder in 1726–7.

190. Alcester Church, Warwickshire, showing the nave as rebuilt by Edward and Thomas Woodward in 1730 (from *Notices of the Churches of Warwickshire*, 1858).

windows and crocketed pinnacles. The west door and window, however, are typical vernacular baroque, and the cornice below the parapet is also of classical character. The result is a rustic hybrid in which the element of Gothic survival is compromised by the intrusive classical features (fig. 189).

Blockley tower was built by the elder Woodward alone. But in March 1729/30 his sons Edward and Thomas appear in partnership in the contract whereby they undertook to rebuild the nave and chancel of Alcester Church in Warwickshire, retaining the existing medieval tower. They agreed

> to rebuild . . . said church of Alcester from the foundation of the same as figured in the Draught hereunto annexed of the said intended New Church . . . and build the walls with Buttresses Battlements and pinnacles with Cross Iron barrs to each pinnacle as figured in the sd. Draught . . . to build and erect . . . new large substantial Pillars or Columns of the Doric Order to support the middle Isle of the said Church [whose roof was to be retained, and to rebuild the chancel] of the same height forme and proportion as the Middle Isle of the said Church.

They were to employ Alcester workmen, and throughout were to 'be under the advise direccion & Government of . . . Mr [Francis] Smith so as to do alter or amend anything of the said worke which hee shall think fitt to have done or altered'.[35] Francis Smith was the great master builder of Warwick, who had designed or erected churches and country houses all over the Midlands, and was probably the most successful provincial architect of the eighteenth century before John Carr of York. It is possible that he made the draughts (now lost) to which the Woodwards were to work, but at a time when there was no such thing as an architectural profession in the modern sense, it was common practice to employ a surveyor or master builder to see that a contract was properly performed, to decide (as the Alcester document itself provides) how far the old materials might be reused, and to measure up the work when it was completed, without going to him for the design, which was often provided by the contractor himself. As rebuilt by the two Woodwards in 1730–3, Alcester Church combined a classical interior with a Gothic shell intended, presumably, to harmonise with the surviving medieval tower. The two-light Gothic windows were replaced in 1870–1, but a lithograph of 1858 shows their original form (fig. 190). The interior, with its 'Doric' (really Tuscan) columns, so far resembles that of the Woodwards' later church at Gloucester as to suggest that they probably designed it themselves, and if so they no doubt designed the Gothic exterior too. To judge from the two surviving west doorways (one at the end of each aisle), the detailing was poor, but, whatever its shortcomings, the Gothic body of Alcester Church was remarkable for its date.

The Woodwards' next contract was for the rebuilding of all but the steeple of the church of St John the Baptist in Gloucester. Here there is no doubt that they were the designers as well as the builders, for in 1729 the churchwardens 'Payd the two Mr. Woodwards for surveying, giving in an Estimation & draught of our church 10–6'. The contract was not signed until 1731, after a year in which the church-wardens had been busy buying timber in Staffordshire, and the foundations were laid on 1 June 1732. The church was reopened for worship on 4 August 1734.[36] The interior of St John's, with its 'Doric' columns and barrel ceiling, is very similar to that of Alcester. There is, however, no suggestion of Gothic in this town church, and its architectural features are concentrated in the east front, which presents a pedimented composition to Northgate Street perhaps suggested by Wren's St Dionis Backchurch in the City of London (fig. 191). The total cost was £1,100, of which the Woodwards appear to have received about £600 for building and masonry: the timber was purchased direct from the owners by the churchwardens, and the fittings were made by Messrs Thomas Nest and John Collett under a separate contract. The original seating has been destroyed, but the admirable reredos given by Mrs Bridgett Price has fortunately been spared.

St John's was scarcely complete before the Woodwards had taken on another contract, the rebuilding of St Swithin's Church, Worcester, which necessitated their becoming freemen of that city in January 1734/5 on payment of a fine of £20.[37] A brass plate over the west door records that 'This church was rebuilt by Ed. and Tho. Woodward in the year of our Lord 1736. Tho. Hoskyns, Tho. Wakeman, churchwardens'. Unfortunately there is a gap in the churchwardens' accounts between 1719 and 1739, but the parish chest contains the Woodwards' bond in £2,000 to fulfil the obligations 'mentioned in certain Articles of agreement bearing date the Thirteenth day of August last past [1733]. . . . concerning the Rebuilding of the Parish Church and Tower of Saint Swithin, and in one deed or Instrument in writing annexed to the said Articles relating alsoe to the rebuilding of the said church and bearing even date with these presents [25 March 1734]'. Attached are several of the receipts for money advanced to the contractors up to November 1736, signed by either Edward or Thomas Woodward.

St Swithin's has sometimes been attributed to Thomas White, the supposed

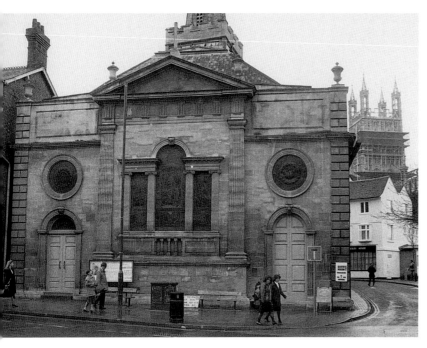

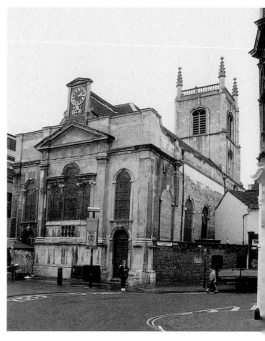

191. (*above left*) St John's Church, Gloucester: the east end of the church as rebuilt by Edward and Thomas Woodward in 1732–4.

192. (*above right*) St Swithin's Church, Worcester: the east end of the church rebuilt by Edward and Thomas Woodward in 1734–6.

193. St Swithin's Church, Worcester: the west tower of 1734–6.

designer of the Worcester Guildhall, and a prolific monumental sculptor,[38] but there is nothing to show that he had any connection with its rebuilding, and the close resemblance between the east front of this Worcester church (fig. 192) and that of St John's in Gloucester is proof that here, as at St John's, the Woodwards were their own architects. There is another feature of St Swithin's which betrays the identity of its designers. Just as Thomas Sumsion repeated Colerne tower at Dursley and Sherston, so the influence of the great tower beside which the Woodwards are buried is clearly traceable in their work. At Blockley it was the tracery of the Chipping Campden belfry windows which the elder Woodward rather clumsily reproduced in his own tower of 1726–7. Here at St Swithin's the pilaster strips that are such a distinctive feature of the Gloucestershire tower (fig. 193) are reproduced, climbing up the walls to embrace the belfry windows and end in ogee arches above, just as they do at Campden.

Externally, St Swithin's is a classical church with a traditional tower. But internally it is prophetic of the Gothic Revival which was so soon to affect English architectural taste (fig. 194). The fittings, happily little altered, are typical examples

194. St Swithin's Church, Worcester: the interior of the church built in 1734–6.

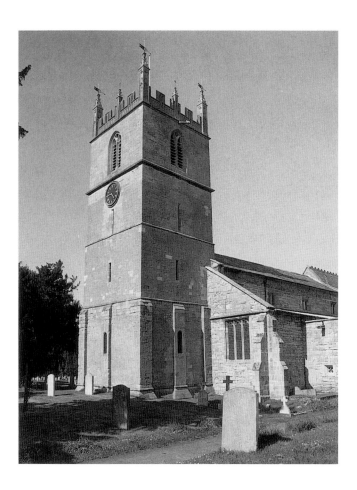

195. Fladbury Church, Worcestershire: the west tower, showing the upper part as rebuilt by the Woodwards in 1750–2.

of eighteenth-century joinery. But the plaster ceiling is in the form of a shallow Gothic vault, with moulded ribs resting on corbels which curiously combine Gothic and classical forms. The identity of the plasterer is unknown, but the ceiling was presumably envisaged by the Woodwards and may have been designed by them. Here, at any rate, the mason's Gothic of the tower and the plasterer's Gothic of the ceiling coexist in the same building.

Another building in which the Woodwards demonstrated their skill as Gothic masons was the tower of Fladbury Church, near Pershore, the upper part of which was rebuilt in traditional Gothic style in 1750–2 (fig. 195). Here no churchwardens' accounts survive to document the work, but a stone inscribed with the name of Edward Woodward's son Richard (who died in 1755, aged thirty-two) came to light in the course of modern repairs.[39]

Much more important for the student of eighteenth-century Gothic is a design made by Edward Woodward in 1752 for rebuilding the church at Preston-on-Stour, then in Gloucestershire, but now in Warwickshire. His patron here was the politician and antiquary James West, the owner of Alscot Park nearby, which Woodward was engaged in rebuilding in a rococo Gothick style under the direction of Messrs Shakespear and Phillips of London, both carpenters by trade and purveyors of a delightfully frivolous Gothic that lacked even Strawberry Hill's modest

236

pretensions to medieval scholarship (fig. 196).[40] For the church, however, Woodward submitted his own designs and estimate, dated 24 June 1752[41] (fig. 197). Unlike most Georgian Gothic churches, which are conceived as single preaching spaces, Woodward's church was to have a structurally distinct nave and chancel and a massive west tower crowned by a lantern supported on flying arches like that of St Nicholas, Newcastle (fig. 198). The panelled surface of the tower was of an established local type. The style and disposition of the windows followed medieval precedent, and the detailing of the porch was authentic. Though unusual, even the chancel buttresses with little pinnacles rising from their offsets have medieval prototypes which Woodward may have noted at Steeple Ashton in Wiltshire or on certain church towers in the south-west (e.g. Bitton, Glos., Taunton, Somerset, Cullompton, Devon, fig. 33). Only in the winged cherubs' heads in the spandrels of the ogee windows has a contemporary detail been introduced.

The estimate for this remarkable building was £1,855. This was clearly more than West was prepared to spend. In fact, all that Woodward was allowed to do was to rebuild the church piecemeal between 1753 and 1757. He began with the chancel, which was rebuilt to the same dimensions as before, but with three

196. Alscot Park, Warwickshire, as rebuilt by Edward Woodward for the politician and antiquary James West in 1750–64 under the direction of Messrs Shakespear and Phillips of London (engraving from J.P. Neale, *Views of Seats*, 1820).

197. Edward Woodward's design for rebuilding Preston-on-Stour Church, Warwickshire, made for James West in 1752 (West family papers).

198. St Nicholas's Church, Newcastle-upon-Tyne: the fifteenth-century steeple.

199. Preston-on-Stour Church, Warwickshire, as reconstructed by Edward Woodward in 1753–7. The chancel was rebuilt with new windows and new windows were inserted in the nave. The medieval tower was retained.

'gothick' windows costing £90. The tower was strengthened by building up the staircase, and the nave was reconstructed with more Gothic windows like 'the great one' in the chancel (fig. 199). Inside, the rococo Gothic wainscotting and the iron screen were supplied by Messrs Phillips and Shakespear and the walls and ceiling

200. Preston-on-Stour Church, Warwickshire: the interior of the chancel, with monuments framed in Gothic panels.

201. Ilmington, Warwickshire: the tomb of Samuel Sansom (d. 1750), attributed to Edward Woodward.

were decorated with plasterwork in a similar style to that in the house. The ogee panels, probably intended as frames for the family monuments which now fill them, and the cornice above, are typical Kentian Gothick of their time, highly decorative, but with no pretensions to authentic medieval forms (fig. 200). So at Preston-on-Stour a church designed in traditional Gothic style was fitted out with 'smart

202. Alnwick, Northumberland: the Pottergate Tower built to the designs of John Bell in 1768, before the removal of the 'crown' in 1812 (from G. Tate, *History of Alnwick*, ii, 1848–9).

203. Alnwick Castle, Northumberland: the Brizlee Tower in the park, designed by Robert Adam in 1777 (Dr David King).

London Rococo Gothick' at the behest of an eminent antiquary. 'Here, if anywhere,' as Mark Girouard has said, 'is the watershed between Gothic survival and revival.'[42]

Though Woodward's vision of building a traditional Gothic church in Georgian England was never to be realised, several features of his design are to be seen on the tomb of Samuel Sansom (d. 1750) in the churchyard at Ilmington, only four miles north-east of Chipping Campden. Rising from a buttressed tomb-chest, a spire-like feature is immediately recognisable as a simplified version of the one envisaged by Woodward for Preston Church, while the panelled battlements are virtually identical with those in his drawing (fig. 201). Wrongly thought by Pevsner to be 'Victorian', this delightful essay in Perpendicular Gothic can confidently be attributed to Edward Woodward.

The Woodwards were not quite the only masons whose continued use of traditional Gothic forms in their own localities overlapped chronologically with the sophisticated antiquarian Gothic of Horace Walpole, Sanderson Miller and Sir Roger Newdigate. In Oxford the Townesends (though best known for the classical buildings they erected under the direction of Dean Aldrich and Dr George Clarke) were capable of building a fan vault (in the Convocation House) as late as 1758–9; in Leicestershire the Wings showed an understanding of Gothic forms that was exceptional for their time, while at Alnwick in Northumberland in 1768 a Durham mason-architect called John Bell (d. 1784)[43] designed the Pottergate Tower (fig. 202), a gateway to the town which was not only detailed in a remarkably convincing manner, but was originally surmounted by just such a 'crown' (based on the one at Newcastle, fig. 198) as Edward Woodward had envisaged for Preston-on-Stour sixteen years earlier (fig. 197). The contrast between Bell's sturdy civic tower and the fantastically attenuated Gothick one in the ducal park (fig. 203), designed by Robert Adam in 1777, shows that, here as elsewhere, fashionable taste took little heed of local architectural tradition, preferring a showy Gothick confection to something characteristically Northumbrian. Once more, Gothick Revival had turned its back on Gothic survival.

NOTES

1 Kenneth Clark, *The Gothic Revival*, 1924, p. 19.
2 R.H. Newton, *Town & Davis Architects*, Columbia University Press, 1942, pp. 211–12.
3 C.L. Eastlake, *A History of the Gothic Revival in England*, 1872, p. 4.
4 *The Gothic Revival*, p. 18.
5 Quoted by W.S. Lewis, 'The Genesis of Strawberry Hill', *Metropolitan Museum Studies*, v, 1934, p. 65.
6 P. Toynbee, *Strawberry Hill Accounts*, 1927, p. 153.
7 See numerous references to Gayfere in Jelfe's letter-book in the British Library (Add. MS 27587).
8 Westminster Abbey Muniments 24836 (paper book of 'Workmen's Bills to the Jerusalem Chamber, and Cloister Gates, 1769').
9 John Newman in *History of the University of Oxford*, iv, ed. G. Tyacke, 1997, p. 169.
10 *The Gothic Revival*, pp. 14, 15.
11 See J. Simmons and H.M. Colvin, 'Staunton Harold Chapel', *Archaeological Jrnl.* cxii, 1955, pp. 173–6.
12 For Hale see Peter Burman, 'Inigo Jones at Hale'?, *Country Life*, 7 Feb. 1974, pp. 263–6.
13 For precursors of the London City churches, see Peter Guillery, 'The Broadway Chapel, Westminster: a forgotten exemplar', *London Topographical Record*, xxvi, 1990.
14 See T.W. Hanson, 'Halifax Builders in Oxford', *Trans. Halifax Antiq. Soc.*, 1928, pp. 253–317.
15 W.G. Hiscock, *A Christchurch Miscellany*, 1946, p. 208.
16 *Archaeologia Cantiana*, xxviii, 1909, pp. 10–13.
17 Derek Linstrum, *Historic Architecture of Leeds*, 1969, p. 12.
18 A. Dale, *James Wyatt*, 1936, p. 2.
19 The last two figures are almost obliterated, but the year of Sumption's death is established by the parish register, which records his burial on 23 October 1744, and by his will, which is enrolled on the court rolls of the manor of Colerne in the archives of New College, Oxford.
20 Although, as F.J. Allen observes in *Great Church Towers of England*, 1932, p. 111, the parapet and pinnacles of Colerne Church 'appear to have been restored', Buckler's drawing of *c.*1809 in the British Library (Add. MS 36391, no. 59) shows that the design of the parapet has not been altered since his

time. The present conical termination to the stair-turret has, however, been substituted for the simple pinnacle shown by Buckler.

21 J.H. Harvey, *Gothic England*, 1947, pp. 24, 97.

22 A pyramidal tomb in Painswick churchyard commemorates 'John Bryan late of this Town Carver', who died in 1787, aged 71, and the name is frequently met with in Gloucestershire building accounts of the eighteenth century.

23 From a transcript of the original contract in a MS history of Great Witcombe in the possession [1948] of Mrs Hicks Beach of Witcombe Park, by whose kind permission I was allowed to copy it.

24 See his deposition in Gloucester Public Library, MS R.R. 300.1. For the story of the rebuilding of Tetbury Church see Marcus Whiffen in *Architectural Review*, July 1944, pp. 3–4 and H.M. Colvin in *Country Life*, 27 Dec. 1946, p. 1263 (Correspondence).

25 Another late Gothic tower of this group is that of Kington St Michael, Wilts. (1725), but as no parish records of this period have survived, nothing is known of its builders.

26 For Palmer's Gothic churches see W. Ison, *The Georgian Buildings of Bath*, 1948, 2nd ed., 1980.

27 A tablet in the church commemorates 'Mr. John Ford Builder / of the City of Bath / died 6 September, 1767 / Aged 56 years. / Whose abilities and Enterprise / In Biusiness in a great Measure / Contributed to the Erection / of the Handsome Buildings / and Streets of that / City', also his son John Ford statuary who died 23 Feb. 1803, aged 67. In the churchyard there is a slab to 'Stephen Ford, of the City of Bath Builder, who died 9 March 1785, aged 72.

28 *Journal of Visits to Country Seats* (Walpole Soc., xvi, 1927–8), p. 76.

29 The inscriptions (now, 1997, almost completely illegible) are given by P.C. Rushen, *History of Campden*, 1911, p. 141. The wills are among the Gloucester Probate records now in the County Record Office.

30 Edward's will (P.C.C. 165 TYNDALL) adds little to our knowledge of the family. He was also a monumental sculptor, and his tablets, signed 'Edwd. Woodward of Campden Fecit' can be seen in several Cotswold churches: see R. Gunnis, *Dictionary of British Sculptors 1660–1851*, 1968, p. 443.

31 Rushen, *Campden*, p. 38.

32 Bundle 31/1. 'The Rebuilding of Blockley Church Tower' is described by E.A.B. Barnard from the original documents in *Evesham Journal*, 8 April 1939, p. 3.

33 In a letter to Sir John Rushout dated 25 Oct. 1725, reviewing the terms of Woodward's contract, Francis Smith of Warwick recites a clause to the effect that the tower was to be built 'according to the Draught given in by Kempster' (presumably of the Burford family of masons of that name) (Worcester CRO, Rushout papers, 705: 66 BA 4221/26, for knowledge of which I am indebted to Prof. Andor Gomme).

34 R. Bigland, *Historical . . . Collections relative to the County of Gloucester*, ed. Frith, Bristol & Glos. Archaeological Soc. 1989–95, pt. i, p. 218.

35 Original contract among parish records of Alcester [1948].

36 From C.H. Dancey's transcripts of the churchwardens' accounts in *Gloucester Parochial Records*, iii, pp. 28 ff. (Gloucester Public Library MS 14261).

37 Information from the Corporation Order Book kindly provided by Mr David Whitehead.

38 For White see my *Biographical Dictionary of British Architects 1600–1840*, 3rd ed., 1995, and Rupert Gunnis's *Dictionary of British Sculptors 1660–1851*, 1968.

39 For information about this discovery I am indebted to Mr Chris Pickford, County Archivist of Bedfordshire.

40 For the rebuilding of Alscot Park see Mark Girouard in *Country Life*, 15, 22 and 29 May 1958. For Shakespear and Phillips see my *Biographical Dictionary* (as above).

41 West family papers, examined by kind permission of the late Mrs Alston-Roberts-West. See also J.H. Bloom, *History of Preston-on-Stour*, 1896, pp. 78–9.

42 *Country Life*, 29 May 1958, p. 1187.

43 John Bell was probably the mason of this name who was admitted a freeman of Durham in August 1730, but another John Bell, a joiner, was admitted in 1752 (Durham CRO, Du 5/1/1).

XIV

THE GRAND BRIDGE IN BLENHEIM PARK

It is only in the present century that Blenheim Palace has come to be generally admired as a work of architecture. In the eighteenth century its baroque rhetoric appealed neither to Palladian nor to neo-classical taste, and in the nineteenth appreciation of its picturesque qualities was nearly always coupled with deprecating remarks about the 'heaviness' of its structure and the 'overloading' of its ornament. Even today, it requires more that a conventional liking for the baroque to under-stand the complex interplay of forms in the north front.

For the Grand Bridge, on the other hand, there has always been genuine, albeit sometimes rather grudging, admiration, especially after Capability Brown flooded the valley which it spans and converted a mere canal into a lake. Springing directly from the water, the great arch satisfied the taste for an *architecture ensevelie* (or in this case *engloutie*) that was fashionable at the end of the eighteenth century, and the spectacular landscape that greets the visitor as he passes through the Triumphal Arch could not fail to impress even those who were deaf to the language of classical architecture as spoken in the reign of Queen Anne. Whether it is seen light against darker water in the morning, or silhouetted against the glittering surface of the lake in the afternoon, the bridge in its setting forms one of the grandest architectural sights in Europe. Nevertheless it is, as Kerry Downes has put it, 'the most mysterious and the least understood part of all Blenheim'.[1] Only one original drawing for it appears to survive, and no written explanation of its puzzling interior spaces has been preserved, let alone any plan. Most of these spaces are now accessible only by boat, and exploring them is an adventure that requires some agility as well as indifference to bats, pigeons and other wild inhabitants of their dark recesses. What follows is an attempt to resolve some of the problems that a study of the Grand Bridge poses for the architectural historian.

Today, the bridge is largely ornamental. But as originally conceived, it had the important function of conveying the principal drive up to the great forecourt. At the present day access to the palace is mainly from the east, either from the Hensington Gate or down the main street of Woodstock, through the Triumphal Arch, and round the eastern side of the lake (or Queen Pool, as this part of it is called). The palace, however, faces north, not east, and it is clear that the original intention must have been for the grand approach to be down the great avenue from the Ditchley Gate, or perhaps, as Professor Downes has suggested, by a circuitous

204. The Grand Bridge, Blenheim, from the west (1991).

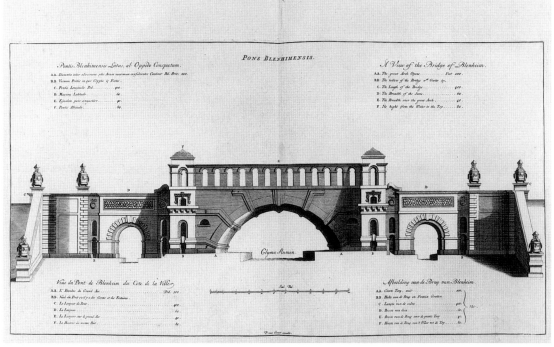

205. The Grand Bridge, Blenheim, engraving by P. van Gunst, published in 1709 (Bodleian Library, Gough Maps 26, ff. 53–4).

206. The Grand Bridge, Blenheim, perspective drawing, probably by Nicholas Hawksmoor (private collection).

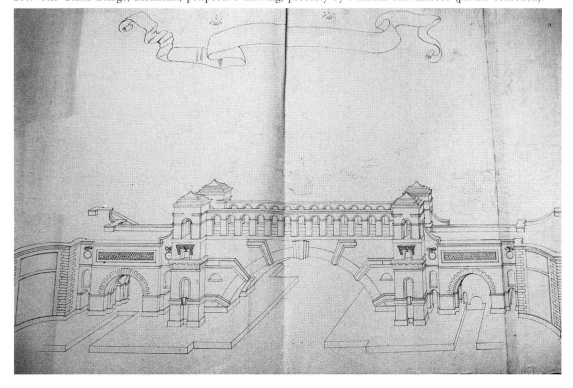

route from Woodstock that went past the site of the old royal manor house on the north side of the Glyme before turning south towards the new palace.[2] In either case a bridge would be needed to cross the valley, whose steep sides and marshy bottom would make difficult going for coaches and other large horse-drawn vehicles. For this bridge and its attendant earthworks not only Vanbrugh and his adjutant Hawksmoor were invited to submit designs, but also Sir Christopher Wren and the landscape gardener Henry Wise. Of Hawksmoor's and Wise's plans nothing is known, but it appears that what Wren proposed was a low bridge only 15 feet high and a pair of curving ramps gradually rising to the level of the forecourt.[3] Vanbrugh, on the other hand, envisaged a bridge – or rather a viaduct – whose carriageway would be almost level with the forecourt of the palace rather than one which involved first descending into the valley and then climbing up again to enter the forecourt. Nothing was to interrupt this triumphal approach save the architectural pomp and circumstance of the bridge itself. In April 1706 there were several meetings at which these alternatives were considered by Lord Treasurer Godolphin and other of the Duke's friends and advisers. Wren's 'Modell', Vanbrugh later recalled, 'was quite rejected, and that I propos'd was resolv'd on'.[4]

Exactly what Vanbrugh's design implied in architectural terms we do not know: it may or may not have incorporated all the features of the grand scheme represented by an engraving made under Hawksmoor's direction in 1709, and by a previously unknown drawing, almost certainly by Hawksmoor, that must have been made about the same time.[5] These agree in showing a huge central arch, two smaller ones to north and south, and four flanking towers linked at the level of the roadway by an arcade on either side (figs. 205–6).

207. The Grand Bridge, Blenheim: the northern arch, showing the splayed junction between the two builds.

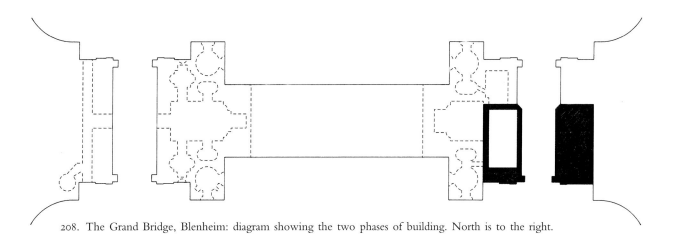

208. The Grand Bridge, Blenheim: diagram showing the two phases of building. North is to the right.

What suggests that the design approved in April 1706 may in fact have been of a somewhat more modest character than the one represented in figs. 205 and 206 is the fact that the northern arch was built in two sections which differ considerably from one another both in dimensions and in other respects. The eastern portion of the arch was intended not only to support the carriageway, but also to shelter a pumping apparatus designed to supply the palace with water drawn from the adjoining spring known as 'Rosamund's Well'.[6] As built by the Oxford mason Bartholomew Peisley in 1706, this arch was only about 36 feet in width from east to west, and was turned in rubble, not ashlar, like the great arch. When work began on the remainder of the bridge in 1708 this northern arch was extended westwards by a second arch built alongside it to make up the full width of the bridge, though to a larger radius and in ashlar masonry. That this was not merely phase two of a structure planned to be built in stages is demonstrated both by the differences in radius and masonry and by the awkward splayed junction between the two builds (fig. 207). Moreover, a glance at the plan (fig. 208) shows that the masonry of 1706 was continued southwards to form an internal space that does not conform to the otherwise symmetrical plan of the northern abutment of the great arch. All this suggests that the grand design as executed from 1708 onwards represented a revised and enlarged version of the one that had been approved in 1706, and that when Sarah, Duchess of Marlborough, complained in later years that designs connected with that 'ridiculous bridge' were being carried out that had never been 'shewn nor understood', her annoyance may have had some justification.[7]

The progress of the works at Blenheim is chronicled fairly fully by regular reports written by Henry Joynes, the clerk of works, to Samuel Travers, MP, who was in charge of the building operations with the title of surveyor-general, as well as by a series of annual accounts extending from 1705 to 1714.[8] At the end of July 1708 Joynes reported that 'the foundations of the Bridge are now Digging, and the first stone was laid the 28th of this instant.' By the end of September the foundations of the south side had all been brought up to the level of the meadow, and 'the foundations of the bridge North side the Great Arch adjoining to the Engine house' were 'bringing up'. The next year saw the 'Arch that answers to the Engine House'

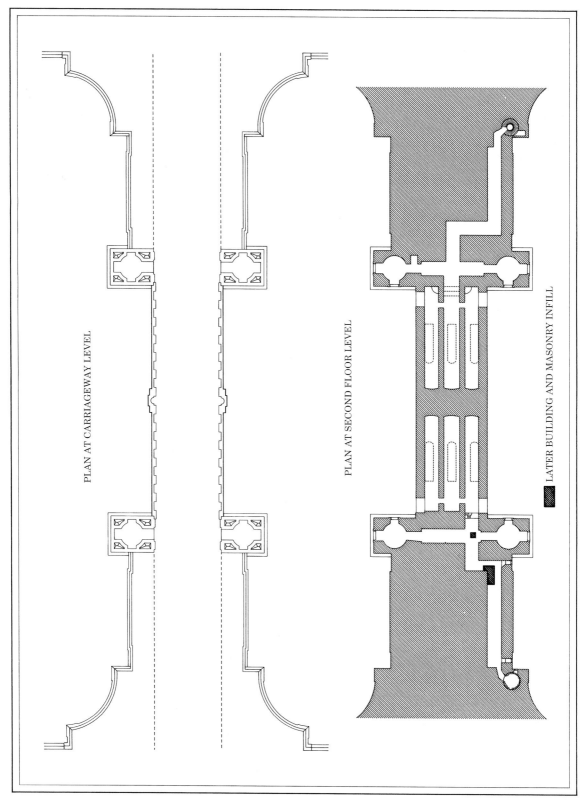

PLAN AT CARRIAGEWAY LEVEL

PLAN AT SECOND FLOOR LEVEL

LATER BUILDING AND MASONRY INFILL

209. The Grand Bridge, Blenheim: plan at carriage-way and second-floor level. North is to the right.

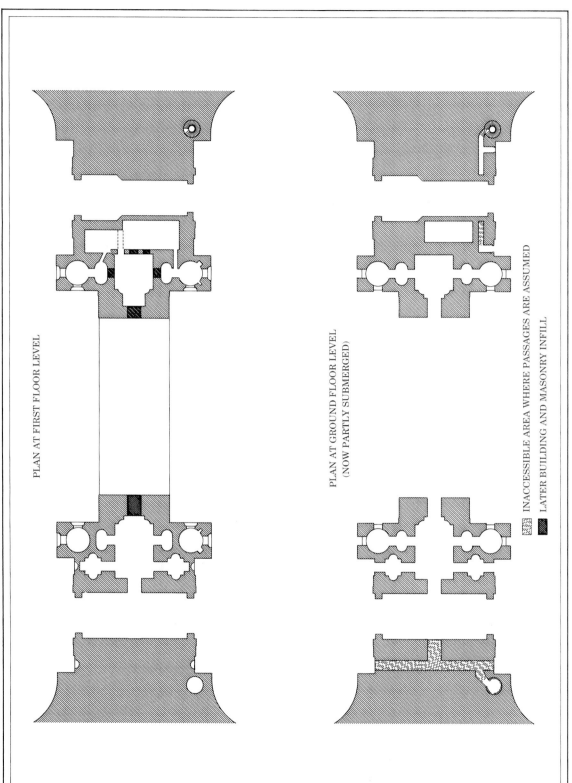

PLAN AT FIRST FLOOR LEVEL

PLAN AT GROUND FLOOR LEVEL
(NOW PARTLY SUBMERGED)

INACCESSIBLE AREA WHERE PASSAGES ARE ASSUMED

LATER BUILDING AND MASONRY INFILL

210. The Grand Bridge, Blenheim: plans at ground-floor and first-floor levels. North is to the right.

(i.e. the western extension of the northern arch) turned and the walls on the south side of the great arch 'considerably advanc'd above the springing of the Rustic Arches'. In 1710 work went on 'very vigorously', the great arch itself being successfully completed by Peisley in December.[9] However, in the absence of the Duke, all works at Blenheim were temporarily stopped by the Duchess in October of that year, and even when they were resumed, she held up work on the towers in the hope of getting the house finished first, so it was not until the autumn of 1711 that the two western towers and the spandrels of the great arch on the west side were in place.[10] The east side was still incomplete, and was to remain so for ten more years. For in December 1711 the Duke of Marlborough was dismissed by the new Tory government and the supply of money from the Treasury stopped, not to be resumed until the accession of George I and the return of the Whigs to power in 1714. Even then it was only the accumulated debt to the workmen that was (in principle) acknowledged by the Treasury. For any new works the Duke and Duchess would have to pay themselves out of their own considerable resources. In 1714 an estimate of £6,994 4s. 2d. was made for the completion of the bridge – £2,643 1s. 8d. for 'The stone and masonry', £851 2s. 6d. for 'The two Grand Acroterias', that is, the two arcades, and £3,500 for making up the ground to north and south with earth.[11]

In fact it was not until September 1721, when the palace was almost finished, that William Townesend and Bartholomew Peisley contracted to complete the east side of the bridge, cope the walls, pave the carriageway and finish the 'slope walls' at either end.[12] By that time the Duke had been incapacitated by a stroke and the direction of the works had passed to the Duchess, for whom the bridge was the maddest of the 'mad things' that Vanbrugh had set in motion either without her knowledge or against her wishes.[13] In November 1716 their epic quarrel had culminated in the architect's dismissal. So in the bridge, as in the palace, all unnecessary frills were now to be dispensed with. The panels of 'frostwork' that are a feature of the west side of the bridge were not to be repeated on the east side. As for the 'Acroterias', they were of course abandoned, and with them the upper parts of the four towers. By 1724 the Grand Bridge had assumed its present appearance as a great flat-topped arch flanked by two smaller ones. Precisely how much it had cost would be difficult if not impossible to calculate from the surviving documents, but contemporary guidebooks mention a figure of 'between 20 and 30,000 £' for bridge and causeway, and there is no reason to doubt that this is a fair estimate.

In Britain the Grand Bridge was unprecedented both in size and in design. Just over 100 feet in span, its central arch was by far the largest in the country at the time. In the 1730s the building of a bridge over the Thames at Westminster with substantially smaller arches was to tax British building technology to the utmost, but there the difficulty lay in constructing piers in the bed of a running river.[14] At Blenheim the masons were operating for the most part on dry land, where normal foundations could be dug without any difficulty, and the structure has never shown any signs of subsidence. Apart from its sheer size, the most striking feature of the design was the architectural superstructure, which again had no precedent in Britain

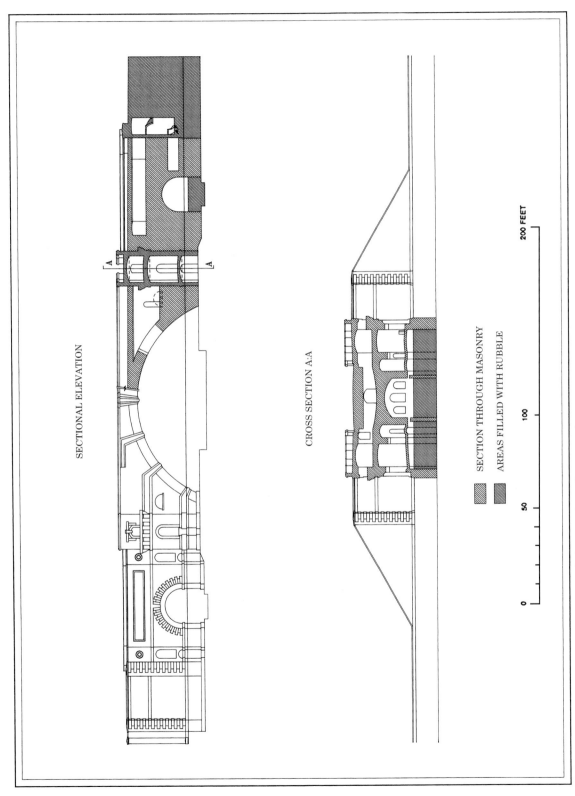

SECTIONAL ELEVATION

CROSS SECTION A:A

SECTION THROUGH MASONRY

AREAS FILLED WITH RUBBLE

0   50   100   200 FEET

211. The Grand Bridge, Blenheim: sectional elevation from the east and cross-section.

apart from the dwellings that had been allowed to encroach on London Bridge. In Venice, however, an arcaded wall framed shops on either side of the sixteenth-century Rialto Bridge, while Palladio's published design for a grander bridge on the same site provided an example of what later in the eighteenth century would be called a 'bridge of magnificence'.[15] Vanbrugh's open arcade owed little or nothing to the Venetian example, but the similarity, such as it was, was enough to earn Blenheim's bridge the name of 'Rialto' in some guidebooks. The beauty of Palladio's bridge would have been the contrast between the enclosed courts at either end and the two open porticos facing up and down the Grand Canal in the middle. Vanbrugh's bridge had no such cross-axis to distract attention as one approached the palace, but the four towers were a characteristic stroke of genius that gave the bridge that 'movement' which Robert and James Adam rightly identified as a characteristic of his architectural compositions.

The most singular feature of the Grand Bridge was the interior spaces. Duchess Sarah claimed to have counted thirty-three rooms inside the bridge,[16] and it is indeed possible to identify some twenty-eight spaces that might just qualify as 'rooms', though some of them have no light and others (in the towers) are open on two sides. There can be no doubt that the basic function of these voids was to save the cost of filling up the spaces between the arches and to reduce the pressure of superincumbent masonry on the latter. Voids were formed in the spandrels of other eighteenth-century bridges for the same purpose, for instance in William Edwards's celebrated one-arch bridge of 140 feet span over the River Taff in Glamorgan (1756) and they figure in at least one of the designs submitted for Westminster Bridge in 1736.[17] In such bridges as these, however, the voids were usually circular and often inaccessible. The complicated sequence of spaces within the mass of the Grand Bridge seems to have been quite without precedent in bridge architecture either British or European. They did, however, have analogies in the perforated-pier type of construction that had haunted the imagination of architects since Bramante's first plan for St Peter's. In the Grand Bridge the mass of each pier is filled at its centre by a large rectangular room, barrel-vaulted and built of dressed ashlar, with a stepped segmental apse on the side towards the springing of the great arch. These two rooms were to have been entered by arches in their north and south walls opening onto the grassed or gravelled walkways bordering the water-courses (fig. 206). They were flanked by a series of minor chambers whose axes crossed the central space. The round and square-headed openings at ground-level seen in Hawksmoor's drawing, blocked since the raising of the level of the lake, mark the extension of these cross-axes onto the face of the building. In the southern pier the cross-axes contain small, almost cruciform chambers, with apsidal recesses, on either side of the main rooms and then a series of narrow oval lobbies leading to circular vestibules in the bases of the two towers. The resulting pattern recalls the fantastical sequences of rooms shown by the Italian architectural antiquary G.B. Montano in some of his reconstructions of Roman temples. His book was in Hawksmoor's library.[18]

In the northern pier the plan, though essentially similar, had to be modified to accommodate the plain rectangular room already built on the south side of the arch sheltering the water-engine. As a result the central room is considerably shorter from north to south and the second series of linked spaces is omitted altogether. Furthermore in the southern pier the subsidiary rooms rose to a considerable height as lofty two-storey chambers, whereas in the northern one it was only the central room that occupied two storeys, the subsidiary spaces (one of which is provided with a fireplace) being half its height. There was also a difference in the way the two suites of rooms were finished. At the lowest level the cross-axis in the northern pier – now only glimpsed as a series of vaulted ceilings a few feet above water level – has been finished throughout in hard wall plaster, still intact below as well as above water level, while the great room with which it connected – also plastered, but probably at a later date[19] – was provided with wooden or metal gratings or overdoors within its connecting arches. There is no trace of plaster in the southern pier, whose rooms can now be explored only by boat. Before flooding their effect as cavernous spaces lit only by light seeping in from the outer chambers may well have been striking. Subtle effects of diffused lighting from the lunette windows in the spandrels of the bridge are also experienced at the upper levels, while the openings in the tower rooms afford dramatic views of the great arch (figs. 212–13).

It is a curiosity of the plan that Vanbrugh did not attempt to link the uppermost floor of the bridge to the rooms below. A small stair might easily have been accommodated within one of the oval rooms or in one of the circular spaces within the towers. Instead he chose to provide access to the top floor by two circular cantilevered stairs constructed within the abutments on their eastern side. These stairs (the southern of which is now ruinous) are connected by long vaulted passages both to the uppermost rooms in the towers and to the six wedge-shaped spaces over the great arch, three on each side, formed by three longitudinal vaults that support the carriageway. In these spaces, light was provided at one end by the lunette windows in the spandrels, and at the other by great sloping openings, eleven feet long, pierced through six feet of ashlar masonry to the soffit of the arch itself. These were the windows out of which, as the Duchess wrote to her friend Mrs Clayton, you may 'set . . . and look out into the high arch, while the coaches are driving over your head'.[20] Now blocked, they are still clearly visible from a boat and even more so from the interior of the spaces they once lit (fig. 214).

What, apart from the saving of weight and money, was the function of these strange speluncar spaces? According to the engraving by P. van Gunst (fig. 205), which shows the complete design, the 'hollow of the Bridge' at ground level was destined to be occupied by 'Grotts etc.' (rendered in the French caption as *Grottes et Fontaines* and in the Latin one as *Cryptae et Fontes*). Grottoes have a long history going back to Antiquity.[21] In the seventeenth and eighteenth centuries they were often constructed in the sides of hills or beneath terraces, and the empty spaces inside the Grand Bridge may well have been planned by Vanbrugh and Hawksmoor as grottoes or nymphaea through which fashionable ladies and gentlemen would wander on warm summer days in the course of a promenade along the banks of the canalised Glyme. Indeed, there is confirmatory evidence of this in the form of a letter that Hawksmoor wrote to the Duchess in 1722, in the course of which he ventured to remind her 'how fine a Grotto may be placed under the bridge finished

212. *following page*: The Grand Bridge, Blenheim: view from one of the openings in the north-west tower, looking south.

214. The Grand Bridge, Blenheim: the underside of the great arch, showing the three blocked-up windows.

with Rocks and Shells and a plentifull command of water', and to suggest that Bernini's fountain might be placed in it, 'being too tender to stand without doors in the Frost and violent weather of this Climate'.[22] A more sympathetic patron than the Duchess of Marlborough might have fallen in with this idea and commissioned not only some rock-work but also an appropriate statue of Thetis, Egeria, Calypso, or even 'Fair Rosamund', presiding over some ingenious water-effects powered by the near-by pumps.

As it is, there is no trace of that rough tufa, or of those patterned shells or glistening spar or quartz with which empty caves or cellars were transformed into magical grottoes. On the contrary, the walls of the large rectangular room on the north side were at some time covered with smooth plaster,[23] and there are clear traces of a collapsed cornice and of some sort of moulding round the arch of the entrance-tunnel on its south side. Was this, perhaps, the 'very large' room which the Duchess sardonically observed might be used 'for a Ball if there were occasion'?[24] As for its southern counterpart, that served as a cold bath, a facility whose value had been emphasised by recent medical opinion.[25] A French traveller called Fougereau who visited Blenheim in 1728 reported that the bridge contained 'deux massifs . . . ou l'on a pratiqué d'un coté un appartement frais pour les bains at de l'autre coté un moulin à l'eau'.[26] The latter was of course the water-pump, which was actually beneath the northern arch rather than in the adjoining *massif*,[27] but Fougereau's reference to fresh-water baths in the southern *massif* is confirmed by an account left by Charles Richardson, a native of nearby Coombe, in which he states that the bridge contained 'a fine bath, the entrance to which is under the small

213. (*preceding page*) The Grand Bridge, Blenheim: view from one of the lower openings in the north-east tower, looking south.

215. The Grand Bridge, Blenheim, engraved view from the west by J. Boydell, 1752 (Bodleian Library, Gough Maps 26, f. 55ᵛ).

south arch and in its north side'. 'I have reason to believe,' he adds, 'that this bath was never used as such owing to the shore [i.e. the sewer] from Blenheim being opposite its entrance.'[28] 'Good accommodations for bathing' are also mentioned as a feature of the bridge in a guidebook of 1748,[29] and some small vents high up in the walls of the southern complex could possibly have been connected with some system of heating now under water.

Whatever facilities the lower spaces provided, they were drowned in 1764 by the rising waters of Capability Brown's lake, which gave the bridge a visual justification that it had previously lacked. No longer would topographers like Defoe or wits like Horace Walpole be able to make quips about a bridge without enough water to justify its existence. What had been the steep sides of a marshy valley were now transformed into 'the bold shores of a noble river'.[30] The loss of the dubious amenities afforded by the interior of the bridge was more than compensated for by the creation of a landscape in which the bridge became the focal point of one of the finest picturesque prospects in Britain.

The flooding of the valley raised the water level by at least fifteen feet. This necessitated some consequential alterations to the bridge. As the pumping engine could no longer function, it was removed, first to 'Queen Elizabeth's Island', and ultimately to Woodstock Mill,[31] and the walls that had screened it (fig. 215) were taken down, opening up the northern arch. In order to protect the foundations and the lower courses of masonry from erosion, the remaining ruins of the manor – already extensively pillaged for rubble with which to build the bridge – were finally levelled to the ground and the stone was 'sunk all round below the foundations at great expense'.[32]

The visual consequences of submerging the lower portions of Vanbrugh's great bridge must have been very much in Brown's mind, and the new water level was calculated with some precision to coincide with the platband between the ground and the first-floor rooms. To allow for seasonal fluctuations in the level of the lake the band was deepened so that it now reads as a plinth extending below water level. At the same time the bold keystones beneath the lower tower windows were removed. On the underside of the great arch the six sloping windows were blocked up with masonry, as were the entrances immediately below them which had led to the rooms in either pier. The floor of the central room on the north side was raised above water level by half filling it with rubble, but the southern one (the former cold bath) found a new use as a boat-house until a new and more convenient one was built on the shore of the lake in 1888.[33] Within, the elegant sequences of interconnected spaces were lost, interrupted either by water or by blocked-up arches, thus creating that 'warren of dark tunnels, oddly shaped rooms and winding stone stairways'[34] that has puzzled those few who have been privileged to explore it ever since.[35]

NOTES

1   K. Downes, *Vanbrugh*, 1977, p. 72.
2   Ibid., pp. 72–3. In a paper criticising the whole scheme, written probably in 1716, Sarah, Duchess of Marlborough, noted that the approach over the bridge was intended to be 'only the way for ourselves to go into the park, and not the way as people come to us from London or Woodstock' (Blenheim Muniment Room, Shelf G, box 10). For the topography of the park in the seventeenth and eighteenth centuries, see the maps in *Victoria County History of Oxfordshire*, xii, pp. 442, 462.
3   L. Whistler, *The Imagination of Vanbrugh and his Fellow Artists*, 1954, pp. 112–13 and Appendix III (this document is now BL, Add. MS 61354, f. 1).
4   *The Complete Works of Sir John Vanbrugh*, iv, *The Letters*, ed. G. Webb, 1928, p. 76.
5   Hawksmoor's account of £45 'For Copper Plates to engrave the plann of Blenheim house . . . and Front of the Great Bridge, and mony disburst to the Engraver' is entered in the Blenheim building accounts under June 1709 (BL, Add. MS 19596, f. 61). A variant form of the engraving is illustrated by David Green (*Blenheim Palace*, 1951), where it is erroneously stated to have been published in *Vitruvius Britannicus*, i, 1717.
6   For the 'Water Engine under the Small North Arch of Blenheim Bridge' see S. Switzer, *Introduction to a System of Hydrostaticks and Hydraulicks*, ii, 1729, pp. 321–2 and *Universal System of Water Works*, 1734. It was capable of raising four tons of water an hour to a height of 120 feet, and was functioning by the end of June 1706 (BL, Add. MSS 19595, f. 20, 19606, f. 5). Screen walls were built on either side of the arch to enclose it, as seen in fig. 215.
7   *The Letters* (as in n. 4), p. 75. She may not always have known exactly what had been agreed between Vanbrugh and her husband. Thus it appears that it was not until September 1711 that she realised that the bridge was intended to have 'four Towers each of which is a little House' (Bodleian Library, MS Top. Oxon. c. 218, f. 56). Yet Vanbrugh had had 'a large drawing' of the Bridge made for the Duke's inspection in August 1710 (*Letters*, pp. 42–3) and the whole scheme had presumably been made public by the print engraved under Hawksmoor's direction in 1709. As late as *c*.1716 the Duchess wrote that she had been told by 'a Man that has looked after the Building of it' (the Bridge) that 'he did not know how many stories there was to be more [in the towers], but he seemed to think two, because that would be necessary to make it look lofty and Great' (Blenheim Muniment Room, as in n. 2).
8   Joynes's reports are in BL, Add. MSS 19608–9, the accounts in Add. MSS 19592–601.
9   BL, Add. MSS 19608, ff. 37, 99, 103, 105, 111, 116, 19609, ff. 9, 10, 15, 19, 20, 34, 35, 40, 41, 45, 46, 67, 80.
10 BL, Add. MSS 19609, ff. 85, 88, 89, 93, 96, 99, 61353 (Travers' reports to Marlborough), ff. 49, 78–9, 107; *The Letters*, p. xxv; David Green, *Blenheim Palace*, 1951, pp. 118–19, 127.

11 BL, Add. MS 61354, f. 29.

12 BL, Add. MS 61354, f. 83. A specification for some further works to be performed by Townesend and Peisley in 1724–5, mostly concerned with watercourses, but including iron railings for the two circular stairs inside the bridge, is in the Berkshire County Record Office (D/ESv (B), F 29/3). The iron railings were never made and the steps of the southern stair have at some date been deliberately destroyed.

13 Bodleian Library, MS Top. Oxon. c. 218, f. 55.

14 R.J.B. Walker, *Old Westminster Bridge*, Newton Abbot, 1979.

15 For Palladio's bridge design see his *Quattro Libri* (1570), Book III, ch. xiii, and Howard Burns, *Andrea Palladio 1508–1580* (Arts Council, London, 1975), pp. 123–8. Well-known designs for 'Triumphal Bridges' or 'Bridges of Magnificence' were made by G.B. Piranesi (1743), Sir John Soane (1779) and Thomas Sandby (*c.*1780). A triumphal arch spanning the roadway like the Roman one still standing at Pola is a feature of the design for a bridge by Vanbrugh which he probably submitted in the Westminster Bridge competition in 1722 (*Architectural Drawings at Elton Hall*, ed. Colvin and Craig, Roxburghe Club, 1964, pl. xxiii b).

16 Letter to Mrs Clayton, probably written in 1716 and printed in W. Coxe, *Memoirs of the Duke of Marlborough*, ed. Wade, iii (1848), pp. 414–15.

17 T. Ruddock, *Arch Bridges and their Builders 1735–1835*, Cambridge, 1979, figs. 4, 49, 52.

18 *Sale Catalogues of Libraries of Eminent Persons*, iv, *Architects*, ed. D.J. Watkin, 1972, p. 103.

19 The plaster, though prior to the rubble filling of the 1760s, is arranged in simple panels whose vertical divisions are unrelated to the lateral openings, which must have been at least partially blocked to accommodate the plaster.

20 Coxe, *Memoirs of the Duke of Marlborough*, pp. 414–15.

21 For grottoes in Antiquity, see H. Lavagne, *Operosa antra*, École Francaise de Rome, 1988, and for more recent ones, Naomi Miller, *Heavenly Caves*, New York, 1982.

22 Printed by David Green, *Blenheim Palace*, 1951, p. 309. For the model for Bernini's fountain in the Piazza Navona in Rome, now in the lower water-terrace garden at Blenheim, see D. Green, 'The Bernini Fountain at Blenheim', *Country Life*, 27 July 1951, pp. 268–9.

23 See note 19 above.

24 In her commentary on the state of the works, probably written in 1716 (n. 2 above).

25 A. Lennard, 'Watering Places', in *Englishmen at Rest and Play 1558–1714*, Oxford, 1931, pp. 74–6.

26 Victoria and Albert Museum Library, MS 86 NN 2, ff. 111–12.

27 A sketch-plan in Fougereau's manuscript in fact shows the pumps in their correct position under the northern arch.

28 Bodleian Library, MS Top. Oxon. d. 173, ff. 176–8. Richardson died in 1827, aged 67 (*Gentleman's Magazine*, xcvii, 1827, pt. 1, p. 571).

29 T. Salmon, *The Foreigner's Companion through the Universities of Cambridge and Oxford and the Adjacent Counties*, 1748, p. 6.

30 T. Whately, *Observations on Modern Gardening*, 1770, p. 78.

31 *VCH Oxfordshire*, xii, p. 466.

32 Charles Richardson in Bodleian Library, MS Top. Oxon. d. 173, ff. 176–8. The carting of rubble from the ruins of the old manor-house is mentioned in the building accounts from 1708 onwards, and numerous fragments of medieval carved and moulded masonry, dating from the twelfth century to the fifteenth, can be seen incorporated in the internal fabric of the bridge.

33 The conversion of the bath into a boathouse is recorded by Richardson as in n. 32.

34 David Green, *Blenheim Palace*, 1951, p. 255. In a letter written to her friend Lady Cairns on 29 Sept. 1721 (BL, Add. MS 61466, ff. 99–102), Sarah, Duchess of Marlborough, tells her of the completion of the bridge, which was 'not to be finished as Sir John intended but only to be made useful to pass over'. 'All those rooms,' she added, 'which he made in the towers . . . are to be stopt up.' No such stopping up is mentioned in the masons' contract of 28 Sept. 1721 (Add. MS 61354, f. 83). Nevertheless it is possible that some of the blockings date from 1721 rather than from 1764.

35 We are grateful to His Grace the Duke of Marlborough, DL, for permission to study the fabric of the Grand Bridge; to his Agent, Mr P.B. Everett, FRICS, and to the latter's assistant, Mr Jonathan Sheppard, for their kindness in facilitating our exploration of its interior, and to Mr Christopher Rayson, FRIBA, for accompanying us on several of our visits, and for providing a set of draft survey plans. For access to a computer for architectural drawing we are indebted to Sir James Dunbar-Nasmith and to his assistant Mr Gordon Piper. Mr Alan Crossley kindly provided several documentary references.

216. Burlington House, Piccadilly, London (*The Builder*, 28 October 1854).

XV

LORD BURLINGTON
AND THE OFFICE OF WORKS

IN 1718, when Sir Christopher Wren was dismissed from the Surveyorship of the Works, the Office of the King's Works had for nearly half a century been the centre of diffusion of the Anglo-baroque architecture which we associate with the names of Vanbrugh, Hawksmoor, Talman and Wren himself. By the 1730s it had become just as closely identified with the Palladian revival of which Lord Burlington was the guiding spirit. How was this revolution in both taste and personnel achieved, and what part did Lord Burlington himself play in the transformation?[1]

In order to answer these questions it is necessary first of all to appreciate that the Civil Service as we know it today is a creation of the nineteenth century. The *laissez-faire* government of the eighteenth century was conducted by a miscellaneous and uncoordinated collection of offices, many, like the Exchequer, medieval in origin and still largely medieval in their operations, others, like the Excise Office or the Lottery Office, the product of more recent financial or administrative expedients. Some were necessary and efficient, others totally useless and anachronistic. Many, but by no means all, were sinecures, and the rewards of office were more often in virtue of the fees and perquisites pertaining to the post than the nominal salaries attached to it. Those posts that were remunerative were generally given to political place-men, who appointed deputies to perform their duties. Whether well-paid or otherwise, absentee or fulfilling his functions in person, the eighteenth-century servant of the Crown was not normally expected to attend more than a few hours a day, a few days of the week, and was free to earn what he could by personal service or private practice. Appointment was by patronage, exercised by the Crown and its ministers in respect of the superior officers, by the superior officers themselves in respect of their underlings.

The Georgian Office of Works was a typical example of this antique but not wholly inefficient bureaucracy. Its responsibilities were limited to the royal palaces, the Houses of Parliament and one or two other buildings, but it was by far the largest and most prestigious concentration of architectural expertise in the country; in fact, since the time of Inigo Jones it had been the heart of the English architectural establishment, and would continue to be so until it fell into disrepute at the hands first of James Wyatt and then of John Nash. Nominally at the head of it was the Surveyor-General of the King's Works, since 1715 invariably a political place-man and the fortunate recipient of an income of some £500, increased in 1726 to £900 a year. The other principal sinecures connected with the Works were the Paymastership, the Surveyorship of the King's Private Roads and the Surveyorship of Gardens and Waters. The real work was done by the Comptroller, the Deputy Surveyor and the Clerks of the Works, one for each palace or group of palaces. The routine of the Office was conducted by a Board consisting of the Surveyor (normally represented by his Deputy), the Comptroller, and men bearing the ancient titles (inherited from the Middle Ages) of Master Mason and Master Carpenter. It was this body that corporately set in motion any works demanded by the Crown through the Treasury or the Lord Chamberlain, that procured the design, engaged the necessary workmen and eventually passed the bills. None of its members were, strictly speaking, professional architects; it was not until 1761 that the existence of an emergent architectural profession was recognised by the appointment of two joint Architects of the Works: William Chambers and Robert Adam. But in the 1720s, the period with which we are concerned, the Comptroller was Sir John Vanbrugh, the Deputy Surveyor was Westby Gill, the Master Mason was Nicholas Dubois and the Master Carpenter was Thomas Ripley: all in practice men of considerable architectural knowledge if not all as able designers as Vanbrugh.

Vanbrugh was a survivor from the great days of Sir Christopher Wren and in no sense a Palladian. But Nicholas Dubois was the translator of Palladio (in Leoni's pioneering edition of 1715–16) and Westby Gill's few recorded architectural works can only be classified as 'Palladian'. Gill certainly, and Dubois probably, owed his place to Sir Thomas Hewitt, Surveyor of the Works from 1719 until his death in 1726. Hewitt, himself an amateur architect, was one of the 'new junta for architecture', which was already trying to steer British architecture in a neo-classical direction before Lord Burlington took charge, so Dubois and Gill were as it were a Palladian advance guard within the Board.

When Vanbrugh and Hewitt both died within a fortnight of one another in 1726 there was, as Hawksmoor told Lord Carlisle, 'prodigious pressing (of) Sir Robert Walpole; by my Ld. Devonshire, Lord Burlington, and many others' on behalf of their own candidates. The man to whom Walpole gave the Surveyorship was the Honourable Richard Arundell, the owner of the Allerton Mauleverer estate in Yorkshire. Arundell had many influential friends, and he did not necessarily owe his promotion to Burlington's good offices. But he would certainly have had Burlington's support, for it was Burlington to whom he was indebted for his seat in Parliament as Member for Knaresborough (he held it from 1720 to 1758). Not only was Arundell a beneficiary of Burlington's patronage. He was a close connection and intimate friend of the 9th Earl of Pembroke, well known as 'the Architect Earl'. He himself was regarded as something of a pundit in matters architectural, and subscribed to works by Leoni, Kent and Ware. So no appointment could have been more favourable to the Palladian cause than Arundell's: and interest and inclination both ensured that he would do his best to oblige Lord Burlington in the exercise of his own patronage within the Office.

As for the Comptrollership, 'Great Endeavours' were made to secure it for

William Kent, but Walpole had reserved this place for a protégé of his own, Thomas Ripley, the carpenter who had married one of his servants, and who had supervised the building of Houghton. Still, Houghton was a Palladian mansion and Ripley could be counted on as a stylistic fellow-traveller, even if he was a poor substitute for Kent. Moreover, Ripley's promotion left vacant the post of Master Carpenter, and this was now offered to Kent. Arundell, anxious to have Kent on the Board of Works, wrote to Burlington to beg him to allow Kent to accept this lesser post: 'They have made my Employment so good by adding 500 pds. per An. to it, that it's impossible for me to decline it & without Kent, that I can depend upon, it will not be very agreeable.' Kent, of course, accepted with Burlington's approval. So by the end of 1726 the entire Board of Works was in the hands of men either actively in favour of Palladianism or at least sympathetic to it.

There remained the Clerkships of the Works. These were in the Surveyor's own patronage; minor posts, it is true, but ones that carried with them modest salaries and official residences and, of course, the expectation of eventual promotion to one of the more prestigious posts on the Board. Eight of them fell vacant in the course of Arundell's Surveyorship, which lasted from 1726 to 1737, and six of them went to men who were sound Palladians. Chief of these was Henry Flitcroft, 'Burlington Harry' as he was called, who in 1726 was given the key Clerkship of the Works at Whitehall, Westminster and St James's. In due course he rose to be Master Carpenter (1746), Master Mason and Deputy Surveyor (1748) and finally Comptroller (1758). But in 1726 Flitcroft was still an obscure ex-joiner who had been taken in hand by Burlington and whose architectural experience was almost entirely limited to acting as his patron's draughtsman. Now the date of Flitcroft's appointment was 4 May 1726 – the same as Arundell's own. But the Clerkships of the Works were normally in the Surveyor's gift, and as we know from a letter written by Arundell to Burlington that he was already in touch with Walpole about another vacancy in the Office (the Comptrollership) some weeks before his own formal appointment, it seems likely that Burlington suggested Flitcroft's name to Arundell and that Arundell then mentioned it to Walpole. Whatever the precise mechanism of patronage may have been in this case, there can be little doubt that it was Burlington who got Flitcroft into the Office of Works, probably with Arundell's help. The same must be true of the appointment in 1727 of Daniel Garrett as Labourer in Trust – a kind of foreman – at Richmond New Park Lodge, where his immediate superior, the Clerk of Works, was none other than Roger Morris. Roger Morris was the architectural adjutant of Arundell's friend, the 9th Earl of Pembroke, and the Lodge itself (the 'White Lodge') had just been built to Pembroke's designs under Morris's direction. But Garrett was another of Burlington's architectural assistants who in 1727 had no independent work to his credit. In 1736, when proposing to bring Garrett to Castle Howard, in order to give advice on the completion of the Mausoleum, Sir Thomas Robinson wrote to Lord Carlisle that 'My Ld. Burlington has a much better opinion of Mr Garret's knowledge and judgment than of Mr Flitcroft's or any person whatever, except Mr Kent, he lives in Burlington House and has had care and conduct of . . . all my Lord's designs he ever gave.' In due course Garrett might have risen to a Clerkship of the Works, but in 1737 he was dismissed for 'not attending his duty'. By now he had begun to build up an architectural practice of his own in the north of England which no doubt proved incompatible with the performance of his duties at Richmond in Surrey.

A scrutiny of the personnel of the Georgian Office of Works shows the names of two other Palladian stalwarts: Isaac Ware and John Vardy. Ware's career in the Office of Works began in 1728 when he was appointed Clerk Itinerant, Vardy's in 1736 when he became Clerk of Works at the Queen's House at Greenwich. As Ware had been apprenticed to Ripley, the Comptroller, in 1721, it is likely that it was the latter who was instrumental in getting him into the Office, but Ware himself is said to have told Roubiliac that he owed his architectural career to a benevolent gentleman who, walking down Whitehall, found him sketching an elevation of the Banqueting House on the pavement with a piece of chalk. Even if the identification of the unknown benefactor with Lord Burlington is probably apocryphal, there are some circumstances in Ware's career that suggest a more elevated mentor than Ripley. We cannot, however, attribute Ware's entry into the Office of Works to Burlington's direct influence, nor can we do so in the case of Vardy, who had close links with William Kent, and was too young to have been a beneficiary of Burlington's patronage.

The exercise of patronage is, of its nature, imperfectly documented. It was a matter of private confabulation, of reciprocal obligations, of tacit but unpublicised understandings. There can, however, be no real doubt that the entry into the Office of Works of all Burlington's architectural protégés, Kent, Flitcroft, Garrett and perhaps Ware, formed part of a deliberate campaign to infiltrate, with Arundell's help, what I have called the heart of the English architectural establishment. From Burlington's point of view the advantages were twofold: on the one hand he was obtaining posts for his protégés, thus providing them with honourable and remunerative but not unduly onerous employment; on the other he was ensuring that future royal buildings would be designed by proved Palladian architects. The Royal Mews at Charing Cross, the Treasury Building in Whitehall, the Queen's Library at St James's, the Horse Guards, were his rewards. All of these buildings were designed by Kent in the Palladian style that Lord Burlington advocated; and as Kent lived in Burlington's household for most of his life it is unlikely that they were designed without his patron's knowledge and approval. There was one other great architectural prize which Burlington nearly secured, and that was a new Palace of Westminster. All through the eighteenth century the idea of rebuilding the Houses of Parliament on a monumental scale was kept alive, and early in the 1730s it came very near to fulfilment. In contemporary journals Lord Burlington's name is repeatedly mentioned in connection with this project, and although the surviving drawings are all in Kent's hand, there can be little doubt that Burlington was in the background, advising and criticising, if not actually drawing.

But in 1733, hurt, it seems, at the King's failure to give him a promised 'white staff' (the symbol of high office in the royal household), Burlington resigned all his posts at Court and went in effect into political opposition. From now on his influence would be at an end. But by 1733 his purpose had been achieved.

Palladians to a man, the personnel of the Office of Works no longer needed his tutelage. Secure in their posts and confirmed in their adherence to Palladian principles, they were architects not only to King George II, but to half the aristocracy of England as well.

APPENDIX

Clerks of the Works appointed during the Surveyorship of the Hon. Richard Arundell (1726–1737):

1726	Whitehall, Westminster and St James's	Henry Flitcroft
1727	Richmond New Park Lodge	Roger Morris
1728 (?)	Richmond and Kew	Henry Flitcroft
1729	Windsor Castle	Isaac Ware
1730	Greenwich (Queen's House)	L. Wooddeson (d. 1733)
1733	Charing Cross Mews	Joseph Phillips
1733	Greenwich (Queen's House)	Isaac Ware
1736	Greenwich (Queen's House)	John Vardy

NOTE

1   This essay is the text of a paper given at a Georgian Group Symposium on 'Lord Burlington and his Circle' in May 1982. All the historical and biographical facts upon which it is based will be found documented in vol. v of *The History of the King's Works* (1976) or in my *Biographical Dictionary of British Architects*. Since it was written a new interpretation has been given to Burlington's resignation of his court offices in 1733 by Jane Clark's claim that he was secretly a Jacobite: see *Lord Burlington. Architecture, Art and Life*, ed. Toby Barnard and Jane Clark, with an introduction by Howard Colvin (Hambledon Press, 1993).

XVI

ARCHITECT AND CLIENT
IN GEORGIAN ENGLAND

THE RELATIONSHIP BETWEEN architect and client has never been an easy one. On the one hand the client is entrusting the expenditure of a large sum of money to another person who may or may not produce the building he wants at a cost he can afford and within a time-scale he can tolerate: on the other the architect is offering a functional and aesthetic concept which perhaps embodies cherished principles of design as well as much hard-won practical experience to someone who may mutilate it by ignorant meddling or ruin it by parsimony.

In Georgian England there were, as there are today, both satisfied and dissatisfied clients, and architects who enjoyed enlightened patronage as well as those who retired hurt from commissions that caused them nothing but frustration. The epic struggle between Vanbrugh and Sarah, Duchess of Marlborough, over the design of Blenheim Palace is well known[1] and at a distance of nearly 300 years we can sympathise with both parties, for if Sarah undoubtedly showed no understanding of Vanbrugh's genius, it is apparent from a reading of the original documents that her high-handed architect was quite capable of altering designs and ordering works at Blenheim without proper consultation.

In the reign of George III Lord Pembroke was only one of many aristocratic clients whose patience was exhausted by the dilatory habits and unbusinesslike methods of James Wyatt.[2] 'When a [new] commission is proposed to him by a Nobleman or Gentleman by whom he has never before been employed,' his nephew Jeffry told the diarist Joseph Farington, 'he will eagerly attend to it till he has got all the instructions necessary for the commencement of the work, but then he becomes indifferent to it, and has lost many great commissions by such neglect.'[3] The letter which Wyatt received from another exasperated client, William Windham of Felbrigg, must be one of the most devastating ever written by a long-suffering client to a delinquent architect.

It is near two years since you undertook a business for me neither requiring, nor admitting of, delay; and which you have not done yet. I have written to you no less than five letters desiring to know, whether you meant to do this, or not: and you have returned no answer. You may perhaps think that this is a mark of genius, and the privilege of a man eminent in his profession: but you must give me leave to say, that it must be a profession higher than that of an Architect, and eminence greater than that of Mr Wyatt, that can make one see in this proceeding anything but great impertinence, and a degree of neglect, that may well be called dishonest.[4]

On the other hand, both Samuel Whitbread, the builder of Southill in Bedfordshire, and Sir George Beaumont, the owner of Coleorton in Leicestershire, were so pleased with the services of their architects, Henry Holland and George Dance the younger respectively, that they were moved to commemorate their satisfaction by inscriptions which in Holland's case pay poetic tribute to 'the labours of thy polished mind' and in Dance's record that he 'has manifested as much friendship, by his attention to the Execution of the work, as he has shown good sense, taste and genius in the Design'.[5]

My purpose in this essay is not, however, to illustrate from eighteenth-century examples those clashes of personality on the one hand, or those harmonious relations on the other, that have always affected the relations between architect and client, but rather to see that relationship in terms of the social and professional conventions of its time. In what ways did the relations between Georgian architect and Georgian client differ from those of the nineteenth and twentieth centuries?

First of all we must remember the physical and geographical constraints that affected architectural practice. In a country without motor-cars, railways, telephones or faxes, the scope for misunderstanding and muddle was enormous. The case of Sir Marmaduke Wyvill, the Yorkshire gentleman who went away for five months, leaving his house to be altered by John Carr of York, and returned to find that 'there had been a mistake' and Carr's workmen had inadvertently pulled down the whole house, was no doubt exceptional,[6] but frantic letters to say that 'the workmen are all at a stand, as not knowing how to proceed one jott farther' for lack of drawings, or that the mason has inexplicably 'lost three feet in one of the fronts'[7] remind us of the difficulty of communication that bedevilled all architectural supervision from a distance and that could so easily embitter relations between an anxious client and an absentee architect.

Often there was a tacit or even an explicit understanding that the architect would visit the site at least once a year, and the diary of the London architect Robert Mylne shows that periodically he set out on a long journey in the course of which he would inspect the slow-moving works at his various commissions in the country.[8] Alternatively, the principal workman, or the clerk of works, if one was employed, might go to London from time to time for instructions. But most communication was necessarily by post, and much depended on the good sense and judgement of the master workmen. As many of these men were quite capable of designing a building themselves, it is easy to see why provincial builder-architects of ability like Smith of Warwick, or Thomas Ivory of Norwich, or Pickford of Derby, were so successful. For they could offer a package, as we should call it — design, supervision and execution — and unlike the architect from London they were only ten or twenty miles away in case of need. For some clients, indeed, it was enough to employ the fashionable London architect just to decorate the interiors of a house designed and executed by an architect-builder. This is one of the reasons why Robert Adam so rarely designed a complete country house, many of his commissions being, as at Hatchlands, Harewood or Croome, for the principal interiors only.

The master builder who designed what he built gained his remuneration mainly from the building contract. The design was an incidental matter for which payment might be expected only if it was not proceeded with. Then, as now, private clients often obtained designs from more than one architect, and in this form the closed competition goes back at least to the early years of the eighteenth century. It was, however, a competition with no rules, and the client would feel himself free to combine features from different designs or even to employ one competitor to carry out another's plans – something that was particularly common in Scotland, where it was not unknown for one architect to provide a design, for a second to be responsible for its execution and for a third to be employed to measure up the completed work.[9] In this way a Scottish client avoided any danger of being exploited by a single builder-architect, but ran the risk of divided responsibility if anything went wrong. Public competition as a way of obtaining designs dates from the latter part of the eighteenth century, but it has never been a method employed by the private client, and it forms a chapter – a fairly scandalous one – in the history of the architectural profession that I cannot attempt to deal with within the limits of this short paper.

Assuming that the client employed what we should call a professional architect to design and supervise the erection of a building either by a contracting master builder or by separate agreements with the various tradesmen, how was that architect remunerated? Remuneration in accordance with a recognised scale of charges is one of the touchstones of professionalism whether in architecture or medicine or law, and in the 1830s the remuneration of architects was one of the first questions to which the newly-founded Institute of British Architects addressed itself in pursuance of its policy of establishing 'an uniformity and respectability in the profession'. In 1845 its Professional Practice Committee recommended that a commission of 5 per cent should be the only recognised remuneration of an architect, 'be the character of the work what it may'. They found that payment on this basis could be traced back as far as 1777, when Sir William Chambers received 5 per cent in connection with the building of Somerset House.[10]

There is in fact abundant evidence that architects had received a 5 per cent commission for their services throughout the eighteenth century. Indeed the practice goes back to the seventeenth century. An abstract of Sir Christopher Wren's account for rebuilding the London City churches after the Great Fire of 1666 shows that Wren and his colleagues Hooke and Woodroffe were paid 'for the management of the whole at 12d per pound for all moneys received and paid'.[11] In 1737, when George Dance was asked by the Mansion House Committee to state what he expected 'for his trouble and care in Surveying, and ordering the intended building . . . he said that the usual allowance was five pounds per cent. on the money laid out.'[12] John Wood of Bath received 5 per cent as architect of Liverpool Town Hall in 1754,[13] James Wyatt charged the same for his work as Shardeloes in the 1770s,[14] and in 1793, when James Lewis modestly asked the Governors of

Christ's Hospital for only $2\frac{1}{2}$ per cent they gave him a gratuity of 100 guineas, observing that 5 per cent 'was the usual charge of gentlemen of his profession upon new buildings'.[15]

But if 5 per cent was the usual charge, it was by no means the only one, and an examination of eighteenth-century building records reveals considerable diversity in the remuneration of architects. Some were content to receive a lump sum which bore no direct relationship to the total cost of the building,[16] others accepted an annual salary in the case of works extending over a long period. In 1730 it was stated in evidence that the architect's fee at Blenheim Palace was '300 a year besides travelling charges', but that 'others [charge] 200 a year, others 5 per cent.'[17] Even if remuneration was on a percentage basis, it might be fixed at anything between 2 and 6 per cent of the total cost. In the same year James Gibbs wrote to the Vice-Chancellor of Cambridge University to say that he was usually paid at the rate of 5 per cent on the total outlay, but that 'out of that respect I have for the University, I only charge the halfe I have from any other person, which is two and a halfe per cent of the whole charge of this building,' that is, the Senate House.[18] In 1720, when he competed for St Martin-in-the-Fields, he was compelled to sign a declaration that he would 'accept of such Reward for his Care pains and Trouble . . . as the Commissioners . . . shall think fit'. What they thought fit was no more than £550, which represented less than $1\frac{1}{2}$ per cent of the total outlay.[19] In 1737 Henry Flitcroft told the committee for rebuilding the church of St Olave, Southwark that 'he would perform his business as a surveyor for 4£ per cent,' while his rival Mr Porter 'offered to perform the same at 2£ per cent'. In view of the 'proved ability' of Mr Flitcroft, the vestry decided to employ him, but then blandly informed him that, 'as they chose him [as] their surveyor, they hoped he would abate somewhat of his proposall.' He replied that he would contract for no less than 4£ per cent; but 'in regard to the parish' he would make a deduction of half per cent, an offer which the parish accepted.[20] On the other hand Nicholas Dubois received a 6 per cent commission for acting as the architect of Stanmer Park, Sussex, between 1721 and 1728, in addition to travelling expenses at the rate of £1 13s. for each journey to and from London. His total remuneration on this basis amounted to £738.[21]

Travelling charges formed a regular part of an architect's remuneration in the case of buildings erected outside London. In 1773 Sir William Chambers informed a client that travelling charges

> are I believe allowed to every Architect of reputation here. I know Mr Wright, Mr Taylor, Mr Adam always charge their Expenses. They have assured me that the article has never been disputed and that excepting some beginners or persons who have not the fortune to be known and are glad on these Accounts to be employ'd on any Conditions, they think travelling expenses are charged by everybody unless in cases of Contract where the profits of the undertaking are supposed to be sufficient to pay all outgoings of this sort.[22]

Some architects charged by the mile, others by the visit or in proportion to the time spent in travelling on behalf of an individual client.

It was the practice for some architects to charge for measuring over and above their commission. In 1795 it was proposed by a committee of the Architects' Club to make a regular charge for measuring in addition to the customary 5 per cent, Soane being the only dissentient.[23] A few years later Henry Holland deposed that 'he was in the habit of charging one, two and two and a half per cent [for measuring] in addition to the usual allowance of five per cent,'[24] but Soane asserted that 'the old-established allowance of five per cent to the Architect or Surveyor' was 'even in these times, an adequate compensation for his best services through all the stages of the work, from the design . . . to the ultimate examination and audit of the accounts of the tradesmen.'[25] He was not alone, for in 1826 the Secretary of the Treasury ascertained that 'upon inquiry of Messrs Soane, Smirke, Cockerell, Seward, Pilkington and Hardwick, they have not in their practice made any charge for measuring the works they have been employed upon, considering this expense to be included in their commission of five per cent.'[26]

However, as the nineteenth century advanced, it became less and less usual for the architect to accept responsibility for the measurement of works carried out under his supervision, for, as the Committee of Professional Practice appointed by the RIBA reported in 1867, 'within the last half century, in consequence of the improvements in many practical points of professional duties originating with the late Sir Robert Smirke, the measuring and bill department has been transferred . . . to the class of measuring surveyors, and is distinctly carried on by them.'[27] Thus the function of the surveyor was at last clearly distinguished from that of the architect, with which it had so long been identified, and architects, though relieved of the onerous if largely mechanical duties of measurement, continued to claim their 5 per cent until the increasingly technical nature of architectural design and supervision was held to justify its increase in 1919.

The general acceptance of 5 per cent as the normal remuneration of an architect in the eighteenth century was only one step towards professional status. The concept of Georgian architects as professional men was still only precariously established in the minds of their clients, for whom most of them scarcely ranked even as gentlemen. Architecture had never been recognised as an academic subject in the English universities, and the fact that so many of its practitioners were involved in the building trades meant that the medieval classification of architecture as a mechanical rather than a liberal art was difficult to shake off. So at Stanmer the Huguenot architect Dubois could be called 'the French son of a bitch' by Henry Pelham's servants,[28] and even Sir William Chambers, a Royal Academician and the Comptroller of His Majesty's Works, complained after a visit to Blenheim Palace that 'I am like the Egiptian Bird who picks the teeth of the Crocodile, admitted and cherished whilst there is any work to be done, but when that is over the doors are shut and the farce is at an end.'[29] The fact that in England so many gentlemen were amateur architects tended no doubt to give architecture a certain degree of respectability, and those gentlemen by birth who became regular architects, like Vanbrugh and Archer, did not lose caste as a result. Robert Adam, whose forebears were minor gentry in Fife, so far succeeded in gaining acceptance in the higher ranks of society that when he died in 1792 his body was buried in Westminster Abbey and the pall-bearers were the Duke of Buccleuch, the Earl of Coventry, the Earl of Lauderdale, Viscount Stormont, Lord Frederick Campbell and William Pulteney of Westerhall.[30]

But for most eighteenth-century architects their relationship to their aristocratic employers was more that of servant to patron than of professional man to client. The idea of patronage, with its implications of subservience on the one side, and of condescension on the other, it not one that appeals to the egalitarian society of the twentieth century. But it operated at every level of eighteenth-century society, and in architecture the search for a wealthy and influential patron was high on every young architect's agenda. If often began in Rome, where clever and ambitious young architects such as Robert Adam, Robert Mylne or John Soane could hope to form the acquaintance of rich young aristocrats on the Grand Tour who were likely to build on their return to Britain. A well-disposed patron might be the making of an architect's career. Writing to Lord Findlater in 1785, James Playfair reminds him of the many architects 'who have accumulated large fortunes in a few years by means of one Patron of Rank. Crunden, Leverton, Holland, and Johnson are all opulent within these ten years by this means, although all of them [he says sourly] possess very slender merits.'[31] Who Crunden's patron was I do not know. Leverton's may have been the Indian nabob, Sir Thomas Rumbold, for whom he designed Woodhall in Hertfordshire. Holland's success stemmed from his employment to design Brooks's Club, a commission that introduced him to a circle of Whig aristocrats which included the Prince of Wales. In John Johnson's case it may have been his work for the Earl of Northampton at Castle Ashby that led to his extensive employment by the Northamptonshire gentry.

Patronage of this sort sometimes had a political bias. Vanbrugh's patrons were nearly all Whigs, Gibbs's largely, but by no means exclusively, Tories. Robert Adam's talents were such as generally to transcend political boundaries, but as a Whig he was never employed in Tory Oxford. Later Sir Robert Smirke had an extensive Tory clientele that included the Prime Minister, Sir Robert Peel.

Benevolent patronage could not only lead to further employment by private recommendation: it could bring the security of salaried office. What Vanbrugh was paid by Lord Carlisle for designing Castle Howard we do not know, but Carlisle was Lord Treasurer, and the office of Comptroller of the Royal Works was Vanbrugh's real reward.[32] In the course of the 1720s Lord Burlington used his influence at Court to infiltrate the Office of Works with his protégés – notably Kent, Flitcroft and Garrett – thus at once providing them with remunerative posts and ensuring that future royal buildings would be designed by Palladian architects.[33] It was to Sir Robert Walpole's patronage that Ripley, the executant architect of his country mansion at Houghton, owed his appointment to the Comptrollership of the Works on Vanbrugh's death in 1726, and when Ripley died in 1758 and Flitcroft took his place, it was by 'the immediate appointment' of the Duke of New-castle (then Prime Minister) that his architect Stephen Wright took Flitcroft's place as Master Mason and Deputy Surveyor.[34] Wright was Newcastle's architect at

Clumber and Claremont, and when, in 1754, the duke gave £500 towards building a new front to the University Library at Cambridge, it was Wright's design that he forced on the unwilling university.[35]

The Office of the King's Works, under the direct patronage of the government of the day, offered the most prestigious posts that Georgian England had to offer to architects. The financial rewards were not enormous, but the senior offices carried with them an official residence in Whitehall or elsewhere, and as daily attendance was not expected, there was time to conduct a lucrative private practice. In London there were other surveyorships – of the Bank of England, the City of London, the East India Company, Greenwich Hospital – that were equally sought after and to which patronage was often the key.

So long as patronage was paramount, there could be no architectural profession as we know it today – no codes of practice nor corporate solidarity, still less any recognised qualifications or system of architectural education. What gradually brought the Georgian system of patronage in architecture to an end was the expanding economy of a country undergoing an industrial and commercial transformation, and the transfer of much hitherto aristocratic patronage to corporations, charities, commissioners (e.g. for new churches) and so forth. Instead of being tied to a party, a family or a region, it was now possible for an architect to specialise, like Mylne in bridges, or like Blackburn in prisons. As J.C. Loudon observed in 1835, 'the time for building palaces, castles and cathedrals is gone by, or nearly so, and that for town halls, schools, museums, libraries, theatres . . . is approaching.'[36] These new types of buildings brought with them a new middle-class clientele of business and professional men and introduced a new era in the relations between architect and client that was to last well into the early years of the twentieth century.

NOTES

1   David Green, *Blenheim Palace*, 1951, tells the story, but Vanbrugh's letters should be read at first hand in Geoffrey Webb's excellent Nonesuch Press edition of 1928.
2   *The Farington Diary*, ed. J. Greig, v, 1925, p. 168.
3   Ibid., iv, 1924, p. 32.
4   *The Windham Papers*, 1913, i, pp. 182–3, letter dated 23 November 1793.
5   *Southill: A Regency House*, ed. Whitbread, 1951, p. 59; inscription at Coleorton.
6   *The Farington Diary*, v, 1925, p. 168.
7   'Letters and Papers relating to the Rebuilding of Combe Abbey, Warwickshire', ed. H.M. Colvin, *Walpole Society* L, 1984, p. 264; British Library, Add. MS 41133, ff. 45–46.
8   A.E. Richardson, *Robert Mylne*, 1955, *passim*.
9   See H.M. Colvin, 'The Beginnings of the Architectural Profession in Scotland', *Architectural History*, 29, 1986.
10 C. Woodward, 'Professional Practice', in *The Growth and Work of the R.I.B.A.*, ed. J.A. Gotch, 1934, p. 118.
11 British Library, Harleian MS 4941, f. 168.

12 S. Perks, *History of the Mansion House*, 1922, pp. 175, 190.

13 J.A. Picton, *Liverpool Municipal Records 1700–1835*, 1886, pp. 158–9.

14 *Shardeloes Papers*, ed. G. Eland, 1947, p. 135.

15 Architectural Publication Society's *Dictionary*, s.v. 'Lewis'.

16 Thus in 1692 Wren accepted £1,000 'for his great Care and paines in Directing and Overseeing the Building of [Chelsea] Hospital and in Stating and Settling the Workmen's Bills relating thereto for ten years past', although the total expenditure was in the neighnourhood of £145,000 (*Wren Society*, xix, pp. 69, 81), and in 1715 the Delegates of the Clarendon Press at Oxford agreed 'to gratifie Mr Hawksmore for his care in drawing and supervising the whole work of the New Printing house', which had cost £6,185, by a gift of £100 (*The First Minute-Book of the Delegates of the Oxford University Press*, ed. S. Gibson and J. Johnson for the Oxford Bibliographical Society, 1943, p. 45).

17 *Vertue Notebooks* (Walpole Society) iii, p. 46.

18 R. Willis and J.W. Clark, *Architectural History of the University of Cambridge*, iii, 1886, p. 55n.

19 Westminster City Archives, MS Minutes of the Commissioners for rebuilding St Martin's Church, f. 27.

20 *The Builder*, ii, 1844, pp. 252–3.

21 Information from the late Arthur Oswald, who had examined the original accounts.

22 British Library, Add. MS 41133. f. 99v.

23 A.T. Bolton, *The Portrait of Sir John Soane*, 1927, pp. 76–7.

24 J. Soane, *A Letter to the Earl Spencer*, 1795, pp. 5–6. James Paine did the same: see his letter to Sir William Chambers stating his professional charges, in British Library, Add. MS 41134, ff. 35–36.

25 Soane, op. cit. Soane gave evidence in 1803 in a case in which R.F. Brettingham was endeavouring to obtain '5 per cent for surveying &c. and 2½ for measuring'. Brettingham lost (*The Farington Diary*, ii, p. 19).

26 J. Noble, *The Professional Practice of Architects*, 1836, pp. 32–3.

27 Report of the Committee of Professional Practice, cited in Architectural Publication Society's *Dictionary*, s.v. 'Measuring'.

28 British Library, Add. MS 33085, ff. 351–2.

29 Heather Martienssen, 'Chambers as a Professional Man', *Architectural Review*, April 1964, p. 281.

30 *Gentleman's Magazine*, 1792 (I), p. 283. All these aristocrats had employed Adam with the exception of Viscount Stormont, who was representing his aged uncle the Earl of Mansfield, Adam's client at Kenwood House.

31 Scottish Record Office, Edinburgh, GD 151/11/32.

32 K. Downes, *Sir John Vanbrugh*, 1987, p. 235.

33 Above, pp. 265–6.

34 J. Mordaunt Crook, 'The Office of Works 1749–1782', in *History of the King's Works*, ed. Colvin, v, 1976, pp. 88–91.

35 Willis and Clark, *Architectural History of the University of Cambridge*, iii, pp. 63–6.

36 Quoted by J. Mordaunt Crook, 'The pre-Victorian architect: professionalism and patronage', *Architectural History*, 12, 1969, p. 72.

XVII

LEASE OR DEMOLISH?
THE PROBLEM OF THE REDUNDANT
COUNTRY HOUSE IN GEORGIAN ENGLAND

SO MANY COUNTRY houses, great and small, have perished during the last sixty or seventy years that the 'demolition sale' may seem as regrettably characteristic of the twentieth century as the urbanisation of the countryside or the destruction of churchyard monuments. Yet the demolition of unwanted houses has been going on relentlessly throughout our history. In the Middle Ages royal houses in particular were constantly being abandoned or demolished at the whim of successive kings or queens. Freemantle (Hampshire) was pulled down in 1276 by order of Edward I; Queen Philippa sold Feckenham (Worcestershire) to the Abbot of Evesham in 1365 for the value of the materials, and Kempton (Middlesex) suffered a similar fate in 1374. When Queen Anne of Bohemia died at Sheen in 1394 Richard II dramatically advertised his grief by ordering the house to be pulled down to the ground. Many more royal houses went in the sixteenth and seventeenth centuries, especially after the Civil War, including Ampthill, Ewelme, Grafton, Havering, Holdenby, Moor Park, Nonsuch, Oatlands, Reading, Richmond, Theobalds and Woodstock.

By the eighteenth century Windsor was in effect the king's only country residence. Elsewhere aristocratic seats proliferated, symbols of the triumph of oligarchy over monarchy. But even they were vulnerable. In 1787, writing to the Duchess of Gloucester in Italy, Horace Walpole reported that 'Claremont [the Surrey seat of the Duke of Newcastle] has just now been sold in parcels, and bought on speculation. Sir Gregory Page's . . . is pulling down; Cannons was demolished a few years ago. Such is sublunary grandeur.' The houses of lesser men were just as expendable. When the Lysons brothers surveyed eight of the English counties for their *Magna Britannia* between 1806 and 1822, they included in several of their volumes a list of former gentlemen's seats which had been pulled down or converted into farmhouses at some time in the past: of these there were 19 in Cambridgeshire, 18 in Cheshire, 24 in Cornwall and 12 in Devonshire. No doubt some of these were long-standing casualties, but demolitions were still not uncommon in the eighteenth and early nineteenth centuries, when so many new mansions were being built. In Buckinghamshire alone, at least a dozen old family residences were pulled down between 1730 and 1830, not in order to rebuild, but because for one reason or another there was no further use for them.★

★ The principal Buckinghamshire houses demolished during these years were Quarrendon (1731–3?), Salden (1738–43), Over Winchendon (1758), Drayton Beauchamp (1760), Haversham (1792), Ascott (Wing) (final demolition *c.*1800), Eythrope (1810–11), Hillesden (1825) and Weston Underwood (1827).

What this essay seeks to explore is the circumstances that lead to country seats becoming redundant and to establish why some houses were demolished while others were sold or let. To understand these circumstances it is necessary to bear in mind the legal arrangements devised to maintain the integrity of a family estate. From the middle of the seventeenth century to the end of the nineteenth most landed estates were governed by a series of legal agreements known as strict settlements. A strict settlement made it possible to tie up the succession to an estate for a generation by ensuring that the titular owner at any time was in fact only a tenant for life with very limited powers to alienate land or to mortgage it. He enjoyed the income, but was not in full control of the capital represented by the landed estate, thus ensuring so far as possible that it would survive mismanagement, a spendthrift owner or a long minority. These settlements could be renewed or dissolved only with the consent of an heir of full age. If an owner died before his son came of age the son might be free to treat the estate as his absolute property. Otherwise a settlement could be broken only by the Court of Chancery or by a Private Act of Parliament. It was usually only the main family estate that was subject to the settlement, so while that remained inviolable, a subsidiary estate might be sold. Capital assets such as buildings and growing timber were normally protected by the settlement and the family mansion would be included. However, as we shall see, the vicissitudes of families were such that by no means every estate was continuously protected by an unbroken series of settlements, and heavy debt, the absence of a male heir and other casualties could lead to the dispersal of the property and the loss of the family seat.

In considering the circumstances which could lead to a family parting with its house permanently or temporarily, we may begin with the *force majeure* of political or financial disaster. In the sixteenth century, especially in the reign of Henry VIII, there were many forfeitures of houses and estates, of which the most spectacular was Wolsey's loss of Hampton Court. After the Restoration these became rare, but involvement in the Jacobite rebellions of 1715 and 1745 did lead to the loss of their estates by many Scots and by a few Englishmen, notably two great Northumbrian landowners, James Radcliffe, 3rd Earl of Derwentwater, who was executed in 1716, and the 4th Lord Widdrington, who was reprieved but lost all his land. Derwentwater's seat was Dilston Hall, near Hexham, Widdrington's Widdrington Castle near Morpeth. The difference between the fates of these two estates is instructive. Because of the terms of a settlement made in 1692, Lord Derwentwater was deemed by the courts to have enjoyed only a life interest in his lands, and it was only that life interest that was forfeited by his attainder. Dilston accordingly passed to his son, a boy who died unmarried in 1731. Unluckily, his heir was his uncle Charles, another Jacobite who had been attainted (though not executed) in 1716. His attainder meant that he could inherit neither title nor estate. So the forfeiture now took effect and the Derwentwater estates fell to the Crown, by which they were given to charity in the form of Greenwich Hospital. Superfluous to the needs of the Hospital, and by then no doubt in decay, Dilston Hall was pulled down in 1765. Lord Widdrington's heir, on the other hand, was not protected by any settlement. Widdrington Castle and its estate were accordingly forfeited in 1716 and were sold in 1720 to the York Buildings Company. The Company sold the estate on to a wealthy victualling contractor called Revell, who lived at Fetcham Park in Surrey and died in 1752. It was his heirs who eventually pulled down Widdrington Castle, which the York Buildings Company had already declared to be 'uninhabitable, save only a small part for the use of the steward of the estate'.

The Scottish Jacobite landowners were usually more fortunate, for in most cases there was no irrevocable forfeiture of their estates. Some were indeeed sold to the York Buildings Company in 1720, but it got into financial difficulties and sold many of the Scottish properties back to the rebels' families at very modest prices. The estates forfeited in 1745 were administered by Commissioners who held them in the name of the Crown until the loyalty of the heirs of men who had been killed at Culloden was demonstrated by their attitude towards the American War of Independence, and in 1784 they were returned. A few mansions in the Highlands had been burned in 1745 by over-zealous Lowland officers in Cumberland's army, but the houses administered by the Commissioners of Forfeited Estates were maintained and the supporting estates kept together. This civilised treatment did much to reconcile the Highlands to becoming part of North Britain and all was forgiven on both sides long before George IV visited Edinburgh wearing Highland dress in 1822.

Catastrophes could, of course, be self-inflicted. Philip, Duke of Wharton, was an extraordinary example of irresponsibility both political and financial. His father having died before he came of age, no settlement had been made to entail the family estates in Westmorland and Buckinghamshire. Wharton was therefore free to mortgage them, and did so in order to live an extravagant and dissolute life. Furthermore, he speculated in the South Sea Bubble and was reputed to have lost as much as £120,000. He might have succeeded his father as a leading Whig magnate, but instead went abroad and became an adherent of the Pretender. He then married the daughter of an Irish colonel in the service of the King of Spain, and was in the Spanish army at the siege of Gibraltar in 1727. For this he was found guilty of high treason and forfeited all his remaining estates. The land and house at Over Winchendon in Buckinghamshire had already been sold to the Duke of Marlborough to pay Wharton's debts, and in 1758 the 4th duke, no doubt finding the house in a state of decay, sold it for demolition.

The demolition in 1791 of the house at Horseheath in Cambridgeshire designed by Sir Roger Pratt for the first Lord Alington was the consequence of financial, though not political, recklessness by its later owners, the 1st and 2nd Lords Montfort. The 1st Lord Montfort, overwhelmed by debt, committed suicide on New Year's Day, 1755. Horace Walpole tells how, after playing cards until one in the morning, he summoned a lawyer 'and executed his will, which he made them read twice over, paragraph by paragraph; and then asking the lawyer if that would stand good, though a man were to shoot himself? and being assured it would, he said, "Pray stay while I step into the next room"; went into next room and shot himself.' The son proved to be as improvident as his father. Having mortgaged the property in 1768, and tried without success to let the house in 1775, he obtained in the following year a Private Act whereby the estate was vested in trustees to be sold. Difficulty was, however, experienced in finding a purchaser, and in 1777 the house was dismantled, everything being sold except the shell, which was finally cleared away in 1792 by a new owner.

The most spectacular case of this kind was that of Sir William Keyte, a Tory gentleman who was for some years MP for Warwickshire, where he had property, but whose ancestral home was at Ebrington, near Chipping Campden in Gloucestershire. In 1716 he acquired a neighbouring estate at Norton, where he built a large baroque house, in which he lived with his wife, the daughter of Viscount Tracy of Toddington, and their three children. In about 1725 his marriage began to break up as a result of his taking his wife's maid as a mistress, and heavy gambling and drinking completed his demoralisation. Finally in 1741, financially ruined, estranged from his family, and deserted even by his mistress, Keyte put an end to his life by setting fire to a pile of linen in the hall and throwing himself onto the pyre. The house (as an observer reported) went up 'like Mount Etna', the interior being almost completely destroyed, while of Sir William nothing was found except a hip and thigh, 'which looked like a loyn of veal burnt very black'. The estate was subsequently sold to Sir Dudley Ryder, Lord Chief Justice, for whom the shell of the house was surveyed in 1749 by the Warwick architect William Hiorne. Hiorne found 'all the outside walls intirely firm and upright' and considered that if 'the floors are properly put in and a well framed Roof on it will be as firm as the first day it was Built'. He and his brother David subsequently drew up a scheme for reconstructing the house with the addition of a Doric portico (fig. 217). However, neither Ryder nor his son Nathaniel chose to rebuild the house and it was at Sandon in Staffordshire that the latter eventually established himself as the first Lord Harrowby. In 1789 the shell of what has ever since been known as Burnt Norton was accordingly demolished, though the surviving seventeenth-century house continues to be used as a secondary family seat.

It is to family problems of a more prosaic kind that the greater part of this essay must be devoted. In what circumstances did ordinary, respectable members of the Georgian aristocracy and gentry find themselves faced with the problem of the redundant country house?

A house might become redundant for one of several reasons. One was the inheritance of a second estate by someone who was already the established owner of a family seat. Thus Thomas Anson, the owner of Shugborough in Staffordshire, who in 1762 inherited the Moor Park estate in Hertfordshire from his brother George, the admiral, promptly sold it in the following year. When, in 1770, Lord Temple, of Stowe in Buckinghamshire, inherited the vast house at Eastbury in Dorset designed by Vanbrugh for his cousin George Bubb Dodington, he first bought more land in Dorset and invited his brother to occupy the house. But when his brother left, he was unable to find a tenant and, needing money for building at Stowe and other purposes, eventually sold most of the Dorset estate and pulled down the great house in 1775 with the exception of one wing and a gateway (fig. 218).

In 1775 Sir Gregory Turner found himself the owner, not only of his father's

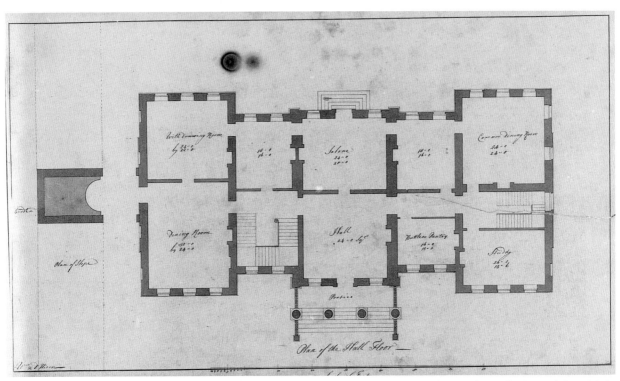

217. Burnt Norton, Gloucestershire: plan and elevation of the burnt-out shell made by William and David Hiorn of Warwick in 1753, with the addition of a portico (Earl of Harrowby's archives).

218. All that is left of Eastbury House, Dorset.

house at Ambrosden in Oxfordshire (fig. 219), but also of Battlesden in Bedford-shire, the property of his deceased great-uncle Sir Gregory Page, and of the latter's huge Palladian house at Blackheath called Wricklemarsh (fig. 220). Preferring to live at Battlesden, he retained the Ambrosden estate, but pulled down the house, which he considered to be unduly large, and sold Wricklemarsh to John Cator, by whom

219. Ambrosden House, Oxfordshire, before its demolition in 1775–9 (Bodleian Library, MS Top. Oxon. a. 37, f. 42).

220. Wricklemarsh, Blackheath, Kent, demolished 1787 onwards (engraving after Samuel Wale in Dodsley's *London and its Environs*, 1761).

it too was eventually demolished. Had he been willing to sell Ambrosden House with the estate, he might have found a buyer for both, but, although probably unconstrained by any settlement, since he had succeeded his father at the age of eighteen, he evidently decided to retain the land without the now unwanted house. As for Wricklemarsh, that was a house without an estate of any size, and when in London Sir Gregory Page Turner, as he now became, understandably preferred a new house in Portland Place by Robert Adam to an old-fashioned Palladian mansion out at Blackheath.

Another contingency that could lead to redundancy was the division of property among co-heiresses. In principle, an estate could be maintained as a unity, only the income being shared, but this presented considerable difficulties, and physical division was more usual, often leading to the sale or demolition of what was now an unwanted house. It was as a result of such divisions that Waldershare House in Kent was sold in 1697 by the heiresses of Monins to Sir Henry Furnese, Chevening in the same county by those of Dacre to the 1st Lord Stanhope in 1717, and Rushton in Northamptonshire in 1828 by the co-heiresses of the last Viscount Cullen to one of the Hopes of Amsterdam. These houses survived in new owner-ship, but similar circumstances proved fatal to the great house at Stowe in North Cornwall built by John Grenville, 1st Earl of Bath, in the reign of Charles II (fig. 221). Its destruction was due to a succession of deaths, one of them self-inflicted. When the Earl died in 1701, leaving the title and estate to his son, the latter inexplicably shot himself, and was buried with his father in the family vault at Kilkhampton. When, ten years later, the grandson died of smallpox at the age of twenty, that was the end of the male line, and the Bath estates were divided among his aunts. The one who inherited the Cornish portion had married Sir George

221. Stowe House, near Kilkhampton, Cornwall, demolished in 1739: copied by John Buckler in 1827 from a lost painting (British Library, Add. MS 36360, f. 167).

Carteret and was the mother of the politician Lord Carteret (d. 1763). The Carterets lived at Hawnes in Bedfordshire and had no use for a remote seat in Cornwall, which they demolished in 1739. The Elizabethan mansion at Salden in Buckinghamshire, built by Sir John Fortescue, Chancellor of the Exchequer (d. 1607), suffered the same fate when it was demolished after a division of the property following the death of the last Fortescue baronet in 1729.

A temporary redundancy might arise when the father died leaving the heir under age. During this period the family mansion was often let, as was Broadlands, for instance, from 1758 to 1760, during the minority of the 2nd Lord Palmerston, the rent being £100 per annum. Hall Place in Berkshire, just across the river from Marlow, built by William East in 1728–35, was let for twenty years (1738–58) during the long minority of his son, but remained in the possession of the family until the middle of the twentieth century.

A family could find itself burdened with surplus houses as a result of acquiring land by purchase, often to expand its nuclear estate. The 11th Duke of Norfolk (d. 1815) bought three small estates adjoining Greystoke, his seat in Cumberland, in order to enlarge his park to 5,000 acres. This was, according to John Martin Robinson, a deliberate challenge to Lord Lonsdale, whose park at Lowther amounted to only 4,000 acres. The houses in question were all small manor-houses which were degraded to the status of farmhouses. The Harlestone estate in North-amptonshire, whose boundaries marched with those of Althorp, was acquired by the 2nd Earl Spencer in 1829 as another piece of territorial aggrandisement. The house, remodelled less than twenty years earlier by Humphry Repton, was let to aristocratic tenants such as Lady Southampton and the dowager Duchess of Grafton, but after the latter's death in 1928, it proved impossible to find another tenant, and according to J.A. Gotch there was a legal difficulty (perhaps a clause in the settlement?) which forbade spending money on its maintenance in the absence of a tenant. Eventually it was pulled down in 1939 by the 7th Earl Spencer, for whom, as for many others in the past, no house was of any consequence but his own.★

A house might sometimes be acquired incidentally as part of a purchase moti-vated primarily by political or financial considerations. Thus in 1775 the Duke of Northumberland bought the Werrington estate in Devonshire and with it the nomination of the four Members of Parliament for the adjoining rotten boroughs of Newport and Launceston. It is safe to conclude that for the duke and duchess holidays in Devon were very much a secondary consideration, but fortunately they did retain the house at Werrington, with its handsome front and interiors evidently designed by some competent London architect in about 1740, and further embel-lished the gallery with portraits of themselves in plaster medallions. Although in 1832 the parliamentary representation of Newport and Launceston was reduced to a single Member, the Dukes of Northumberland kept Werrington until 1864. Another house which went with a rotten borough was Gatton in Surrey. When the Indian nabob Sir Mark Wood bought his way into Parliament by acquiring it in 1801, he does not appear to have taken up residence there, and, as we shall see, from 1808 to 1812 or '13 the house was certainly let to Sir Henry Harpur of Calke Abbey in Derbyshire.

Investment, rather than residence, was what determined the history of Abington Hall in Cambridgeshire throughout most of the eighteenth century. In 1709, through default, the Abington estate became the property of one Thomas Western, to whom it had been mortgaged by its hereditary owner, John Bennet. Western was a wealthy London ironmonger whose son Maximilian was the only member of the family who seems to have had any aspirations to becoming a country gentle-man. After his death in 1754 the house was let and eventually sold to a merchant called Pearson. It was presumably Pearson who built the existing late Georgian house. But in 1800 he resold it to a banker for whom the estate was an investment rather than a country seat. So for many years the house was let, in the 1770s to the immensely wealthy Sampson Gideon, Lord Eardley, to the Earl of Chatham up to 1820, and to the Duke of Wellington's brother Lord Maryborough thereafter. Gideon, the son of a stockbroker, acquired extensive estates in the Cambridgeshire area and sat in the House of Commons as Member for that county from 1770 to 1780, but his purchases were likewise motivated by investment considerations rather

---

★ According to Horace Walpole (*Letters*, ed. Toynbee, iii, p. 446), it was 'lest it should interfere with the family seat, Deene' in Northamptonshire, that the 3rd Earl of Cardigan (d. 1732) pulled down another house he owned at Kirkstall in Yorkshire.

222. Worksop Manor, Nottinghamshire, sketched by Emma Elizabeth Wilmot in course of demolition in 1842 (Mr Robin Fryer).

than by territorial ambition, and it is significant that he rented a house rather than built one for himself. He had, in any case, inherited his father's seat at Belvedere, near Erith in Kent.

Finally, there was the rationalisation of an overextended estate. A good example of this, which led incidentally to the demolition of two notable country houses, is afforded by the 12th Duke of Norfolk. Having inherited in 1815 as the third cousin of the 11th Duke, he was in a position to look at his inheritance with fresh eyes. He decided to enlarge his southern estates at the expense of those in the north Midlands. In 1827 he doubled the Arundel estate by purchasing the Shelleys' family seat of Michelgrove, whose very interesting sixteenth-century house he pulled down five years later, and in 1839 he sold the Worksop estate in Nottinghamshire to the Duke of Newcastle for £375,000. At Worksop was the vast unfinished house designed by James Paine for the 9th Duke, for which its new owner had no more use than its vendor, and in 1842–4 that too was demolished (fig. 222).

The demolition of Kiveton (pronounced 'Keeton'), halfway between Worksop and Sheffield, was the result less of deliberate estate policy than of necessity. By the early eighteenth century the Dukes of Leeds were the paramount landowners in south Yorkshire, with their seat at Kiveton, built by the first Duke in 1694–1704 to the designs of an as yet unidentified architect, whose very grand baroque interiors boasted ironwork by Jean Tijou, painting by Louis Laguerre and wood-carving by Jonathan Maine (fig. 223). His descendants' finances were severely strained by the

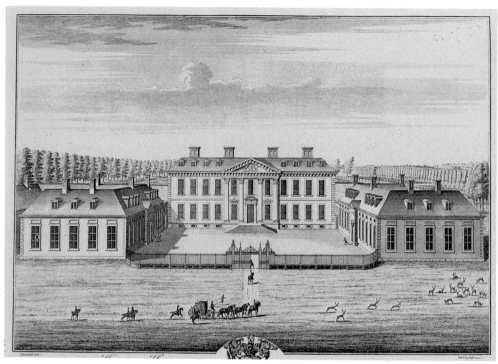

223. Kiveton House, Yorkshire, the seat of the Duke of Leeds, demolished in 1812 (engraving in Badeslade and Rocque, *Vitruvius Brittanicus volume the Fourth*, 1739, pls. 11–12).

longevity of the 3rd Duke's widow (she was his third wife), who enjoyed her jointure of £3,000 a year for no less than sixty-three years. This represented not far short of one-third of the annual income of the entire estate. No wonder that in 1756 Horace Walpole should describe Kiveton as 'an ugly neglected seat of the Duke of Leeds' (though with 'noble apartments and several good portraits'), and that when in 1778 the duke's eldest son inherited Hornby Castle through his marriage to the heiress of the last Earl of Holderness, Hornby replaced Kiveton as the family's Yorkshire seat. By then Kiveton was probably unfit to be let and was pulled down in 1812, no doubt to take advantage of the high price of building materials, especially timber, then prevailing owing to the Napoleonic Wars.

Looking at these cases of selling and leasing and pulling down from the point of view of their owners' wealth and standing as landowners, one can see that the really and persistently rich – such as the Buccleuchs, Carlisles, Devonshires, Norfolks, Northumberlands – could afford to acquire or shed subsidiary seats as the need arose without ever endangering their main estate. They could even have more than one capital seat – Boughton and Drumlanrig, Castle Howard and Naworth, Chatsworth and Hardwick, Greystoke and Arundel, Alnwick and Syon, none of which (so far as I am aware) were ever let. From time to time a subsidiary seat might be bought or sold or demolished, but (with the notable exception of Kiveton) few of the grandest houses were ever in serious danger. Even among the less rich, multiple houses were still quite often listed in *Burke's Landed Gentry* in the nineteenth

286

century. One does not know how many of them were let or occupied by other members of the family, though this could no doubt be ascertained by diligent inquiry. But, as we have seen, secondary seats were naturally the first to go when money was needed or maintenance became a burden. Those in serious difficulty who had only one seat might in the last resort lose even that, as the Andrews did at Harlestone and the Bennets at Abington. But the will to retain an ancestral home could be strong. One house that has remained in the possession of the same family despite being let for the greater part of the nineteenth century is Broughton Castle in Oxfordshire, the seat of the Lords Saye and Sele since the fifteenth century. Broughton was regularly let at least from 1810 onwards, but the family's finances were temporarily improved by the marriage in 1794 of the 14th Lord to one of the daughters and co-heiresses of that Sampson Gideon, Lord Eardley, whose wealth we have already noted. On the latter's death in 1824 Lady Saye and Sele inherited a substantial amount of land in Lincolnshire and (for her life and that of her son) the Gideon seat at Belvedere in Kent, where she and her husband lived in preference to Broughton. Their son the 15th Lord proved to be a fashionable spendthrift, but despite further lettings in the late nineteenth and early twentieth centuries, the 21st Lord Lord Saye and Sele is still at Broughton today.

What were the mechanics of letting? In the eighteenth and early nineteenth centuries the chief medium for advertising that a country house was to let seems to have been the major regional newspaper, such as the *Hampshire Chronicle*, the *Norfolk Chronicle*, the *Norwich Mercury*, *Jackson's Oxford Journal* or the *Yorkshire Gazette*. In the late nineteenth and early twentieth centuries it is said to have been common for the letting of country houses to be advertised on the notice-boards of the London clubs, and in the early twentieth century many advertisements to let, as well as to sell, appeared in *Country Life*. At all times, no doubt, the 'grapevine' of private information was important.

In Norfolk between 1771 and 1824 at least twenty mansion houses, besides a number of villas and smaller country residences, were advertised for letting in the local newspapers, including Bixley, Hethel, Honingham, Oxburgh, Rackheath and Rainthorpe Halls, and in Suffolk, Baston and Brandon Halls, Oakley House and Oulton High House. Some were offered furnished, others unfurnished, some with the whole estate, but most with only the gardens, though often with shooting over a wider area. Shooting, in fact, seems to have been the chief reason for taking a house in Norfolk. In September 1802 the *Bury and Norwich Post* had a news item: 'Lord Paget has hired the Mansion and Manor, late Mr Colhoun's, at Wretham, for a sporting residence. – Sir George Wombwell Bart. also occupies Hilborough Hall.' In the Midlands hunting rather than shooting would have been the incentive, and here there were several smaller houses, without land attached, which were regularly lent or let for hunting purposes. Such were Stroxton Hall and Hanby Grange, both near Grantham, and, at least in the 1830s, Lowesby Hall in Leicestershire. Pitsford Hall in Northamptonshire, the property of the Money Kyrles of Much Marcle in Herefordshire, was in the early nineteenth century regularly let to a succesion of Masters of the Pytchley Hunt, while Quorndon Hall in Leicestershire, having been first rented and then bought in the middle of the eighteenth century by Hugo

Meynell, the founder of the Quorn, was subsequently passed down, apparently by sale, from one Master to another, until in 1856 Lord Stamford, himself a Leicestershire landowner with his own seat in the county, took over the mastership of the hunt and the house was sold to a businessman.

In the Home Counties round London the reason for having a secondary seat, or leasing someone else's, was often social. It was a base from which one could to some extent enjoy the amenities of both town and country life. It was for this reason that, as Hasted wrote of north-west Kent, it was 'interspersed throughout with handsome seats and buildings, mostly inhabited by persons of fashion and opulence'. Here my chief witness is that very unsociable person, Sir Henry Harpur (later Crewe) of Calke Abbey, Derbyshire. Although he hated society to such an extent that in Derbyshire he was known as the 'isolated baronet', he was a man of sensibility and taste who wanted to be able to visit shops and theatres and exhibitions in London, provided that did not involve him in entertaining or being entertained. So he sold the Harpur family house in Grosvenor Street, but regularly hired a country house near London. Before doing so he inquired minutely into its amenities, employing agents to inspect eligible properties and provide him with plans and often with elevations as well. It is from this source that we discover just how many houses were available to let in and around London in the early years of the nineteenth century. As the Norfolk advertisements make clear, to view a house one had to get a ticket from the solicitor or agent, and a number of these are preserved among the Harpur Crewe papers. So are his agents' bills for inspecting properties to let. Here are some extracts from a bill submitted for inspections carried out between June and December 1816:

June 6   To going to Lord Ellenborough's at Roehampton to ascertain respecting the House to let &c.

7   To Journey to Wandsworth to view Mr Morris House &c. to Tooting Common, Vicinities, &c.

10   To journey to Eltham, to Foots Cray, Chiselhurst and Vicinities and to Beckenham to view Rectory House, &c, &c.

11   To making Sketched Plans of House at Beckenham, &c.

12   To journey to Putney Heath, to Roehampton & Vicinity to mark the surrounding roads, and to take particulars of Lord Ellenborough's House, &c.

17   To Coach Hire to Old Brompton to view Lady Fleming's Villa

18   To my journey to Ham Common about Sir P. Sinclair's house, to Ewell, to Sutton Common about Mr Kinnersley's, to Carshalton & Vicinities

22   To Journey to Croydon, to Bromley abt. Mr Harrison's House, Wigmore; to Eltham, to Shooters Hill about Shrewsbury House & Vicinities.

26   To Journey with Mr. Smith to Dulwich to view Mr Evans' House, to Norwood, Bloomfield House & Vicinities.

29   To going to Knightsbridge to view Mr Erskine's House, sketching Plans & round by Fulham searching.

And so it goes on to the end of the year, when the agent submitted an account amounting to £54 5s. od. for 'my various Attendances and applications from June to December at various Offices and to different Persons respecting Country House, prosecuting Enquiries, framing advertisements, writing about 60 various letters in correspondence with you and others respecting Houses, &c. &c.'

Sir Henry appears to have taken none of these particular houses, but in the 1790s he leased Stone House, near Margate, and from 1801 to 1805 Stourfield House near Christchurch in Hampshire. In 1808 he took Gatton Park in Surrey for four or five years, and from 1812 to 1815 he had May Place near Dartford as well. In 1818 his choice fell on Mereworth Castle, but in the following year he removed to Barham House near Elstree in Hertfordshire. At Stone House and at Stourfield ('a neat mansion, with sylvan grounds, on an acclivity overlooking Pool Bay') the attraction must have been the seaside rather than the metropolis, but numerous bills for coach-hire show that visits to London were a regular feature of his summer holidays in the south of England, and it was while driving a carriage from Marylebone to Barham House in Hertfordshire that there occurred the fatal accident that terminated his life on 5 February 1819.

Another regular leaser of country houses until he had one of his own was Sir Robert Peel. In 1818 he took Cluny Castle in Scotland for six weeks or more, in 1821–2 Lulworth Castle in Dorset, and in 1827 Maresfield House in Sussex. In fact it is clear that, at least in areas with either sporting, social or scenic attractions, the practice of letting country houses was general. One is reminded, too, that two of Jane Austen's novels, always a good guide to contemporary social practice, begin with leases of this sort: in *Pride and Prejudice* it is the letting of Netherfield Park that brings the eligible Mr Bingley into the Bennets' life, and in *Persuasion* Sir Walter Elliot, under the necessity of economising, is finally persuaded to let Kellynch Park to an Admiral, 'who having acquired a very handsome fortune, was wishing to settle in his own country [Somerset], and had come down to Taunton in order to look at some advertised place in that neighbourhood'.

To be let, for a longer or shorter period, furnished or unfurnished, was therefore part of the history of many British country houses, from family seats like Broadlands, Lulworth, Heythrop and Tixall, or grand villas like Mereworth in Kent or Duddingston near Edinburgh, all of which were let in the late eighteenth or early nineteenth centuries, down to innumerable smaller houses and villas, including parsonages belonging to non-resident clergymen. Only in the twentieth century, for reasons beyond the scope of this essay, has leasing, rather than demolition, subdivision or conversion to other than residential purposes, ceased to be a common solution to the problem of the redundant country house.

APPENDIX

Sources and Bibliography

For the strict settlement and every aspect of the sale, acquisition and inheritance of estates in the eighteenth and nineteenth centuries, the essential work is Sir John Habakkuk, *Marriage, Debt and the Estates System, English Landownership 1650–1950* (Oxford, 1994). Sir John has been kind enough to make some very helpful comments on a draft of this paper.

For the demolition of royal houses see *The History of the King's Works*, ed. H.M. Colvin, ii (1963) and iv (1982), *passim*.

The papers of Sir Henry Harpur (later Crewe) are in the Derbyshire Record Office (especially D 2375/89/2) and are quoted by kind permission of Miss Airmyne Harpur-Crewe.

For the hiring of houses by (Sir) Robert Peel, see N. Gash, *Mr Secretary Peel* (1961), pp. 237, 269, 270.

For the extracts from the Norwich newspapers I am indebted to Mr David Cubitt.

The principal sources for the vicissitudes of the houses mentioned in the text are:

Abington Hall, Cambs.: *VCH Cambridgeshire*, vi, p. 6.

Ambrosden House, Oxon.: *VCH Oxfordshire*, v, pp. 15–18.

Broughton Castle, Oxon.: *VCH Oxfordshire*, ix, p. 91; Habakkuk, *Landownership*, p. 386.

Broadlands, Hants.: B. Connell, *Portrait of a Whig Peer* (1957), pp. 23, 27.

Burnt Norton, Glos.: *Gentleman's Magazine*, xliv (1774), pp. 171–2; Edward Malins, 'Norton Hall', *Garden History*, vii(1), 1979, pp. 78–85.

Dilston Hall, Northumb.: *History of Northumberland*, x (1914), pp. 286–96.

Eastbury House, Dorset: John Beckett, *The Rise and Fall of the Grenvilles* (1994), pp. 54–7.

Gatton Park, Surrey: E.W. Brayley, *Topographical History of Surrey* (1841–8), iv, p. 311; *History of Parliament: the Commons 1790–1820*, ed. R.G. Thorne, ii (1986), p. 380.

Greystoke Castle, Cumberland: J.M. Robinson, *The Dukes of Norfolk* (1982), p.177.

Hall Place, Berks.: *VCH Berks.*, iii, pp. 156–7.

Hanby Grange, Lincs.: Joan Wake, *The Brudenells of Deene* (1953), p. 221.

Harlestone Hall, Northants.: Habakkuk, *Landownership*, pp. 382–3; J.A. Gotch, *Squires' Homes . . . of Northamptonshire* (1939), p. 36.

Horseheath Hall, Cambs.: Catherine E. Parsons, 'Horseheath Hall and its Owners', *Proceedings of the Cambridge Antiquarian Society*, xli (1948).

Kiveton Hall, Yorks.: Habakkuk, *Landownership*, pp. 84–5; P. Roebuck, *Yorkshire Baronets 1640–1760* (1980), p. 307.

Lowesby Hall, Leics.: W.C.A. Blew, *The Quorn Hunt and its Masters* (1899), p. 177.

Michelgrove, Sussex: *VCH Sussex*, vi(1), p. 13; Habakkuk, *Landownership*, p. 390.

Moor Park, Herts.: Habakkuk, *Landownership*, p. 393.

Over Winchendon, Bucks.: *Dictionary of National Biography*, s.v. 'Wharton'; Habakkuk, *Landownership*, pp. 380–1; J.J. Sheahan, *History and Topography of Buckinghamshire* (1862), p. 440.

Pitsford Hall, Northants.: *VCH Northants.*, ii, p. 361.

Quorndon Hall, Leics.: W.C.A. Blew, *The Quorn Hunt and its Masters* (1899), pp. 82, 129, 234, etc.

Salden House, Bucks.: *VCH Bucks.*, iii, pp. 401–4; *Records of Bucks.*, i (1854), p. 97.

Stowe House, Bucks.: John Beckett, *The Rise and Fall of the Grenvilles* (1994).

Stowe House, Cornwall: M. Trinick, 'The Great House at Stowe', *Journal of the Royal Institution of Cornwall* (1979). For the site see *Cornish Archaeology*, 32 (1993), pp. 112–27.

Stroxton Hall, Lincs.: *The Letters of Daniel Eaton*, ed. Joan Wake and D.C. Webster (Northants. Record Soc. 1971), p. xlix and *passim*.

Werrington Park, Devon: Habakkuk, *Landownership*, pp. 394–5; *History of Parliament: The Commons 1790–1820*, ed. R.G. Thorne (1986) ii, pp. 65–6, 74.

Widdrington Castle, Northumberland: J. Hodgson, *History of Northumberland*, ii(2) (1822), pp. 239, 244–5.

Worksop Manor, Notts.: Habakkuk, *Landownership*, p. 390; B. Connell, *Portrait of a Whig Peer* (1957), p. 427; Marcus Binney in *Country Life*, 15–22 March 1973, pp. 678–82, 750–3.

Wricklemarsh, Kent: Habakkuk, *Landownership*, pp. 430–1; *Hasted's History of Kent*, ed. H.H. Drake, i (Hundred of Blackheath) (1886), p. 125.

XVIII

WRITING A BIOGRAPHICAL DICTIONARY OF
BRITISH ARCHITECTS★

IT WAS IN 1938 or 1939 that the idea of writing a biographical dictionary of English architects – or something very like it – first occurred to two students of History at University College London: David Young and myself. My interest in architecture went back almost to my childhood. At first it was mainly medieval buildings that appealed to me. As a schoolboy I was a great visitor of churches, castles and ruined abbeys both in my native Kent and in Derbyshire, where I was a boarder at Trent College, a minor public school midway between Nottingham and Derby. Fortunately Trent took only one game (rugby football) seriously, and in the summer I was allowed to opt out of cricket and bicycle round the Midland countryside in search of medieval architecture. It was in the Market at Derby that I made my first purchases of architectural books, from the stall of a bookseller called Frank Woore, whose main shop was in Nottingham. Some fifteen years earlier John Summerson had done the same on trips to Derby from his prep school at Matlock – the 'unromantic castle' of his collected essays. By the late 1930s I had begun to appreciate the classical architecture of the seventeenth and eighteenth centuries and found a kindred spirit in David Young. David Young was an odd, diffident man whose ineffectual career ended in his working as an agricultural labourer in Norfolk, but he was a keen student of Georgian architecture and my earliest ally in investigating its history. The Georgian Group had been founded in 1937, but we had no contact with its members, or indeed with anyone else with similar architectural tastes. Needless to say, architectural history formed no part of the curriculum in the History Department at UCL.

David and I soon began to realise the deficiencies of what John Summerson, perhaps rather unkindly, called 'the muddled vapourings which passed for architectural history between the wars'. Unlike Summerson, we did not then appreciate to what extent those shortcomings were due to ignorance of continental art-historical scholarship, but as budding historians we did realise that the factual basis of English architectural history was hopelessly amateurish, and we concluded that the way to remedy the deficiency was to apply to architecture the ordinary processes of historical scholarship that we were learning in the History Department at UCL. At that stage what we had in mind was a handbook which, though chiefly bio-

★ Based on a talk given at a party held in 1995 to launch the third edition.

graphical, would also provide information about selected types of buildings, such as villas or prisons or Palladian bridges. There were also to be dated plans of some important buildings like Greenwich Hospital. It was to be a reliable work of reference for the architectural history of England from the seventeenth to the early or mid nineteenth century, based throughout on the relevant printed and documentary sources. The realisation of our scheme was interrupted, first by the necessity of getting our respective degrees, and then by the Second World War.

So far as I was concerned, the war proved rather less inimical to the progress of the handbook than might have been expected. One basic requirement was a copy of the Architectural Publication Society's celebrated *Dictionary*, a rare and expensive work published in parts between 1852 and 1892. Batsford's, then the leading architectural booksellers in London, had a set, and, fearful of losing their stock in the Blitz, sold it to me for a bargain price. Even a two-year stint in an embattled Malta was not wholly unproductive. Not only did it introduce me to Mediterranean Baroque. In Valetta there were then three libraries: the Royal Malta Library founded by the Knights in the eighteenth century, the Garrison Officers' Library founded by the British in the nineteenth century, and the British Institute Library maintained by the British in the twentieth century, all of which remained open and all of which fortunately escaped damage. From my point of view the most useful was the Garrison Officers' Library, which catered for military gentlemen of literary and antiquarian tastes who could solace themselves in exile by reading books such as Horace Walpole's *Letters* and Nichols's *Literary Anecdotes*, both primary sources, of course, for the study of English culture in the eighteenth century. And not only such literary sources as these: to my surprise I found many essential architectural books ranging from Stuart and Revett's *Antiquities of Athens* to Loudon's *Encyclopaedia of Cottage, Farm and Villa Architecture*. These had evidently been acquired for the benefit of the Royal Engineers, who in the nineteenth century formed an important element of the British garrison, and were responsible both for the maintenance of the fortifications and for new buildings such as the neo-classical Main Guard in Valetta. So it was in the rather curious context of a beleaguered Mediterranean island that I first discovered some important sources for English architectural history. By the time I returned to England in 1943 I had done quite a lot of the basic reading in printed sources.

By the end of the war David Young had effectively dropped out of the enterprise, but academic posts, first at UCL (1946) and then at Oxford (1948), gave me time to pursue architectural history alongside the medieval history which I taught, until in 1965 my architectural interests were officially recognised by a personal Readership in Architectural History. Before the end of the war I had been to the Soane Museum and met its newly-appointed Curator, John Summerson, whose help and encouragement were of enormous importance. He introduced me to Jock Murray, who had already had the idea of publishing a dictionary of English architects to cater for the new interest in architectural history. The contract was signed in 1949 and the first edition was published in 1954.

The first edition was, of course, extremely imperfect, but getting the basic biographical facts into print provided a nucleus of properly authenticated information upon which others could build besides myself. Its purpose was, in any case, almost as much negative as positive. One of my chief aims was to discourage the kind of irresponsible attributionism that had been so prevalent in the past. Sir Albert Richardson, then head of the Bartlett School of Architecture, was a prime offender. Seeing himself as an architectural Berenson, he signed certificates of authentication which one used to find hanging in churches and country houses. Anything at all baroque was apt to be given to Hawksmoor, anything elegantly neo-classical to Henry Holland. My *Dictionary* helped to put an end to what I described in the foreword as 'the widespread but unscholarly habit of attributing even the most commonplace buildings to one or two well-known architects of the appropriate period'.

The second edition of 1978 was a much more considered affair. It also extended the coverage chronologically to its logical starting-point at 1600 instead of 1660, thus bringing in Inigo Jones, and topographically to Scotland. My move into Scotland was at the invitation of a group of Scottish architectural historians which included David Walker, Kitty Cruft and Colin McWilliam. Their help in initiating me into the mysteries of Scottish archives – so different both in character and in vocabulary from English ones – was invaluable, and the kindness first of Alistair Rowan and then of Alan Tait in lending my wife and myself their respective houses enabled me to get to grips with the great accumulations of records, both public and private, in the Register House and the National Library, as well, of course, as familiarising myself with Scottish architecture.

The third edition (1995) breaks no new ground, but, thanks largely to Tom Lloyd, it does justice for the first time to local Welsh architects, and it has, I hope, kept pace with the enormous amount of research that has gone on in the intervening years. A great many scholars have contributed to it directly or indirectly and I am immensely grateful for the generosity with which many of them have sent me news of their latest discoveries, often well before publication. This is perhaps the place to say that, although the *Dictionary* has assimilated a great deal of other people's work – always, I hope, with proper acknowledgement – its form and content have always been those that I have chosen to impose upon it. Had individual architects been given to others to write, some of the articles would no doubt have been better, others possibly worse. But collaborative works are notoriously difficult to bring to the point of publication, and consistency is not easy to enforce on others, so I have no regrets about writing every entry myself. I would not like to assert that there are no inconsistencies, but I believe they are very few. One of my nightmares is to discover that I have inadvertently given the same building to two different architects!

One aspect of the book that I hope has been kept strictly under control is the stylistic attributions. Attributions on stylistic grounds are perfectly legitimate provided they are responsibly made, but the prime object of the *Dictionary* was to provide a firm basis of properly ascertained fact uncompromised by the sort of irresponsible attributions mentioned above. So such attributions as I have admitted are all in my judgement very strong ones, often supported by historical as well as stylistic evidence, and they are always clearly indicated as such. In the first edition there were sixty such attributions. Of these fourteen had been confirmed (by documentary evidence) by 1978 and only three proved to be wrong. In the second edition there were 128 such attributions, of which fourteen have since been confirmed and twelve abandoned (though not necessarily shown to be wrong).

Writing a dictionary of this sort depends very much on serendipity – on noticing an interesting house among the advertisements in *Country Life*, on accidental discoveries made while looking for something quite different, on drawings briefly exposed to view at Sotheby's or Christie's, and so on. But, however opportunist in practice, my research has always had an underlying strategy. That strategy has been, before writing a single biography, first, to concentrate on exploiting all the major sources of architectural information in turn (by major sources I mean such things as the catalogues of exhibitors at the Royal Academy and other societies of artists, contemporary periodicals such as Loudon's *Architectural Magazine*, the *Builder* and the *Gentleman's Magazine*, the major collections of architectural drawings at the RIBA, Soane Museum, Victoria and Albert Museum, National Monuments Record of Scotland, Register House, etc.) and second, to identify as far as possible the authorship of certain categories of important buildings such as churches, town halls and country houses, whether surviving or demolished. In this way, the names of many hitherto unknown architects were discovered which would never have come to light had my research proceeded on a purely biographical basis.

Some of the sources in question were of course printed, and I was lucky to start work at a time when many of the books in question could be acquired for ridiculously low prices. I have already mentioned the *APS Dictionary*. Other essential acquisitions were the early volumes of the *Builder* and sets of Pigot's and other directories from which the names and addresses of architects and their clients could be ascertained. So little were such books valued in the fifties that the bookseller from whose catalogue I ordered the first fourteen volumes of the *Builder* rang me up to make sure that I really wanted to pay the postage on this to him almost worthless periodical.

But most of the basic sources were in manuscript, and were to be found in the British Museum (now the British Library), the National Libraries of Scotland and Wales, the Public Record Office and the Scottish Register House, and in the new County Record Offices that were established after the war, with many of whose archivists I established friendly relations. Few of these sources had ever been used by anyone interested in architectural history, and the excitement of discovery was enough to sustain me in many tedious searches through long unindexed lists in record offices or the contents of piled-up boxes in private muniment rooms. In the Public Record Office, for instance, I found that there was something called the Chancery Masters' Exhibits (papers produced in evidence in Chancery lawsuits, but never reclaimed by their owners), which when I first gained access to them were an almost unknown archive, or rather collection of archives, housed with, but legally not part of, the Public Records, and which proved to include, among much else, such treasures as the business letter-book of Mrs Coade's artificial stone manufactory and the records of the commissioners for rebuilding the town of Warwick after its destruction by fire in 1694.

In the 1940s and 1950s many more of the documentary sources for British architectural history were still in private hands than is the case today, and then, as now, a good deal of diplomacy was needed to get into private muniment rooms. For, as a Cheshire historian called Stewart-Brown wrote in 1912, 'the history of celebrated or interesting private places frequently lies buried in collections of deeds and documents either hard to come at, ill-arranged, carelessly guarded, churlishly hoarded, or lost for ever.'[1] Here my great ally was Rupert Gunnis.[2] Well-connected and well-liked in aristocratic circles, he rarely failed to get access to the muniment room of any eligible country house, where his search for sculptors and mine for architects went hand-in-hand. Research with Rupert was a continuous adventure – social as well as historical – and as he never believed in booking hotels one never knew whether one was going to spend the night (as we did once) in a former railway-carriage in the middle of a field in Lincolnshire, or (on another occasion, when every bed in York was taken) at Castle Howard. Rupert himself had a magnificent library in his house in Tunbridge Wells, and visits there, surrounded by sculpture bought for a song or given to him – like some porphyry busts of Roman emperors which he found in a chicken-run at Goodwood – by their uncaring owners, were immensely profitable and enjoyable. In return for friendly recommendations, Pratley, the Tunbridge Wells bookseller, allowed Rupert to buy any book he wanted for a nominal sum. This privilege was extended to me as Rupert's guest, and every visit to Tunbridge Wells resulted in a car-load of books for my own library.

In approaching the aristocracy in those days a visiting card was essential and a Christ Church tie was a great help. The former I had but the latter I was not entitled to wear. Luckily my other ally in getting access to private archives was. This was Lawrence Stone, later a Professor at Princeton, then a History Tutor at Wadham, as I was at St John's. He was collecting material for his book *The Crisis of the Aristocracy*, and our archival objectives often coincided. Not only did Lawrence wear a Christ Church tie on suitable occasions: he also drove an enormous black sports car in which we made a dashing entry into the courtyards of Arundel, Belvoir, Castle Ashby and other great houses whose papers we wanted to examine. Another student of country-house architecture was Arthur Oswald, the most scholarly of the *Country Life* team at a time when that magazine was a more important vehicle for architectural research than it is today. He and I met regularly for lunch at Rules Restaurant in Maiden Lane to exchange information.

For church archives I hunted in collaboration with the Revd B.F.L. Clarke, the author of *Church Builders of the Nineteenth Century*, whose knowledge of English parish churches was encyclopaedic and whose visual memory of them was remarkable. He could sketch virtually any church he had ever seen on the back of an envelope. Ecclesiastical archives in those days – I am speaking of the late forties and fifties – were often in a deplorable state. Only two lots of diocesan archives were freely available to students – those of Lincoln and Oxford. The Chancellor of the diocese of London was the sworn enemy of historians and would not admit a Regius Professor of Ecclesiastical History to the records in his care, let alone a mere don like myself. The records of the Incorporated Church Building Society (a most important source for nineteenth-century church building) were in total chaos in a filthy cellar in Queen Anne's Gate, and many parish records were in no better case.

In 1949 I found the verger of Malmesbury Abbey tearing out pages from the churchwardens' accounts to light his pipe, and many other vestry minutes and churchwardens' accounts were lying about in unlocked parish chests or in the cellars or attics of rectories and vicarages. Much coaxing was sometimes needed to discover the whereabouts of long-forgotten parish documents that might reveal the name of an architect employed in the eighteenth or early nineteenth century.

I forbear from wearying you with further horror stories – of drawings being filched from the Dean of Guild records in Edinburgh, of funerary monuments to architects being destroyed, on one occasion literally before my eyes, of buildings being all too often pulled down unrecorded before one had a chance to see them – all these added a melancholy excitement to the pursuit of architectural history in the earlier years of this century and are not wholly unknown even today.

So the *Dictionary* has occupied me, on and off, for much of my life, and writing it – conceived originally as an essentially documentary exercise – has in practice meant engaging also in those art-historical studies in which I had not had any formal training. Its basic aim was quite a simple one – to establish who the architects practising in Britain during the 240 years from 1600 to 1840 were, and exactly what they designed. At the same time I hoped to throw some light on the history of architectural practice, so different in the past from what it became in Victorian Britain, and of course already different now from what it was then. It was important to do so because most architectural historians of the late nineteenth and early twentieth centuries were themselves architects by profession and tended to think that architectural practice in the past had been much as it was in their own time. So provincial builder-architects like the Smiths of Warwick or the Woodwards of Chipping Campden were apt to be ignored, and the role of the gentleman-architect (which could, as we now realise, sometimes be crucial) was discounted in the belief that every amateur had behind him a professional 'ghost' who was really responsible for the designs for which his master took the credit. The rediscovery of the craftsmen architects on the one hand and of the amateurs on the other was something that gave me particular satisfaction.

The biographical was only one of many possible approaches to British architectural history, though one fairly basic to its study in the state of knowledge prevailing in the 1950s. If, as I think most would agree, the second half of the twentieth century has been much more fruitful for architectural history in this country than the first, much of the credit is due to those who, like Pevsner and Summerson, either brought with them, or absorbed, the continental art-historical scholarship particularly associated with the Warburg Institute. But, together of course with the *Buildings of England*, *Scotland* and *Wales*, the *RIBA Drawings Catalogue*, and Eileen Harris's magisterial bibliography of British architectural books, I hope that the *Dictionary* has played its part.

NOTES

1 R. Stewart-Brown in *Lancashire and Cheshire Historical Society*, 64, 1912, p. 82.
2 Author of the *Dictionary of British Sculptors 1660–1851*, 1953; died 1965.

XIX

THE AUTHOR'S PRINCIPAL WRITINGS ON ARCHITECTURAL HISTORY

★Items marked with an asterisk have been reprinted in this volume of essays

1945 'Aberystwyth's Architecture', *Wales*, iv, no. 6.

1946 'Victorian Malta', *Architectural Review*, 99, pp. 170–80.

1947 'The Architectural History of Marlow', *Records of Buckinghamshire*, xv.
'The Bastards of Blandford, architects and master-builders', *Archaeological Journal*, civ.

1948 'Abbey Dore', *Transactions of the Woolhope Naturalists' Field Club*, xxxii (1946–8), pp. 235–7.
★'Gothic Survival and Gothick Revival', *Architectural Review*, 103, pp. 91–8.

1950 'Fifty New Churches', *Architectural Review*, 107, pp. 189–96 (reprinted as an introduction to E.G.W. Bill, *The Queen Anne Churches*, 1979).

1951 'Roger North and Sir Christopher Wren', *Architectural Review*, 110, pp. 257–60 (incorporated into the introduction to *Of Building: Roger North's Writings on Architecture*, with John Newman, 1981).
'The rebuilding of Woodstock church tower (1770–1786)', *Oxfordshire Archaeological Society's Reports and Papers*, 87 for 1949.

1952 *Architectural Drawings in the Bodleian Library*, Bodleian Picture Book No. 7.
★'The Architect of Thorpe Hall', *Country Life*, cxi, 6 June 1952, pp. 1732–5.

1953 'The rebuilding and repair of Berkshire Churches during the seventeenth, eighteenth and early nineteenth centuries', Part I, with Basil F.L. Clarke, *Berkshire Archaeological Journal*, 53.

1954 *A Biographical Dictionary of English Architects 1660–1840*, John Murray (new edition in 1978 under the title *A Biographical Dictionary of British Architects 1600–1840*).
'The Clarendon Building', *Victoria County History of Oxfordshire*, iii, pp. 43–55.
'The Architects of All Saints Church, Oxford', *Oxoniensia*, xix.
Ackermann's Oxford (King Penguin series, edited by Nikolaus Pevsner).
★'The South Front of Wilton House', *Archaeological Journal*, cxi.
'The Bishop's Palace, Lichfield', with Arthur Oswald, *Country Life*, cxvi, 30 December 1954, pp. 2312–15.

1955 'The rebuilding and repair of Berkshire Churches during the seventeenth, eighteenth and early nineteenth centuries', Part II, with Basil F.L. Clarke, *Berkshire Archaeological Journal*, 54.

'Architectural History and its Records', *Archives*, II, no. 14 (republished as *A Guide to the Sources of English Architectural History*, Pinhorns 1967, 2nd ed. entitled *English Architectural History. A Guide to Sources*, 1976).

'Staunton Harold Church', with Jack Simmons, *Archaeological Journal*, cxii, pp. 173–6.

'Roubiliac's Bust of Isaac Ware', *Burlington Magazine*, xcvii, no. 626, May 1955, p. 151.

★'Chesterton, Warwickshire', *Architectural Review*, cxviii, pp. 115–17.

1958 'Domestic Architecture and Town Planning', in *Medieval England*, ed. A.L. Poole, 1.

'The Architects of Stafford House', *Architectural History*, i.

1959 'The Building of St Bernard's College', *Oxoniensia*, xxiv.

'Four fourteenth-century building contracts', *Architectural History*, 2.

1961 'Haunt Hill House, Weldon', *Studies in Building History: Essays in Recognition of the Work of B.H.St J. O'Neil*, ed. E.M. Jope, Odhams Press.

'Henry Bell of King's Lynn', with L.M. Wodehouse, *Architectural History*, 4.

'Dorchester Abbey', *Victoria County History of Oxfordshire*, vii, 1961, pp. 56–61.

1962 'A Georgian Architect in Cornwall', with H. Dalton Clifford, *Country Life*, cxxxii, 4 and 18 October, pp. 774–7, 959–62.

'Discoveries in Eton College Chapel', *Records of Buckinghamshire*, xvii, part 2.

1963 *The History of the King's Works*, I–II. *The Middle Ages*, General Editor and part author with R. Allen Brown and A.J. Taylor, HMSO.

A History of Deddington, Oxfordshire (with sections on the parish church and other buildings), SPCK.

1964 *A Catalogue of Architectural Drawings of the 18th and 19th Centuries in the Library of Worcester College, Oxford*, Clarendon Press.

Architectural Drawings in the Library of Elton Hall by Sir John Vanbrugh and Sir Edward Lovett Pearce, edited with Maurice Craig, Oxford University Press for the Roxburghe Club.

The Sheldonian Theatre and the Divinity School (guidebook), Oxford University Press (reprinted 1974).

'Eythrope House and its demolition in 1810–11', *Records of Buckinghamshire*, xvii.

1965 'The Howard Tombs at Framlingham, Suffolk', with Lawrence Stone, *Archaeological Journal*, cxxii.

1966 'Views of the Old Palace of Westminster', *Architectural History*, 9.

1968 *Royal Buildings*, RIBA Drawings Series, Country Life Books.

'Castles and government in Tudor England', *English Historical Review*, lxxxiii.

★'Aubrey's *Chronologia Architectonica*', in *Concerning Architecture: Essays on Architectural Writers and Writing presented to Nikolaus Pevsner*, ed. J. Summerson, Allen Lane, The Penguin Press.

'Georgian Architects at Badminton', *Country Life*, cxliii, 4 April 1968, pp. 800–4.

1969   Introduction to reprint of D. King, *The Cathedrall and Conventuall Churches of England and Wales* (1672).

1970   Edited with John Harris, *The Country Seat: Studies in the History of the British Country House presented to Sir John Summerson*, Allen Lane, the Penguin Press, and contributed 'Peter Mills and Cobham Hall' and 'Grimsthorpe Castle, the North Front'.

1971   Edited *Building Accounts of King Henry III*, Clarendon Press, Oxford.
'Edward VI at Hunsdon House', *Burlington Magazine*, cxiii, April, pp. 210–11.

1973   'Francis Smith of Warwick 1672–1738', *Warwickshire History*, ii, no. 2 (winter 1972–3)
Edited *The History of the King's Works*, vi, *1782–1851*, by J. Mordaunt Crook and M.H. Port, HMSO.

1974   'A Scottish Origin for English Palladianism?', *Architectural History*, 17.

1975   *The History of the King's Works* III, *1485–1660* (part 1), General Editor and part author with D.R. Ransome and John Summerson, HMSO.
★'Robert Hooke and Ramsbury Manor', *Country Life*, clvii, 23 January, pp. 194–5.

1976   *The History of the King's Works*, V, *1660–1782*, General Editor and part author with J. Mordaunt Crook, Kerry Downes and John Newman, HMSO.

1978   *A Biographical Dictionary of British Architects 1600–1840*, John Murray (new edition 1995).
'A monument by Robert Adam', *Architectural History*, 21.
'The origins of the Gothic Revival', in *Il neogotico in Gran Bretagna*, Accademia Nazionale dei Lincei, Rome, quaderno 241.

1980   *Architectural Drawings from Lowther Castle*, with J. Mordaunt Crook and T. Friedman, Society of Architectural Historians Monograph II.

1981   Edited with John Newman, *Of Building: Roger North's Writings on Architecture*, Clarendon Press.
★'The Church of St Mary Aldermary and its rebuilding after the Great Fire of London', *Architectural History*, 24.

1982   *The History of the King's Works*, IV, *1485–1660* (part 2), General Editor and part author with John Summerson, Martin Biddle, John Hale and Marcus Merriman, HMSO.
★'Lord Burlington and the Office of Works', in *Lord Burlington and his Circle*, papers given at a Georgian Group Symposium, 22 May 1982.
'An Architect for Tredegar House?', *Architectural History*, 25.

1983   *Unbuilt Oxford*, Yale University Press.
'Calke Abbey, Derbyshire', *Country Life*, clxxiv, 20, 27 October, 3 November, pp. 1062–5, 1162–5, 1242–5.
★'The Court Style in Medieval English Architecture: a review', in *English Culture in the Later Middle Ages*, ed. V.J. Scattergood and J.W. Sherborne, Duckworth.

1984   'Letters and Papers relating to the rebuilding of Combe Abbey, Warwick-shire 1681–1686', *Walpole Society*, 50.

Introduction to *An Exhibition of 18th and 19th century British and Continental Architectural Drawings*, Clarendon Gallery and Fischer Fine Art.

1985   *Calke Abbey, Derbyshire. A Hidden House Revealed*, National Trust and George Philip.

'Beaudesert, Staffordshire', *Transactions of the Ancient Monuments Society*, NS 29.

1986   ★'Royal Gardens in Medieval England' in *Medieval Gardens*, ed. E.B. Macdougall, Dumbarton Oaks, pp. 7–22.

'Architecture' in *History of Oxford University*, vol. 5: *The Eighteenth Century*, ed. L. Sutherland and L. Mitchell, Oxford University Press.

'The Beginnings of the Architectural Profession in Scotland', *Architectural History*, 29.

'Inigo Jones and the Church of St Michael le Querne', *London Journal*, 12 (1).

1987   Introduction to *Georgian Arcadia*, exhibition catalogue of paintings of garden buildings by John Piper, Georgian Group and Marlborough Fine Art.

1988   *The Canterbury Quadrangle, St John's College, Oxford*, Oxford University Press.

1989   *All Souls, An Oxford College and its Buildings*, with John Simmons, Oxford University Press.

'Calke Abbey, Derbyshire' (report on its restoration by the National Trust), *Country Life*, clxxxiii, pp. 138–45.

Calke Abbey, National Trust, chapter 3 ('Architectural History').

1991   *Architecture and the After-Life*, Yale University Press.

★'Architect and Client' in *Georgian Architectural Practice*, a Georgian Group Symposium.

'A Roman Mausoleum in Gloucestershire. The Guise Monument at Elmore', *Georgian Group Journal*, 1991.

1992   'A Collection of seventeenth-century architectural plans', with Alison Maguire, *Architectural History*, 35.

1993   'Bell Guttae and the Woodwards of Chipping Campden', *Georgian Group Journal*, 1993.

★'The Grand Bridge in Blenheim Park', with Alistair Rowan, in *English Architecture Public and Private. Essays for Kerry Downes*, ed. J. Bold and E. Chaney, Hambledon Press.

'What we mean by Amateur', in *The Role of the Amateur Architect*, a Georgian Group Symposium.

1994   'The Pomfret Portrait', *The Ashmolean*, no. 26 (Pomfret House, London), pp. 6–7.

1995   *A Biographical Dictionary of British Architects, 1600–1840*, 3rd ed., Yale University Press (paperback reprint, 1998).

'Introducing Alexander Roos', in *Scottish Country Houses 1600–1914*, ed. I. Gow and A. Rowan, Edinburgh University Press.

Introduction to *Lord Burlington, Architecture, Art and Life*, ed. T. Barnard and J. Clark, Hambledon Press.

1996   Edited, with Susan Foister, *The Panorama of London by Antonis van den Wyngaerde*, London Topographical Society.

Introduction to *Memorial Inscriptions in St John's College, Oxford*, ed. Reginald H. Adams, published by the College.

Memoir of Sir John Summerson, *Proceedings of the British Academy*, 90 for 1995, with bibliography (bibliography reprinted in *Architectural History* 40, 1997), pp. 467–95.

'Gothic Survival' (in Western Europe), *Macmillan Encyclopaedia of Art*, 13, pp. 209–12.

1997   'The Architect of Foots Cray Place', with John Harris, *Georgian Group Journal*, vii.

'The North Front of the Royal Exchange' in *The Royal Exchange*, ed. Ann Saunders, London Topographical Society.

★'Lease or Demolish? The problem of the redundant country house in Georgian England', *The Later Eighteenth Century Great House*, ed. Malcolm Airs, University of Oxford, Dept. for Continuing Education. 1997.

1998   'Capability Brown and Croome Church', *Georgian Group Journal*, viii.

SOURCES OF ESSAYS

The following essays are published here for the first time: 3, 4, 5, 6 and 18. The others originally appeared in the following publications:

1 *Medieval Gardens*, ed. Elizabeth B. Macdougall, Dumbarton Oaks, Washington DC, 1986.

2 *English Court Culture in the Middle Ages*, ed. V.J. Scattergood and J.W. Sherborne for the Colston Research Society, Duckworth 1983.

7 *The Archaeological Journal*, xci for 1954 (extensively revised).

8 *Country Life*, cxi, 6 June 1952 (extensively revised).

9 *The Architectural Review*, cxviii, 1955.

10 *Country Life*, clvii, 23 January 1975.

11 *Architectural History*, 24, 1981.

12 *Concerning Architecture: Essays on Architectural Writers and Writing presented to Nikolaus Pevsner*, ed. John Summerson, Allen Lane, the Penguin Press, 1968.

13 *Architectural Review*, ciii, 1948 (extensively revised).

14 *English Architecture Public and Private. Essays for Kerry Downes*, ed. J. Bold and E. Chaney, Hambledon Press 1993.

15 *Lord Burlington and his Circle. Papers given at a Georgian Group Symposium on 22 May 1982*.

16 *Georgian Architectural Practice. Papers given at a Georgian Group Symposium*, 1991, ed. Giles Worsley.

17 *The Later Eighteenth Century Great House*, ed. Malcolm Airs, Oxford University Department for Continuing Education, 1997.

INDEX